The Development of Consumer Credit
in Global Perspective

Worlds of Consumption

Published in association with the German Historical Institute, Washington, D.C.

Series Editors: Hartmut Berghoff and Uwe Spiekermann

Worlds of Consumption is a peer-reviewed venue for the history of consumption and consumerism in the modern era, especially the twentieth century, with a particular focus on comparative and transnational studies. It aims to make research available in English from an increasingly internationalized and interdisciplinary field. The history of consumption offers a vital link among diverse fields of history and other social sciences, because modern societies are consumer societies whose political, cultural, social, and economic structures and practices are bound up with the history of consumption. *Worlds of Consumption* highlights and explores these linkages, which deserve wide attention, since they shape who we are as individuals and societies.

Published by Palgrave Macmillan:

Decoding Modern Consumer Societies
By Hartmut Berghoff and Uwe Spiekermann, eds.

The Development of Consumer Credit in Global Perspective: Business, Regulation, and Culture
By Jan Logemann, ed.

The Development of Consumer Credit in Global Perspective: Business, Regulation, and Culture

Edited by Jan Logemann

THE DEVELOPMENT OF CONSUMER CREDIT IN GLOBAL PERSPECTIVE:
BUSINESS, REGULATION, AND CULTURE
Copyright © The German Historical Institute, 2012.

First published in 2012 by
PALGRAVE MACMILLAN®
in the United States—a division of St. Martin's Press LLC,
175 Fifth Avenue, New York, NY 10010.

Where this book is distributed in the UK, Europe and the rest of the World,
this is by Palgrave Macmillan, a division of Macmillan Publishers Limited,
registered in England, company number 785998, of Houndmills,
Basingstoke, Hampshire RG21 6XS.

Palgrave Macmillan is the global academic imprint of the above
companies and has companies and representatives throughout the world.

Palgrave® and Macmillan® are registered trademarks in the United
States, the United Kingdom, Europe and other countries.

ISBN: 978–0–230–34105–0

Library of Congress Cataloging-in-Publication Data

The development of consumer credit in global perspective : business,
    regulation, and culture / edited by Jan Logemann.
        p.   cm. — (Worlds of consumption series)
    ISBN 978–0–230–34105–0 (alk. paper)
    1. Consumer credit.   2. Consumer credit—Law and legislation.
    I. Logemann, Jan L.
    HG3755.D48 2012
    332.7′43—dc23   2012011382

A catalogue record of the book is available from the British Library.

Design by Integra Software Services

First edition: July 2012

10 9 8 7 6 5 4 3 2 1

Printed in the United States of America.

Contents

List of Figures

List of Tables

Contributors

Rebecca Belvederesi-Kochs, Social Media Aachen and belvederesi Kommunikations- und Unternehmensberatung

Lawrence Bowdish, Department of History, The American Public University System

Lendol Calder, History Department, Augustana College, Rock Island, Illinois

Sabine Effosse, Department of History, François Rabelais University de Tours and Institute universitaire de France

Larry Frohman, Department of History, State University of New York, Stony Brook

Isabelle Gaillard, Department of History, Pierre Mendès France University of Grenoble

Andrew Gordon, Department of History, Harvard University

Charles Yuji Horioka, Institute of Social and Economic Research, Osaka University

Jan Logemann, German Historical Institute, Washington, D.C.

Silke Meyer, Department of History and European Ethnology, University of Innsbruck

Sean O'Connell, School of History and Anthropology, Queen's University, Belfast

Gunnar Trumbull, Harvard Business School

Introduction: Toward a Global History of Credit in Modern Consumer Societies

Jan Logemann

D uring the late 1920s, many German retailers vigorously fought the spread of new installment sales methods as an "Americanism," an unwelcome import from what was widely regarded as the "classic land of consumer credit." Germany, one trade journal commentator observed, was not an "economic colony" of the United States and should uphold "German methods" of solid cash payment rather than kneel before the "American idol of prosperity" with its seductive credit schemes.[1] More than eighty years have passed, and Germany is now unquestionably a developed consumer society, yet the topic of consumer credit still reveals deep anxieties about economic and cultural change brought from the outside. Reports about rising household indebtedness in Germany and elsewhere in Europe still frequently invoke the image of European societies approaching "American conditions" of unsustainable consumer debt.[2]

Throughout the twentieth century and across developed countries in Western Europe, East Asia, and North America, a lively debate occurred over the institution of consumer credit and its implications for retailers, consumers, and economies as a whole. This debate was frequently cast in comparative, international, and what we would now call transnational terms. In Germany, elsewhere in Europe, and Asia, the American case frequently took on special significance as both a model for emulation and a foil for national contrasts. Although Europeans and Asians discussed new consumer credit forms as "American imports" during the interwar period and even before World War I, the debate over household indebtedness in recent years—still in terms of "Americanization"—indicates that patterns of consumer lending and borrowing have by no means completely converged in modern consumer societies, notwithstanding a century of rhetoric lamenting such a development. Instead, a variety of cultures of credit appears to have prevailed despite the growing importance attached to consumption and consumer credit across the globe.

The financial crisis of 2007–2009 once again underscored the centrality of consumer credit for modern economies. Lavish lending and the overextension of many American households with mortgages and other consumer loans stood at the epicenter of a financial earthquake whose ripple effects extended across the globe. Subsequent contractions in the consumer credit market might also have added to the severity of the crisis and impeded recovery. Although some Europeans were quick to point fingers at an unsustainable American culture of credit and consumption, consumer indebtedness became a growing problem elsewhere, as well. In 2006, for example, the ratio of household debt to disposable income in traditionally "frugal" Japan was only slightly smaller than that in the United States, while the United Kingdom's ratio even exceeded the American one.[3] Still, important differences in cultures of credit were discernible in the seemingly so globally homogenized world of finance and consumption.[4] There were differences in lending practices and institutions, differences in consumer attitudes toward borrowing, and differences in regulatory approaches toward the consumer credit market. These historically contingent differences call for comparative study as well as careful analysis of adaptation processes in transnational transfers. Developments in consumer credit need to be situated within the story of a multifaceted, global world instead of in a linear narrative of homogenizing modernization and globalization.[5]

The present volume aims to give the issue of consumer borrowing and indebtedness historically comparative and transnational dimensions by addressing a series of questions.[6] How did the American experience with consumer credit—frequently seen as globally formative—compare to those in other parts of the world? What did changes in lending practices—from easy access to credit cards to increasingly refined credit scoring—mean for consumers as economic and social actors in various countries? To what degree did transnational exchanges of lending practices promote these transformations? Although a general shift from face-to-face credit relations (with neighborhood retailers or local pawn shops) to institutionalized lending (by banks and specialized financial institutions) was increasingly discernible over the course of the modern era, what breaks and continuities characterized this development under various regional and national circumstances? Finally, how significant was the frequently drawn line between consumer loans made under conditions of affluence and household debt incurred because of poverty and destitution? Did debt really become less "problematic," as many believed during the boom years of the mid-twentieth century, when overall standards of living rose across developed economies?

To answer these and other questions, this volume brings together contributions from history, economics, anthropology, and other disciplines by scholars from Europe, East Asia, and North America.[7] As a result, it offers not just comparative, but also interdisciplinary perspectives on the development of cultures of credit, a term that here refers holistically to both the economic and political structures that framed consumer lending as well as the social and cultural meanings that attached to this form of household financing.

The history of consumer credit is part of a broader history of consumption, which has been a growing field over the past few decades.[8] In part, the vitality of consumption history draws from its ability to bring together and combine the diverse perspectives of business history, economic history, cultural history, social history, and political history. The story of consumer credit adds to each of these perspectives.

For business historians, developments in consumer credit offer a key to understanding changes in retailing, ranging from modes of price calculation to interactions with customers. The history of consumer credit also sheds light on innovations in marketing new products such as sewing machines and television sets.[9] Credit cards have helped revolutionize shopping patterns in recent decades, for example, while the automobile and other high-priced durables achieved considerably faster market penetration through the increasing availability of installment credit that began in the interwar period. Research on credit practices can also illuminate the acquisition of marketing knowledge—about consumer shopping habits and preferences, for instance—by various market actors, as Josh Lauer's work on department store credit offices shows. Their mining of credit data even before World War I for direct advertising foreshadowed today's individualized and segmented marketing.[10]

Economic historians have long recognized consumer credit as a central element of the macroeconomics of demand under the Keynesian paradigm during the middle decades of the twentieth century. For example, with the so-called Regulation W instituted in the United States during the 1940s and adapted by several European governments during the 1950s, states attempted to steer consumer credit volume and aggregate demand by adjusting minimum down payments and maximum repayment periods. Credit use is also of vital importance to the study of household finances and consumer spending behavior. Already by the 1960s, behavioral economists such as George Katona used borrowing patterns as a major indicator of broader consumer attitudes toward the economy at large and consumer spending in particular.

Meanwhile, borrowing has become a key indicator of consumer confidence.[11] Despite several common patterns among national credit policies, however, Katona and others have shown significant national variations in credit use, and they have underlined the unique centrality of credit and consumption to America's postwar model of growth—a finding that several chapters in this volume underscore.[12]

Cultural historians point out that practices of credit use can reveal not only consumer attitudes and expectations with regard to their finances, but also deeper webs of meaning that underlie consumer culture more broadly. Most pronouncedly, literary scholars in the field of "new economic criticism" have recently begun to challenge existing disciplinary divides between cultural and economic perspectives on credit.[13] While much of the effort to contextualize credit relationships socially and culturally has focused on emerging market societies of the nineteenth century, many of the questions raised are relevant for twentieth-century consumer societies as well.[14] What significance did consumers invest in goods, money, and certain consumption practices in various cultural contexts? How did their attitudes change over time? This line of historical inquiry has especially profited from the introduction of anthropological perspectives to the history of consumption.[15] While much research has focused on the symbolic significance of material objects and their uses, credit financing adds another layer of complexity to our understanding of consumer economies. The questions of trust and trustworthiness that arise in credit financing relate to perceptions of social respectability, making creditworthiness a marker of social status that transcends relations based on simple economic exchanges.

In other words, studying the history of credit use raises questions about value that are not merely monetary, but also of broader cultural import.[16] While the chapters in this volume eschew a reductionist link between credit patterns and "national cultures," they suggest regional peculiarities and changes over time in the cultural meanings that adhered to consumer loans. For example, a culture of spending restraint that produced moralizing critiques of new credit forms prevailed in Japan and many Western European countries well into the postwar era—much longer than in the United States.

Credit use was always embedded in specific social contexts. For social historians, this circumstance leads to questions about class, social mobility, and related practices of social distinction or emulation through credit-financed consumption. In the United States, liberal credit access offered a pathway into a broadening middle class in ways unfamiliar to more socially stratified European consumer societies across the twentieth century. Because of this connection to social mobility, questions of discrimination and equal access in modern consumer societies along the lines of race, class, gender, and ethnicity also became salient.[17] Even in societies with liberal access to credit, women faced severe obstacles in securing loans well into the 1970s. To this day, "subprime" markets for the credit needs of the economically marginalized also continue to exist and are served or exploited by pawn shops and payday lenders.

The shift to increasingly standardized and institutionalized methods of establishing trust offers a window onto changing relationships between individuals and their communities in modern societies.[18] Whereas personal relationships between retailers and customers—or one's reputation within the community—once determined creditworthiness, modern economic identities frequently rest on credit scores and centrally collected credit histories. Although recent scholarship has rightly complicated linear narratives of modernization and rationalization in credit markets, creditworthiness, largely expressed in numbers and reports, is clearly a key to economic citizenship in today's consumer societies.[19] Therefore, historians of the political economy of consumption need to consider the creation and impact of credit regulations. Credit policies were often a central arena for negotiating the political and economic frameworks underlying our consumer societies, and political scientists, too, can understand them not only as a key link between politics and economics, but also as part of broader social policy strategies in the twentieth century.[20]

The history of consumer credit also speaks to a growing interest in global and transnational history. Increasingly, the study of consumption more generally is informed by a global perspective that rejects popular notions of a homogenizing "McDonaldization" of the world. Instead, scholars now carefully trace transnational exchanges, hybridity in consumption forms, as well as the international organization of market actors and consumer activists.[21] Complementing our questions about the development of consumer credit is recent comparative research on overindebtedness and cross-national efforts toward personal bankruptcy regulation, as well as a transnational study of household savings programs.[22] The present volume will contribute to this growing body of transnational scholarship on consumption and household finances by offering new comparative perspectives on central aspects of credit development. In many ways, then, research in the history of consumer credit has a lot to offer to a variety of disciplines and historical subfields.

* * *

Despite its significance for twentieth-century mass consumption, consumer credit long did not receive the scholarly attention it deserved from historians of consumption in many countries. Instead, the historiographical focus has been far more on areas such as advertising or specific products such as automobiles, but much less on how consumption was financed. This neglect is surprising, given the public attention historically paid to credit use and abuse in political, economic, and cultural debates surrounding new consumption patterns. To be sure, significant monographs on the economic and cultural history of credit in the United States have appeared, and more are forthcoming.[23] For Britain, too, a substantial amount of historical research is available that focuses in particular on the social contexts in which lending was embedded.[24] For many other European countries, however, the historiography is more circumscribed and usually focuses on the immediate post–World War II period. For Japan, as well, the few existing historical studies are of recent vintage.[25]

A truly global history of consumer credit development is still missing—as are sufficient regional studies upon which to base such a project. Interest in the subject appears to be growing, however. In the United States, *Business History Review* recently published a special issue on the history of consumer credit, and in Europe, *Entreprises et histoire* devoted an issue to European perspectives on the history of consumer lending.[26] The present collection seeks to contribute to these efforts by examining developments in the United States, Great Britain, France, Germany, and Japan. In doing so, it raises a number of broad questions that are relevant to consumption scholars beyond specialists in the field of consumer credit.

The chapters in this volume offer new comparative insights and point out transnational connections in four key areas of inquiry regarding the history of consumer credit and consumption since the late-nineteenth century. The first area concerns the relationship between *credit and individual freedom* in modern consumer economies. In many ways, the credit card has become the symbol of individual freedom in today's world of consumption. Any credit card advertisement worth its salt will play on this image, as Silke Meyer's chapter reminds us, promising instant gratification of highly individualized needs and desires.[27] At the same time, however, credit illustrates—like few other aspects of consumption—the disciplining side of the modern consumer cornucopia. The weight of contractual payments can tie down and sink the finances of consumer households, which has been the focus of much recent sociological research on household debt.[28] Furthermore, increasingly refined mechanisms of credit screening and scoring have turned today's consumer into an easily readable "glass" customer whose household finances and buying habits are laid bare, as Larry Frohman's chapter illustrates, using debates about the German Schufa agency as a telling example.[29] To what degree is his or her spending truly more unrestrained and private than that of consumers in earlier eras, who for their credit needs had to rely on the trust and goodwill of neighborhood retailers or on doorstep credit agents like in Sean O'Connell's account of working-class credit in the United Kingdom? Access to credit has also remained riddled with inequalities and structural discrimination along gender lines. As Lawrence Bowdish's chapter discusses, such inequities have been commonplace in the development of credit markets across the globe. By probing the balance between consumer rights and opportunities, on the one hand, and the structural restraints to individual freedom that consumers encounter, on the other hand, research on credit markets can help accentuate and elucidate the conundrum of consumer agency and the true extent of consumer choice that has driven much recent research on modern consumerism.[30]

The second area of inquiry in this book is so-called *Americanization* or, more generally, cross-national convergence and the role that the American credit and consumption model played in consumer societies globally. As Andrew Gordon observes in his chapter on Japan, both proponents and opponents of new credit methods perceived them as something "foreign" or "American." The term "Americanization" suggests economic and cultural homogenization in a "globalized" world, and it still enjoys widespread currency among historians of consumer markets and popular culture alike. Lately, however, much scholarship in this vein has qualified the concept by emphasizing processes of selective local adaptation and hybridization. This research underlines the limits of "Americanization" as a heuristic device for understanding the development of modern consumer societies around the world.[31]

The chapters by Isabelle Gaillard and Sabine Effosse on postwar France, for example, illustrate the attention that French businesspeople and state regulators paid to American developments. Both groups did not directly import U.S. practices, however, but instead adapted them to French conditions in different ways. Consumer credit appears ideally suited to trace American influences on economic developments in other countries more generally and to gauge the reception of American economic and cultural practices.[32] Installment sales schemes pioneered by Singer, revolving charge accounts, and regulatory frameworks for credit are among the transatlantic and transpacific examples explored in this volume. At the same time, however, transnational links did not always directly involve the United States. Exchanges and networking among companies and policy makers also took place within Europe, as well as between Europe and Asia, as the chapters by Sean O'Connell and Sabine Effosse demonstrate.[33] Comparative perspectives on credit also reveal the limits of international convergence and the degree to which the American consumption model remained distinct, if not exceptional, from a global perspective. More comparative and cross-regional research on consumption practices along the lines sketched out in this volume is needed—with particular attention to transnational and transcultural transfers.

The third area of inquiry that this book addresses is *periodization* and the question of when "modern" consumer societies came into their own. While much American research on the history of consumer credit focuses on the late-nineteenth century and the first half of the twentieth, this volume pays special attention to the post–World War II era. This emphasis appears justified by the dramatic expansion of consumer credit in this period, especially in Europe and Asia. Several chapters suggest a significant shift in both lending practices and attitudes toward consumer debt under conditions of postwar prosperity. Rebecca Belvederesi-Kochs's chapter on the lending practices of public savings banks (*Sparkassen*) in postwar West Germany exemplifies this trend. At the same time, however, there is a much longer trajectory of credit development to consider, even outside the United States. O'Connell and Gordon remind us that consumer lending was not simply a postwar innovation, but could also build on older institutional and cultural traditions, as the cases of Great Britain and Japan show.

Modern consumer cultures began to take off in most of the countries under consideration here by at least the end of the nineteenth century. Moreover, the rise of modern, formalized credit for durable goods in many of these countries must be situated within a longer history of credit forms that included informal retailer book credit (the practice of running up a bill at the neighborhood store), pawn shops, and even loan sharking, all of which date back to the preindustrial era. In fact, cash business was historically an anomaly in important ways, and it was rarely the "normal" state that some mid-twentieth-century opponents of installment credit made it out to be.[34] Instead, as Lendol Calder's chapter points out, even "respectable" Victorian-era Americans were often hopelessly overindebted. Although consumer lending became increasingly institutionalized and formalized over the past century, the development of credit and the continued coexistence of a myriad of lending forms defy narratives of linear "progress" as much as they do cultural jeremiads about a continuous decline of thrift.[35] Nonetheless, the recent financial crisis raises the question of whether increased institutionalization of lending has made individual consumer households ever more vulnerable to the cycles of boom and bust in global financial markets.

The fourth and final area of inquiry that this volume deals with entails *delimiting the field of consumer credit*. What does it include? Which forms of "getting and spending" by private households should historians of consumption consider more generally? Installment loans have been the subject of perhaps the most sustained research on the history of consumer credit. Some work has also been done on the history of salary lenders, small loans banks, credit unions, credit cards, and revolving charge accounts.[36] By contrast, we know much less about the development of informal retail credit, specialized hire-purchase stores, and pawn shops despite the continued (and partially resurgent) prominence of these credit sources for much of the modern era.[37] While the above-mentioned areas of credit use have been neglected in the historiography, others have been consciously excluded. Unlike car loans, which are widely regarded as an essential aspect of contemporary consumer credit, mortgage credit is frequently treated separately. Does it make sense to ignore this most significant form of household debt, especially in times when home equity loans are routinely used to make all manner of consumer purchases? Although most contributors to this volume focus on banks and retailers, installment and credit card loans, several essays also probe the fringes of the credit economy, including "gray" and "black" markets for loans such as credit societies and loan sharks. Finally, Jan Logemann's chapter argues for a more comprehensive understanding of consumer credit that would even include student loans and medical debt, while economists like Charles Horioka quite seamlessly discuss mortgage debt and retail loans as equally important parts of household liabilities.

Forms of consumer credit changed over time, and so did the circumstances under which consumers borrowed. Common distinctions between "productive" and "consumptive" credit are historically arbitrary and misleading, just as the line between debt incurred because of destitution and loans made under conditions of affluence quickly blurs. Such distinctions were often generated in the debates that accompanied the very formation of contemporary credit patterns. Hence, they are burdened with historically contingent assumptions about what constituted necessities and luxuries, needs and wants. For example, proponents of installment credit in the mid-twentieth century actively reframed the debate by arguing that household durables—long seen as luxuries—should be considered rational and productive "investments" rather than mere consumption goods.[38] Sabine Effosse offers a telling example of this phenomenon in her discussion of semantic shifts in French postwar policies aimed at legitimizing expanded consumer borrowing. British credit regulators similarly enumerated goods deemed "creditworthy," compiling a list that would appear curious and arbitrary to many present-day consumers. By the same token, when Singer pioneered installment schemes for its sewing machines in the nineteenth century, these machines were not only consumer goods but also investments, especially for the many women who used them as a source of additional household income. How wide is the difference, then, between such consumer loans and the much celebrated microcredits to women entrepreneurs in Bangladesh and elsewhere today, which are not commonly considered consumer credit?

Whereas mid-twentieth-century consumption models focused primarily on increased access to consumer durables, today other expenses from education to medical spending are increasingly important to consumer household budgets. In the United States, at least, they certainly count among the leading causes of personal bankruptcy. Like the recent spread of payday lenders, this fact serves as a reminder that—contrary to the predictions of postwar prophets of prosperity—debt incurred in destitution has by no means been eradicated, but is instead on the rise, especially in the United States. In this particular regard (recalling the question of Americanization), American patterns of consumer debt appear as anything but a global "model" from the perspective of the early twenty-first century.

* * *

The issues raised by the four lines of inquiry discussed above played out in different ways in the national cases considered in this volume and took on various forms, depending on the perspectives of the actors involved. The chapters in this book are therefore organized in four sections that emphasize particular actors and perspectives on credit development, focusing on the respective roles of the lenders, borrowers, state regulators, and cultural discourses. The first section traces developments among lending institutions from banks and retailers to consumer goods companies. In the second section, the social context in which consumers borrowed comes into view with essays that examine lending in working-class communities, credit discrimination against women, and debates over privacy concerns in credit rating. The third section takes a comparative look at state regulatory approaches to consumer credit. The last, most explicitly interdisciplinary section combines and contrasts the perspectives of an economist, an anthropologist, and a historian on the question of culture's role in influencing the development of consumer credit.

The first section focuses on the lenders and transformations in lending practices across different countries in Europe as well as in Japan and the United States during the latter half of the twentieth century. Who were the innovators or driving forces behind change? How did the relationship among retailers, producers, and financial institutions evolve in the consumer credit business? To what extent can we trace transnational transfers of lending practices? In assessing transfers of the American credit model, we must also keep in mind that it was by no means static but underwent dramatic changes during the postwar decades, as Louis Hyman's recent work has underscored. Hyman posits a transition from an installment credit economy of the "Fordist" era to a revolving credit economy of the "post-Fordist" era, when profits derived from credit financing became an end in themselves for retailers and manufacturers alike.[39]

The revolving credit regime that Hyman discusses as increasingly central to postwar America did not attain the same significance in Europe and Asia. Instead, the growth of installment credit from retailers, manufacturers, and financial institutions dominated the postwar decades there. Isabelle Gaillard discusses the central role that the electronics industry—especially television manufacturers—played in the development of consumer credit in postwar France. Specialized lenders such as Cetelem engaged a frequently skeptical French public and greatly expanded the consumer credit market in an effort to grow the overall sales of electronic appliances. Rebecca Belvederesi-Kochs's essay turns to the changes in marketing and business ethics that resulted from bringing an institution peculiar to Germany, the public savings bank or *Sparkasse,* into the consumer loans market. These banks had long emphasized the importance of savings and "German thrift," retaining this stance well into the 1960s. However, they also emerged as reluctant pioneers in the consumer loans business at a time when most commercial banks in Germany did not yet consider ordinary consumers creditworthy. Andrew Gordon's essay on the Japanese case emphasizes the combination of American influences (for example, through the Singer company) and indigenous developments in retail credit for the growth of consumer lending in Japan. Although Japanese consumers "caught up with" Americans in some measures of credit use, the structure of their credit system remained significantly different. As in Europe, revolving credit lines were much less common here. In Japan and elsewhere, transfers and "modernization" rarely meant convergence toward a uniform business model of consumer lending. Instead, each country under consideration developed its own particular array of lending institutions and loan forms.

The second section turns from the lenders to the borrowers and to questions about credit access, privacy concerns, and the changing social context of credit. Sean O'Connell opens with an essay on the long and especially developed tradition of working-class credit in the United Kingdom, which dated back to the nineteenth century. In a market segmented by class, working-class consumers were supplied with access to credit by tallymen and check-trading companies such as Provident. Their agents were deeply embedded in the fabric of local communities and continued to collect money on the doorstep well into the second half of the twentieth century. While largely unknown in the

United States, this business model of installment-credit checks redeemable at local retailers and geared toward less affluent consumers was prominent in various European countries and Japan for much of the twentieth century. Like poorer consumers, women as a group also faced frequent challenges in the consumer credit market. Lawrence Bowdish chronicles the push for credit rights for women in the United States that ultimately led to the Equal Credit Opportunity Act of 1974. Drawing on a large repository of letters from affected women, he shows how especially middle-class women rallied around the cause of credit access as a way to gain economic independence and "economic citizenship."

Consumer self-determination and agency also stood at the center of debates over credit reporting and privacy rights in West Germany during the 1970s, which Larry Frohman analyzes. He describes the rise of the Schufa agency, which in some ways functioned as an equivalent to American credit bureaus but did not employ credit scores. Overall, the section uncovers similar trends toward expanded access to credit for various social groups, as well as an increase in contractual and institutionalized lending forms that relied on the scientific mapping of consumers rather than on social ties. Even so, national distinctions in credit practices—including the degree of class stratification in credit markets and approaches to determining creditworthiness—remained palpable throughout the twentieth century.

State regulation and credit policies are the subject of the third section, which explores differences in the macroeconomic significance of consumer credit in France and the United States. French postwar policy was in many ways reflective of a more reluctant European approach to credit, so the two countries form a particularly sharp contrast in their approach to regulation. Gunnar Trumbull presents a truly comparative perspective on the two countries by analyzing the impact of regulatory policy and the relative economic incentives for lenders. Trumbull explains the high American rates of indebtedness in the United States as compared to France. He considers regulatory and especially deregulatory approaches in both countries and ultimately traces the roots of national differences to the structures of the financial sector and the policies that shaped them. Here, he underscores the role played by commercial banks in expanding credit access in the United States. By contrast, Sabine Effosse finds that French governmental attitudes toward expanded consumer credit long remained reserved at best. Like elsewhere in Europe after World War II, developing industry and fighting inflation outweighed interest in expanding credit. Although the French government adopted more liberal regulations modeled after American examples during the mid-1950s, the overall significance of credit-financed consumption still paled in comparison to the

United States even toward the end of the postwar boom or *trente glorieuses,* a nearly thirty-year span of sustained economic growth.

Jan Logemann's essay explores the motives behind American policies that favored credit expansion. He argues that credit expansion in the United States was not just tied to neoliberal market deregulation, but also to long-standing attempts to expand credit access as a form of social policy. From mortgages and student loans to credit cards and installment loans, making various forms of credit affordable and widely available to consumer households was of peculiar importance in twentieth-century America, which lacked European-style welfare systems but tied social mobility closely to consumption possibilities. Thus, although state actors repeatedly engaged in cross-national exchanges about policy approaches, nationally specific regulations and policy making still influenced consumers and shaped credit markets even in the latter half of the twentieth century.

The final section of this volume probes the extent to which cultural differences can explain variations among national credit patterns. While the previous chapters point to market innovations, social structures, and policy incentives to explain credit development, anthropologist Silke Meyer suggests that a cultural shift in attitudes toward the use of credit has been a major contributing factor to growing household indebtedness in recent decades. Spurred on by advertising and aggressive marketing, debtors, who were the subject of Meyer's field research in Germany, have come to view credit-financed consumption and instant gratification of personal desires as integral to notions of social inclusion and self-realization. The social ties that once governed traditional credit exchanges have changed, she argues, and loans and debts are increasingly embedded within the cultural logic of modern consumerism.

Economist Charles Horioka approaches the question of culture in household finances from a different angle. Comparing cross-national data from the Organization for Economic Cooperation and Development (OECD) on household liabilities and assets, he probes the conventional notion of the "frugal" Japanese. Surprisingly, household liabilities became relatively high in Japan in recent decades, at times even surpassing those in the United States. These liabilities, however, were more than offset by high household assets. Although this circumstance seemed to vindicate standard assumptions about Japanese household budgeting, Horioka cautions against purely cultural explanations by pointing to the significant rise in debt over the postwar decades, which counters assumptions about deeply ingrained or immutable cultural patterns.

Finally, looking at American debt cultures, historian Lendol Calder again underscores the importance of historical contextualization that reaches back at least into the nineteenth and early twentieth centuries. He rejects simplistic narratives of a decline of thrift or a Victorian "golden age" of responsible budgeting. Although traditional notions of thrift enjoy less currency today, even "respectable" nineteenth-century Americans were no strangers to financial irresponsibility. Thrift was never the only game in town, Calder argues. Furthermore, modern forms of debt often have a financially disciplining character that merits consideration as its own form of thriftiness, for they force households to budget more carefully and over longer periods of time. Thus, while cultural patterns clearly influence credit use, arguments about "national cultures" of thrift or credit-fueled hedonism are rarely borne out by the historical record. Indeed, the comparative view suggests that the nation may well be an unsuitable unit for gauging cultures of credit. Attitudes to credit between, for example, urban and rural consumers in any given country may well have been more disparate than those between metropolitan consumers in Berlin, New York, and Tokyo for much of the century.

* * *

Overall, the contributions to this volume emphasize the importance of several factors for understanding the development of credit. Ranging from cultural processes to public policies and market incentives, these factors defy easy characterization and stereotyping. Although the influence that American developments have had on other nations is undeniable, the twentieth century was hardly characterized by Americanization or the global homogenization of consumer borrowing and lending practices. Instead, transfers went in multiple directions. Economists, historians, and other social scientists repeatedly note that the American model of consumer credit remained peculiar to the United States in important ways. Still, comparing experiences from numerous countries suggests that fundamental problems of twentieth-century credit development remain central to all modern consumer societies. The challenge, raised especially by the American case, of how to provide "democratic" access to credit under safe and affordable conditions while avoiding irresponsible lending and overindebtedness, for example, has thus far defied easy solutions.

Despite clear differences across the globe, several factors emerge from the studies in this volume that can help us understand how credit came to play such a central, yet precarious role in today's economies. Consumer credit institutions and practices grew in the context of emerging consumer societies from the late-nineteenth century, which also saw an increasing cultural acceptance of debt for material consumption. Postwar affluence and a rise in living standards helped to change attitudes toward consumer debt in most countries even further, albeit with variations in timing and degree. Credit-extending businesses—from specialized lending institutions and retailers to, increasingly, commercial banks—discovered consumer loans as a lucrative market and promoted their spread through advertising and marketing. Larger lenders overcame their reservations about lending to "average consumers," as these attained regular salaries and bank accounts and as more refined data on their financial circumstances became available. Nonetheless, the revolving credit lines that are so important to modern U.S. credit cards did not find widespread reception in Europe and Japan, where more "conservative" forms of loans continued to predominate. State regulation also added to the puzzle, especially as several European countries eased restrictions and regulations since the 1950s and further liberalized markets by the late 1960s (in the Japanese case, during the early 1990s). Few countries went as far as the United States, however, where deregulation was especially prominent during the 1970s and early 1980s. Across the board, credit fueled hopes among politicians, administration officials, and consumers for the continuous growth of businesses, while questions of sustainability tended to take a back seat—in some countries more than others.

The recent credit crisis may have shattered these hopes, but it should be seen neither as the inevitable culmination of previous developments nor as the end of growth in consumer credit. As sociologist Martha Poon points out, credit scores, the innovation that drove many of the U.S. and global financial developments in recent decades, were still rooted in traditional notions of predicting and avoiding default. Future scores, she avers, may well transcend this perspective and focus solely on lending profitability instead. Although such a shift would perhaps promote even further depersonalization and commoditization of lending relations, the history of consumer credit suggests that face-to-face lending and the neighborhood loan shark are not likely to vanish any time soon.

* * *

This book originated in a workshop entitled "Cultures of Credit: Consumer Lending and Borrowing in Modern Economies," which was held at the German Historical Institute in Washington, D.C., in February 2010.[40] I would like to thank the GHI for supporting both the workshop and this volume. I would also like to thank the participants of the conference for many stimulating discussions amid an epic snowstorm. Besides the contributors to this volume, I would especially like to thank Hartmut Berghoff, Michael Easterly, Sheldon Garon, Martina Grünewald, Louis Hyman, Christina Lubinski, Martha Poon, and Uwe Spiekermann. Next, I am grateful to Mark

16 • Jan Logemann

Stoneman for his extensive editorial efforts and Bryan Hart for his work on the graphs. Finally, my thanks go to Chris Chappell and Sarah Whalen at Palgrave Macmillan for guiding this manuscript to publication.

Notes

1. See, for example, "Diskussion über das Abzahlungsgeschäft," *Handelsschutz* 24 (1929): 169.
2. One example among many: "Privathaushalte: Sorgen wegen Schulden," *Frankfurter Rundschau Online,* November 11, 2009, http://www.fr-online.de/in_und_ausland/wirtschaft/aktuell/2074255_Privathaushalte-Sorgen-wegen-Schulden.html.
3. "Indebtedness of Households," *OECD Economic Outlook,* no. 85, http://www.oecd-ilibrary.org/economics/household-wealth-and-indebtedness-2010_207438 4x-2010-table18.
4. For inter-European differences in "cultures of credit," see Lucia A. Reisch and Wencke Gwozdz, "Finanzkulturen in Europa: Ähnlichkeiten und Unterschiede," in *SCHUFA Kredit-Kompass 2010* (Wiesbaden, 2010), 139–57.
5. Recent global history approaches reject notions of a uniform globalization process and instead focus on the "links and flows . . . [of] people, ideas, products, processes and patterns that operate over, across, through, beyond, above, under or in-between politics and societies." Akira Iriye and Pierre-Yves Saunier, eds., *The Palgrave Dictionary of Transnational History* (New York, 2009), xviii.
6. A good overview of recent scholarship on the transnational turn in the historical profession: Ian Tyrrell, "Reflections on the Transnational Turn in United States History: Theory and Practice," *Journal of Global History* 4 (2009): 453–74.
7. The present volume, to be sure, while global in its approach, is by no means all-encompassing, as it lacks contributions on the development of credit in Africa, Eastern Europe, Latin America, and large parts of Asia. In part, these omissions follow from the book's focus on those "developed" consumer societies in which assumptions about convergence appear most prominent and existing differences are perhaps most surprising. The omissions are also rooted, however, in a dearth of research on the credit history of these areas despite some exceptions. See, for example, Grietjie Verhoef, "Informal Financial Service Institutions for Survival: African Women and Stokvels in Urban South Africa, 1930–1998," *Enterprise & Society* 2 (2001): 259–96.
8. Recent stocktaking of the state of the field of consumption history: Hartmut Berghoff and Uwe Spiekermann, eds., *Decoding Modern Consumer Societies* (New York, 2012).
9. See, for example, Martha Olney, *Buy Now, Pay Later: Advertising, Credit, and Consumer Durables in the 1920s* (Chapel Hill, NC, 1991); Britta Stücker, "Konsum auf Kredit in der Bundesrepublik," *Economic History Yearbook,* no. 2 (2007): 63–88; Uwe Spiekermann, *Basis der Konsumgesellschaft: Entstehung und*

Entwicklung des modernen Kleinhandels in Deutschland 1850–1914 (Munich, 1999), 337–54.

10. Josh Lauer, "Making the Ledgers Talk: Credit Management and the Origins of Retail Data Mining, 1920–1940," in *The Rise of Marketing and Market Research,* ed. Hartmut Berghoff, Philip Scranton, and Uwe Spiekermann (New York, 2012).

11. George Katona, Burkhard Strumpel, and Ernest Zahn, *Aspirations and Affluence: Comparative Studies in the United States and Western Europe* (New York, 1971).

12. On postwar economic growth policies in the United States, see Robert Collins, *More: The Politics of Economic Growth in Postwar America* (Oxford, UK, 2000).

13. Mary Poovey, *Genres of the Credit Economy: Mediating Value in Eighteenth- and Nineteenth-Century Britain* (Chicago, IL, 2008).

14. See Mischa Suter, "Jenseits des 'cash nexus': Sozialgeschichte des Kredits zwischen kulturanthropologischen und informationsökonomischen Zugängen," *WerkstattGeschichte* 53 (2009): 89–99.

15. This line of inquiry was pioneered by Mary Douglas and Baron Isherwood in *The World of Goods: Towards an Anthropology of Consumption* (London, 1979).

16. On the cultural history of credit in the United States, see esp. Lendol Calder, *Financing the American Dream: A Cultural History of Consumer Credit* (Princeton, NJ, 1999) and Daniel Horowitz, *The Morality of Spending: Attitudes towards the Consumer Society in America, 1875–1940* (Baltimore, MD, 1985).

17. There is a particularly rich literature on working-class credit in Britain: Melanie Tebbutt, *Making Ends Meet: Pawnbroking and Working Class Credit* (Leicester, 1983); Margot Finn, "Working-Class Women and the Contest for Consumer Control in the Victorian County Courts," *Past and Present* 161 (1998): 116–54; Avram Taylor, *Working Class Credit and Community since 1918* (Basingstoke, 2002); and Sean O'Connell, *Credit and Community: Working-Class Debt in the UK since 1880* (Oxford, UK, 2009). On the social history of credit from a comparative perspective, see Jan Logemann, "Different Paths to Mass Consumption: Consumer Credit in the United States and West Germany during the 1950s and '60s," *Journal of Social History* 41 (2008): 525–59. On the question of credit access for women and African Americans in the United States, see Lizabeth Cohen, *A Consumer's Republic: The Politics of Mass Consumption in Postwar America* (New York, 2003).

18. See, for example, Gilles Laferté, "De l'interconnaissance sociale à l'identification économique: vers une histoire et une sociologie comparées de la transaction à crédit," paper presented at "Consommer a crédit en Europe au XXe siècle," Université de Paris Ouest Nanterre La Défense, January 21, 2010.

19. See Suter, "Jenseits des 'cash nexus' " for a critical discussion of modernization narratives in credit history.

20. See, for example, Cohen, *Consumer's Republic* and, with somewhat less pronounced attention to the role of consumer credit, Meg Jacobs, *Pocketbook Politics: Economic Citizenship in Twentieth-Century America* (Princeton, NJ, 2005).

21. See Victoria de Grazia, *Irresistible Empire: America's Advance through Twentieth-Century Europe* (Cambridge, MA, 2005); Sheldon Garon and Patricia Maclachlan, eds., *The Ambivalent Consumer: Questioning Consumption in East Asia and the West* (Ithaca, NY, 2006); and Matthew Hilton, *Prosperity for All: Consumer Activism in an Era of Globalization* (Ithaca, NY, 2009).
22. Iain Ramsay, "Comparative Consumer Bankruptcy," *Illinois Law Review*, no. 1 (2007): 241–74; Sheldon Garon, *Beyond Our Means: Why America Spends while the World Saves* (Princeton, NJ, 2011).
23. Olney, *Buy Now Pay Later*; Calder, *Financing the American Dream*. A significant new contribution to the history of postwar consumer credit: Louis Hyman, *Debtor Nation: The History of America in Red Ink* (Princeton, NJ, 2011). See also the abstract of Michael Easterly's dissertation, "Your Job Is Your Credit: Creating a Market for Loans to Salaried Employees in New York City, 1885–1920," *Enterprise & Society* 10 (2009): 651–60.
24. See Suter, "Jenseits des 'cash nexus'...."
25. For Germany, see esp. Peter Horvath, "Die Teilzahlungskredite als Begleiterscheinung des deutschen Wirtschaftswunders," *Zeitschrift für Unternehmensgeschichte* 37 (1992): 19–55, and Stücker, "Konsum auf Kredit in der Bundesrepublik." For France, see Isabelle Gaillard, "Il credito al consumo in Francia," in *Credito e nazione in Francia e in Italia; XIX-XX secolo*, ed. G. Conti, O. Feiertag, R. Scatamacchia (Pisa, 2009), 457–71; and for Japan, Andrew Gordon, "From Sewing Machines to Credit Cards: Consumer Credit in 20th Century Japan," in *The Ambivalent Consumer*, ed. Garon and Maclachlan, 137–62. For postwar consumer credit in the United States, see also Lendol Calder, "The Evolution of Consumer Credit in the United States," in *The Impact of Public Policy on Consumer Credit*, ed. Thomas Durkin and Michael Staten (Boston, MA, 2002), 23–35.
26. *Consumer Finance*, special issue of *Business History Review* 85, no. 3 (2011): 459–575; Sabine Effosse and Isabelle Gaillard, eds., "Consommer à crédit en Europe au XXe siècle," special issue of *Entreprises et histoire* 59 (2010): 1–134. In Fall 2010, the Harvard Business School's Baker Library put on an exhibition that highlights and contextualizes their collections pertaining to credit; see "Buy Now, Pay Later: A History of Personal Credit," http://www.library.hbs.edu/hc/credit/.
27. On the history of the credit card, see Robert Manning, *Credit Card Nation: The Consequences of America's Addiction to Credit* (New York, 2000) and Lewis Mandell, *The Credit Card Industry: A History* (Boston, MA, 1984).
28. See, for example, Teresa Sullivan, Elizabeth Warren, and Jay Westbrook, *The Fragile Middle Class: Americans in Debt* (New Haven, CT, 2000). From a historical perspective, the case for the disciplining force of installment debt has been made by Calder, *Financing the American Dream*, 297–99.
29. On the development of modern consumer credit scoring, see Martha Poon, "From New Deal Institutions to Capital Markets: Commercial Consumer Risk Scores and the Making of Sub-Prime Mortgage Finance," *Accounting,*

Organizations and Society 34 (2009): 654–74, as well as Josh Lauer, "From Rumor to Written Record: Credit Reporting and the Invention of Financial Identity in Nineteenth-Century America," *Technology and Culture* 49 (2008): 301–24.

30. For a thoughtful sketch of the historiographical debate over the role of consumer agency in consumption, see David Steigerwald, "All Hail the Republic of Choice: Consumer History as Contemporary Thought," *Journal of American History* 93 (2006): 385–403.

31. The most important recent contribution to this debate has perhaps been de Grazia, *Irresistible Empire*. See also Harm Schröter, *Americanization of the European Economy: A Compact Survey of American Economic Influence in Europe since the 1880s* (Boston, MA, 2005) and Dominique Barjot, *Catching Up with America: Productivity Missions and the Diffusion of American Economic and Technological Influence after the Second World War* (Paris, 2002). For the realm of mass culture, see Robert Rydell and Rob Kroes, *Buffalo Bill in Bologna: The Americanization of the World, 1869–1922* (Chicago, IL, 2005).

32. On credit and Americanization in the German case, see Michael Wildt, "Amerika auf Raten: Konsum und Teilzahlungskredit im Westdeutschland der fünfziger Jahre," in *Westbindungen: Amerika in der Bundesrepublik,* ed. Heinz Bude and Bernd Greiner (Hamburg, 1999), 202–30, and Jan Logemann, "Americanization through Credit? Consumer Credit in Germany, 1860s–1960s," *Business History Review* 85 (2011): 529–50.

33. On transfers within Asia and between Europe and Asia of policies regarding household spending, see, for example, Sheldon Garon, "The Transnational Promotion of Saving in Asia: 'Asian Values' or the 'Japanese Model'?" in *The Ambivalent Consumer,* ed. Garon and Maclachlan, 163–87.

34. On this point, see Jan Logemann and Uwe Spiekermann, "The Myth of a Bygone Cash Economy: Consumer Lending in Germany from the Nineteenth Century to the Mid-Twentieth Century," *Enterprise et histoire* 59 (2010): 12–27.

35. On the shift from face-to-face to institutional credit and the "banking" of consumers, see, for example, Gilles Laferté, "Formalization of the Economy: From Face-to-Face Credit to Automated Consumer Credit," paper presented at the annual meeting of the American Sociological Association, Boston, MA, July 31, 2008. For a long-term perspective on the development of consumer credit, see Rosa-Maria Gelpi and Francois Julien-Labruyère, *The History of Consumer Credit: Doctrines and Practices* (London, 2000).

36. On the history of early twentieth-century pawnshops, credit unions, and efforts to regulate the small loans market, see, for example, Bruce G. Carruthers, Tim Guinanne, and Yoonseok Lee, "Bringing 'Honest Capital' to Poor Borrowers: The Passage of the Uniform Small Loan Law, 1906–1930," *Journal of Interdisciplinary History* 42, no. 3 (2012): 393–418.

37. A recent exception is Wendy Woloson's rich history of the American pawn shop, *In Hock: Pawning in America from Independence through the Great Depression* (Chicago, IL, 2009).

38. See, for example, Carl Dauten, *Financing the American Consumer* (St. Louis, MO, 1956).
39. Louis Hyman, "Retail Financing and the Origin of the Post-Fordist Transition," paper presented at the annual meeting of the American Historical Association, New York, January 5, 2009.
40. See the conference report by Jan Logemann, "Cultures of Credit: Consumer Lending and Borrowing in Modern Economies," *Bulletin of the German Historical Institute* 47 (Fall 2010): 102–6.

PART I

Lenders and Lending Practices

CHAPTER 1

Selling Televisions on Credit: The Rise of Consumer Loans in Postwar France

Isabelle Gaillard

In 1957, Henry Davezac, president of the French electrical manufacturing labor union, commented on the sizable role that consumer credit should play in the market for television sets in France: "We have to take all measures suitable for expanding the market. Making it easier for customers to get credit constitutes the most effective of these . . . It represents not only additional sales that would not otherwise be made, but also an essential stimulant to commercial activity, because it brings about an important growth in cash sales."[1] Davezac defended consumer credit against its critics as a major way to increase the sales of new television sets and help the whole electronics industry grow. But rhetoric and reality are not always identical. What role did consumer credit really play in the market for television sets in postwar France?

After World War II, the implementation of a consumer credit system benefited from the dual context of modernization of banking techniques and the emergence of new and simpler forms of credit, mainly inspired by the United States. A modern and efficient installment system emerged based on credit organizations that were frequently connected to manufacturers and that specialized in financing household appliances, among which the television was an especially profitable item. Installment purchases partly explained the massive growth of credit-financed television sales during the period. Credit helped to widen the clientele base for television sets, much to the pleasure of industry leaders, who saw credit as a powerful support for their market and industry, because it greatly accelerated the expansion of mass production.

Still, only families in middle-income groups could gain access to consumer credit and become television owners during the immediate postwar decades. Indeed, consumer credit in postwar France faced many challenges, particularly in contrast to other European and North American countries. Born of a desire to protect the borrower and the economy, a rather tight credit policy—which Sabine Effosse discusses in chapter 9—worked to limit this expansion, particularly for television sets. Loan companies selected their customers and retailers in a rigorous fashion. At the same time, credit proponents had to overcome some cultural resistance to consumer credit.

Creating Credit

The birth and the development of Cetelem, a private consumer credit company (initially called Crédit à l'équipement électroménager) that specialized in household appliances, exemplified the postwar growth of modern installment systems. Cetelem's success underlined the new importance attributed to consumer credit for durable goods by organizations anxious to find a profitable niche and operating with close ties to the manufacturing sector. But such financing schemes did not come out of nowhere.

The Emergence of Modern Institutional Structures for Consumer Credit

Installment payment plans dated as far back as the Neolithic period, according to Rosa-Maria Gelpi and François-Julien Labruyère.[2] Not until the nineteenth century, however, was a "modern" credit system introduced in France. It arose with the growth of department stores and was dedicated to the purchase of consumer durable goods. In 1865, a furniture retailer, Jacques-François Crespin, promoted sales in his store "by subscription," and he convinced other retailers to adopt his system. A former partner of Crespin's, Georges Dufayel, developed the system further.[3] As Sean O'Connell describes, "it involved the purchase of vouchers, via installments collected by Dufayel's travelers. Vouchers were spent in the numerous stores that accepted them."[4] In 1913, some of Dufayel's former employees created La Semeuse, a sales financial company that was based on this credit system, as were the so-called economic unions.[5] This credit model was characterized by monthly payments, door-to-door sales, and consumer credit dedicated to household equipment.[6] During the interwar period, installment credit was increasingly associated with the purchase of new durable goods such as cars, household appliances, and radio receivers, whereby manufacturers' installment loan subsidiaries became much more involved in this business than retailers.[7]

Like so much else, consumer credit had to be rebuilt after World War II. As early as 1949–50, Philips, through its installment loan subsidiary Radiofiduciaire, advertised consumer credit while marketing television sets.[8] Still, one had to wait until 1954 for consumer credit for televisions to truly expand in France. Modernization of banking techniques and the development of monthly salary deposits helped sustain a modern institutional structure for consumer credit.[9] New methods simplified the process, and Cetelem helped pioneer their introduction.

These methods were mainly inspired by the United States.[10] From 1950 until the company's creation in 1953, Boris Mera, who was a close collaborator of Jacques de Fouchier (Cetelem's chair and chief executive officer), had been in the United States, from where he brought back new techniques of consumer credit such as notebooks with money orders. Whereas the old system of drafts put the initiative for covering debts on the lender, this new method transferred it to the borrower. Borrowers could now conveniently pay each monthly installment by check or money order. By shifting considerable postage costs to the customer, this method lowered the cost of payment collections for the company.[11]

Such methods did not always transfer across the Atlantic smoothly, however. Although the system worked in the United States, where customers routinely paid by check, it initially ran into problems in France, where only 6.5 percent of payments were drawn on a bank in 1958. Only in the 1960s did the number of personal bank accounts begin to expand in France.[12] In 1965, Cetelem decided to create what it termed "pocket credit." It, too, was inspired by the American experience with revolving credit. Pocket credit was essentially a credit card that allowed customers to have a certain sum at their disposal for purchases. The expenses of credit were then added to the remaining monthly balance. Yet such revolving credit represented only a small percentage of the total outstanding loans made by Cetelem to private individuals even as late as 1981.[13] Consumer credit in France remained predominantly installment credit. Still, such new methods—in the context of sustained economic growth during the postwar boom—helped credit sales grow by facilitating procedures and reducing costs.

Specialized Consumer Credit Companies Invest in the Market

Several companies that specialized in financing household appliances emerged in this context. As in Japan and the United States, consumer credit in France partially emerged from specialized lending institutions.[14] Imitating or diversifying the activities of sales financing companies born during the interwar period, manufacturers set up installment loan subsidiaries, in order to sell their products and develop their own markets. Indeed, as far as consumer credit for television sets was concerned, three main organizations dominated the market in France.

There were two television makers' credit companies, CREG (Crédit Electrique et Gazier) and Radiofiduciaire. Based on the model of sales financing companies for cars, they had already been founded during the interwar years.[15] CREG, from the French Thomson group, was founded in 1927, and Radiofiduciaire, an organization of the French subsidiary company of Philips, La Radiotechnique, was born in 1933. Both credit companies were created in connection with banks so as to finance the sales of radio receivers on credit. CREG's activities were stopped during World War II and only resumed in 1954.[16] Now the focus shifted to financing television sets, because radio receivers were no longer expensive and the market for them was increasingly saturated. Even if it was a subsidiary of Thomson, CREG was allowed to finance all manufacturers' brands that had a quality label. It shared 50 percent of television installment loan financing—risks and profits—with the Society for the Development of the Television (SODETE), which was registered as a financial institution by the Bank of France in 1954. Aside from Thomson, banks and insurance companies were among its main shareholders.[17]

Cetelem was also affiliated with SODETE, but unlike its competitors, it had originated more directly from banks.[18] Cetelem was a subsidiary company of the Compagnie Bancaire from Paribas, although electrical engineering firms also held a minority stake of about 35 percent in it.[19] The company's founder, Jacques de Fouchier, initially wanted to focus on household appliances. In a note to close coworkers in 1953, he wrote, "M. de Buron, Minister of Economic Affairs, asked me to prepare to extend our activities to television...I confirmed to him, however, that we do not intend to concern ourselves with financing televisions or radios in the beginning, only later."[20] Cetelem started with washing machines, but had to wait until early in 1954 for permission from public authorities to sell television sets on credit.[21] By 1958, the magazine *Consommation* indicated that the company was—after automobile lenders, whose market Cetelem entered the next year—"one of the leading private consumer credit companies in France."[22] This trend continued in the following decades; Cetelem financed between a quarter and a third of all consumer credit during the 1960s and 1970s. For radio and television financing, it held a market share between 30 and 40 percent.[23] Television sets were a large part of its success.

Televisions: Profitable Consumer Goods for Private Credit Companies

In 1953, it took about three months and eighteen days of average wages to buy a black-and-white television. By 1977, it took only eleven days for a black-and-white set, but still over a month for a color one.[24] Not surprisingly, then, television purchases became one of the major targets of Cetelem's installment system during the postwar boom. As big-ticket items that could potentially last for more than ten years, far longer than it took to pay them off, they represented a good investment in the eyes of consumers. At the same time, however, the characteristics of this technological durable good were always changing, so that the newest model was more expensive but also more attractive. This circumstance fostered the ongoing contradiction between the desires and the ability of consumers to pay that credit financing promised to resolve. As the "better argument against the [high] price," consumer credit offered a way to obtain faster access to goods. This was at least what Cetelem suggested to its retailers in 1975.[25] The company asked them to speak "about [the] monthly payment" *(mensualité)* instead of the "purchase price" *(prix d'achat)*. It invited them not to forget that "the term of a loan (up to twenty-one months) allows a customer to make a more important purchase painlessly. A color television doesn't cost more than six francs a day or two packs of cigarettes . . . The price of an ordinary black-and-white television largely corresponds to the down payment intended for the purchase of a color television."[26] Customers were not encouraged to evaluate the real cost of their acquisition. Instead, by comparing the initial cost of their color set on the installment system to the cash price for a black-and-white set, they felt that they were getting a good deal and could enjoy their purchase, which no longer seemed so dear.

But buying on credit was quite expensive for most households. In 1954, the price of a standard model television was about 90,000 francs. Paying for the same set over a period of fifteen months raised its price to 103,730 francs, which was 15 percent higher. Televisions purchased over an eighteen-month period cost 17.5 percent more than their original cash price.[27] In other words, consumers who had limited means to pay cash ended up spending 15 to 20 percent more to buy financed television sets that they could not really afford. According to a report of the Ministry of Industry, however, evaluating credit charges was not only a matter of monetary costs. Credit charges also accounted for the rendered service, which entailed more than a loan of money.[28] In addition, a 1974 market study from Cetelem found that inflation considerably reduced credit charges: "buying on credit is much cheaper than you think."[29] Yet the cost of such a financing service remained high. If a color television cost 4,500 francs, for example, 1,400 francs was paid in cash, and the monthly installments were about 185.40 francs for twenty-one months, which resulted in a total cost of 5,293.40 francs—about 17.6 percent more than the television's original price. That did not look bad against an annual increase in general prices of 11.1 percent between 1974 and 1980; however, between 1967 and 1985, the retail prices of color televisions rose by only 1.2 percent annually on average, which was far less than the general rate of inflation.[30] Seen in this light, the finance charges appear to have been rather high, especially considering that the television set was a technological good whose technical characteristics might change within six months.[31] Still, as Gunnar Trumbull suggests in chapter 7, consumer borrowers in France were "highly insensitive to price" and, in particular, to the importance of interest rates, even when inflation declined. Thus, installment plans for televisions remained a big part of the companies' turnovers.

From 1954 to 1961, televisions accounted for some 20 percent of Cetelem's business. This figure increased to about 25 percent by the middle of the 1960s—even though the company also began financing cars in 1959—and peaked at 36 percent in 1966,[32] before slowly declining to 12 percent in 1983.[33] Even if its competitors, Radiofiduciaire and CREG, were created by their parent corporations more as means than ends, television sales still accounted for 35 to 50 percent of their turnovers at the end of the 1960s.[34] Indeed, by considering the massive growth of credit sales in the television set market, we can understand why manufacturers chose to develop their own credit companies in the first place.

A Piece of the Marketing Puzzle

As a way to increase television sales, consumer credit became an impor-tant piece of the marketing puzzle, even though it expanded in France on a much smaller scale than in most other Western countries. On the other hand, because customers came predominantly from middle-income families, consumer credit remained quite limited in scope.

Massive Growth of Television Sales on Credit

Consumer credit for televisions expanded rapidly in the postwar boom years and thereby helped to promote demand in the television market. The figures of the market leader Cetelem were revealing. The company started to grant consumer credit for televisions in December 1953 and financed the sale of 2,569 in 1954.[35] By comparison, it financed the sale of 115,600 in 1971, a fortyfold increase in fewer than twenty years.[36] Between 1953 and 1983, about 3,308,000 borrowers bought televisions on credit through Cetelem.[37]

According to *Entreprise* magazine, about 50 percent of all radios and televisions sold in 1954 were financed by consumer credit.[38] Similarly, *Consommation* magazine found that credit financed 50 percent of the televisions and 25 percent of the radios purchased at the end of the decade.[39] Furthermore, although these devices represented only 5 percent of total household expenditures in 1958, for example, they represented 9 percent of the consumer loans for durable goods.[40] As the television market grew, this last figure reached some 30 to 40 percent in the 1960s.[41] The demand for credit-financed televisions continued in the 1970s, and about 30 percent of color television sales were credit sales at the end of that decade.[42] By this time, color receivers had partly replaced black-and-white sets in French households, but they were still three times more expensive.

Representing a quarter to a half of the sales of television sets over the period, consumer credit played a major role. Indeed, as early as the 1950s, a report dedicated to consumer credit by the Ministry of Industry commented on the relationship between consumer credit and economies of scale: "we admit generally that credit sales contribute to an increase in purchasing power by expanding production series and by [consequently] lowering prices."[43] A survey by Cetelem in 1962 tried to evaluate how many new customers consumer credit actually brought to television manufacturers. According to this study, it was possible, thanks to credit purchases, to obtain a fivefold increase in purchasers. Only 11 percent of customers had been able to pay cash for their sets, which cost between 130,000 and 140,000 old francs on average. This price required a monthly investment over eighteen months of 7,500 francs, which could be saved by only 55 percent of the population at the time.[44] On the other hand, the availability of credit alone did not drive the sale of televisions. As the Ministry of Industry observed in the above-quoted report, consumer credit "can help in the development of the sales of a given product only insofar as this product is in demand by the consumer."[45] Consumer credit could help the product to diffuse more rapidly only if it was selling anyway. But who bought a television set on credit?

Limited Expansion among Households

The social groups that used credit—especially the working classes—were also the ones that saw their durable equipment expand most quickly. However, installment credit was confined to specific social milieus. The greatest opportunity for expanding its use lay in the middle-income ranges, especially among the better-off working-class and white-collar families. According to a 1961 survey,[46] white-collar employees represented 11 percent of television purchases. And among these, 31.4 percent were on credit. For blue-collar workers, the figures in the same survey reached 28 and 39.3 percent, respectively. Working-class consumers appear to have preferred televisions to washing machines and refrigerators, and they were the best customers for credit companies as far as televisions were concerned. Farmers, by contrast, did not purchase more than 3 percent of the television sets, and only 1.5 percent of those were bought on credit. The liberal professions also used less credit. They represented 12 percent of the total of television set purchases, but only 4 percent of credit purchases. Taking marital status into account, the survey indicated that mid-range families with one or two children were the most strongly represented group among loans granted for televisions (43.6 percent).[47]

The majority of customers, thus, earned a salary or steady wages, and indeed it was easier for such people to obtain credit in the first place. The reasons behind this circumstance looked much the same as in other countries. Talking about the creation of consumer credit for household appliances in Japan during the 1950s, for example, Simon Partner affirms, "the finance companies would generally lend only to customers who had salaried employment, with the payments automatically deducted from the borrower's bank account."[48]

People using credit came mostly from average and well-to-do segments of the population. SODETE indicated in 1956 that the social categories interested in credit were the ones "whose family incomes vary between 50,000 and 150,000 francs a month: miners, skilled workers, middle managers."[49] By comparison, the average monthly income in 1956 was 40,000 francs.[50] This profile of consumer credit clients changed very little over the next three decades. Sandrine Bertaux draws up the model portrait of the Cetelem customer: a male employee earning 7,000 francs or more a month and rather young (between twenty and thirty years old), younger, according to her, than at the end of the 1950s, when the price of a color television set was about 4,500 francs.[51] If consumer credit was a way to democratize the television set market, then it did so only on a quite limited scale. Furthermore, as extraordinary as the growth of credit purchases for televisions was, only 35 percent of electronic goods (including television sets) and major appliances in France were bought on credit in 1962, when the market was booming. By contrast, this figure reached 55 percent in West Germany, 60 percent in Great Britain, and even 70 percent in the United States and Canada in the same year.[52]

Highly Regulated and Feared Consumer Credit

Did distrust of consumer credit lay behind its limited expansion in France? In short, yes. Concerned especially about increasing inflation and also worried about poverty and financial destitution, the attitudes of public authorities, credit companies, and consumers toward consumer credit were marked by skepticism and reluctance.

Restrictive Credit Policies

Highlighting the major role that he believed consumer credit had to play, Henry Davezac, the representative of the set makers' trade union, complained about credit rationing, which, according to him, "dissuades the customer from entering a retail outlet."[53] As Sabine Effosse shows, the legitimacy of consumer credit was highly debated in postwar France. If, since 1953, the French government intended to boost the economy by encouraging consumer credit while simultaneously fighting black-market credit, French monetary authorities were slow to subscribe to this policy—in particular because of concerns about inflation risks.[54] Gunnar Trumbull notes that policy makers on the labor left and Catholic right alike considered consumer credit—and the growing household indebtedness resulting from it—a threat to social solidarity.[55] Yet, at the end of the 1950s, household indebtedness represented 12 percent of consumer spending in the United States, 6 percent in Great Britain, 2.5 percent in West Germany, and only 1.2 percent in France.[56] From 1959 to 1978, according to the French statistical institute INSEE, a related economic indicator, the level of personal savings, had even increased from 15 to 20 percent of available income.[57]

A rather tight credit policy resulted from such doubts about consumer credit. Created in 1945, the National Council of Credit was responsible for regulating credit sales and devised many restrictive rules concerning the maximum length and minimum down payment for consumer loans, the ratio of capital stock to incurred credit on company balance sheets, the number of loan companies in the market, and their licensing.[58] These restrictions heavily affected television. Initially, credit sales were limited to "useful durable goods."[59] According to an internal Cetelem document from February 25, 1953, public authorities advised the company not to immediately declare its intention to offer loans for radios and televisions,[60] because these were not considered "useful" possessions.

Indeed, not until 1954 was consumer credit authorized for television sets.[61] And from 1950 to 1984, despite some easing of credit restrictions, other limits remained in place. During the 1950s, especially from 1957 to 1959 (times of a short recession, the war in Algeria, and subsequently high growth in France), the term of a consumer loan was limited to twelve months, and a 35 percent down payment had to be made. According to a 1958 piece in *Consommation* magazine, such restrictions had an impact on more than the television set market: "Other statutory measures intervened in 1957 (especially the striking increase of the VAT on certain consumer goods) and certainly provoked a reaction in the behavior of the consumers; it is difficult to measure the real effect of the restrictive credit measures, [but] it is very clear that the credit purchases of domestic appliances, furniture, and diverse other goods (clothing in particular) underwent a sensitive regression as a whole . . ."[62]

There was an ease of this restriction in May 1959. During the following two decades, the lengths of loans varied from fifteen to twenty-one months (at the end of the 1960s), whereas down payments averaged between 20 and 25 percent of the purchase price. To put these conditions in perspective, in 1960 a French consumer needed to pay 25 percent of a television's purchase price down and had 18 installments to make, whereas a British consumer paid only 5 percent down for the same item with a twenty-four-month loan, a German consumer paid 10 percent down for the same twenty-four-month period, and an Italian consumer paid about 5 percent down for a consumer loan with a thirty-six-month term.[63] In 1968, a household was not supposed to have monthly repayments that exceeded 15 to 25 percent of its income, which was far from today's limit of one-third.[64] In April 1979, obligatory cash down payments were eliminated, but not until 1984 were credit restrictions totally abolished.[65] Whether a cause or a consequence of this policy, the overall volume of credit sales remained extremely low. Even if there was an increasing liberalization in French economic policy, it did not affect credit regulations.

Claire Andrieu wonders if the time and energy expended on regulating consumer credit bore any relationship to its importance in the economy as a whole and concludes, "It does not seem so because, between 1958 and 1971, the volume of credit sales represent[ed] only 2 to 3 percent of all bank loans."[66] In 1983, consumer credit still represented less than 3 percent of all loans and only 3 percent of the disposable income of French households.[67] This low figure was not alone a consequence of state credit policies, however. At the same time that consumer credit was highly regulated by public authorities, private consumer credit companies used rigorous criteria to select the retailers and consumers that they worked with.

Rigorous Selection of Retailers and Customers

It might sound surprising, but consumer credit companies rarely complained about restrictive public credit policies. In 1961, they even agreed with public restrictions and complained about English abuses in credit. According to them, English consumer lending was absolutely out of control in 1958, which led "to absurd competition and price drops." They believed that such circumstances could not occur in France, where the number of credit institutions in television was practically limited to three big companies—CREG, Radiofiduciaire, and Cetelem—that did not aggressively compete with each other. Moreover, "the industrialists accumulate their stocks at levels such as the development of credit transactions and resumption of their business can come only from the digestion of the previous operations by buyers whose resources are blocked today."[68] Liberalizing consumer credit would thus damage manufacturers, so that the conclusion was clear: "18 months for a television is good."[69]

Despite Cetelem's leading position in the consumer credit market in France, it did not succeed in significantly expanding the number of retailers eligible to use its services. The requirements it set were stringent. The report of a visit to a retailer for Sonora televisions in late 1953 illustrates Cetelem's strict selection process. Having chosen to approve the establishment in question at the request of the manufacturer, the inspector in charge of the visit declared, "We would not know how to please 1500 Sonora retailers," however, insofar as "this figure seems to him exaggerated, if we take into account that there were [only] 240 receivers sold in the month." Even if, according to Sonora, retailers of its products were numerous, they could only obtain Cetelem's approval if their sales were strong.[70]

Indeed, according to a study undertaken for Cetelem, "the quality of the loan, according to the American experience, depends on the quality of the salesman."[71] Jean Acquier's article on consumer credit also insists on the rigor of Cetelem in this respect. The finance company avoided "the dynamic, but unserious salesmen and the very serious, but undynamic storekeepers." Cetelem retailers were supposed to sell only "quality devices," and they had to have good after-sales service.[72] On top of an "initial sorting, which [led] to the retention of fewer than 40% of the candidate storekeepers, Cetelem followed their activity individually and in particular the delays, the disputes, or the outstanding payments financed for each of them."[73] Cetelem shared some financial responsibilities with the distributor: "so that the retailer is interested in sharing reliable customers with us, it always carries a part of the risk. This . . . is limited in principle to 20% of the cash price of the device in our company."[74] Cetelem also set a ceiling for the outstanding discounted bills of every retailer proportional to its turnover. In return, it "support[ed] its retailers with important advertising and help[ed] them with good statistical information on the market and its development."[75]

Like with its retailers, Cetelem selected its customers in a rigorous way. It sought information on their social status and income, as well as on the guarantees they could offer. The company compiled statistical surveys of their past customer records to help decide which loans would make good business sense. And it was able to base credit decisions for former customers on their old records, if they applied for another loan; such repeat customers accounted for 30 percent of the credit applications that Cetelem received.[76] French companies had to develop their own internal consumer credit reporting systems, because there was no private "national" consumer credit reporting agency like Schufa in West Germany, whereby this circumstance seemed to limit their knowledge about new borrowers.[77]

Yet the limitations caused both by restrictive state credit policies and the conservative lending practices of credit companies might not be the only elements that explain the relatively limited use of consumer credit in France. The nature of the debate that still accompanied the use of consumer credit seemed to suggest that there was also broad opposition to it among the French population more generally.

Resistance to Consumer Credit?

The ways in which credit companies like Cetelem and Radiofiduciaire tried to convince people to use consumer credit indicates that, at least until the end of the 1960s, there was still much to do to convince consumers. In 1953, Cetelem intended "to decrease the prejudices of the buyers" by means of an "educational and propaganda campaign," that is, advertising.[78] According to the company, credit purchases, as seen by the French people, were doubly open to criticism: the goods purchased were inessentials, and consumers squandered money on them that they did not even have.[79] In 1955, the Philips magazine *Phil à Phil* dedicated an article to the company's credit subsidiary, Radiofiduciaire. This article talked about consumers in a way reminiscent of speeches in interwar France on how the working class spent its free time: the miner who bought a television set "instead of spending his leisure activities in the tavern . . . stays at home and we can say that, around the TV set, family life is reborn and organized."[80] It appeared that consumer credit was still morally suspect in France after 1945. Manufacturers knew how they could counter such attitudes. So did the credit companies.

In the 1960s, Cetelem insisted on the salutary character of credit, which would teach people how to save. The company did not hesitate to play on the long-lasting character of credit purchases by encouraging its salespeople to speak not about price but rather "investment" *(placement)*,[81] a term that clearly aimed at reassuring potential customers by presenting credit as something productive. This tactic revealed still powerful hesitations and prejudices in a France that was saving less but that still distrusted debt. *Entreprise* magazine also advocated consumer credit. While assuring readers that using credit was a way to promote economic growth, the article regretted "the hostility of official circles and the distrust of the private individuals," and it carefully noted that credit was not "an inflationary stimulant." Even if this piece was aimed first and foremost at public authorities, it also addressed "consumers" and "private individuals" seen as unwilling to buy on credit.[82]

In fact, however, there appears to have been a gap between stated attitudes and actual practices.[83] This was particularly the case for the main users of consumer credit, the working classes. From the beginning of the 1950s, sociologist Paul Henry Chombart de Lauwe indicated that if 39 percent of the workers of his sample of 132 working-class households bought on credit, the credit purchase was nonetheless seen in a negative light by many households.[84] And if unskilled workers were just a little less likely (33 percent) to use installment credit and vouchers than qualified (40 percent) and highly qualified workers (45 percent), unskilled workers were generally the least willing to buy on credit.[85]

Sociologist Gérard Noiriel also observes this difference for 1969. The group of 35-to-49-year-old workers, who were firmly rooted in the company, closely linked to its factory and its region, and highly skilled, displayed "the clearest reservations towards the use of credit."[86] Noiriel underlines, however, the important role played by complexes in the distribution of credit—as well as the diffusion of new standards of consumption. Speaking about subsidized housing, he writes,

> HLM buildings are conceived for standards of consumption quite other than those of the previous popular district. In a survey of inhabitants of a housing complex of the Parisian suburb, 60 percent of the households considered that their furniture was insufficient and 44 percent had to take out a loan, just after their moving in, to equip themselves. Very quickly, the change of housing entails a restructuring of the budget—with an increase of spending on rent, transportation, and loan payments.[87]

In his study of the working classes in northern France in the mid-1970s, sociologist Olivier Schwartz shows that there was still resistance to credit. Most of the people he studied preferred saving up for a television set over using credit to buy one. Even if their financial circumstances were precarious, some people preferred to save up for certain things rather than even consider using credit. This was the case with Jean-Louis and Gilberte, a couple with four children whose main income consisted of welfare payments. They paid 8,000 francs cash for their color television and the piece of furniture that housed it "with the sum received upon the birth of the fourth child." Schwartz takes care, however, to underscore the privileged status of the television, "the total object, the fetishistic object in the universe of Jean-Louis," purchased at a time when such an acquisition went against the couple's principles of economy.[88] Yet they did not try to acquire this object faster by credit—had they even been able to. Reporting on her purchases during a temporary job, Martine Trouvé, a wife with three children, displayed a similar attitude: "My color television, I bought it when I was working at the hospital . . . I always bought just a little of what I wanted. Everything is paid for in cash, nothing on credit, because when I work, I easily earn 400,000 francs a month."[89] Such a comment suggests that credit was used only in the last resort.

Paradoxically, however, even among those who were most averse to credit—farmers—a change took place after the beginning of the 1960s. In a rural area like Plodémet in the Bretagne, according to sociologist Edgar Morin in 1967, "the traditional psychology that had condemned credit purchases doubly because of the immorality (living above one's means) and the dishonor (because it signifies indebtedness, that is, alienation) . . . has not yet disappeared."[90] Nonetheless, Morin observed, "some already use shameful credit: they go to Quimper to post their money order so that nobody knows anything about it in Plodémet." Lawrence Wylie, an American sociologist studying Roussillon, a small village in the Vaucluse, observed in 1951 that numerous villagers were hostile to credit and that nobody knew television. When he returned to Roussillon in 1961, however, most of the villagers had bought their televisions on credit.[91]

There was thus indeed a kind of paradox of consumer credit in France during the postwar period: even if they availed themselves of it, the French appear to have been critical of installment lending, and credit still continued to be discredited and hidden, even by its main users. The postwar culture of credit in France was thus still very different from, for example, the consumerist cultural logic that Silke Meyer describes for Germany after the 1970s.[92]

* * *

As constraining as consumer credit terms in France were, credit purchases of televisions expanded and contributed to a dramatic change in consumer spending. During the period under consideration, 30 to 40 percent of television sets were bought on credit. Installment credit certainly made it possible for workmen and employees to obtain one—and to do so sooner. The television set was one of only a few durable goods that spread relatively quickly and evenly across all social classes. In 1970, workmen were even better equipped with televisions than senior executives.[93]

But as a representative of the French Ministry of Industry had already observed in the mid-1950s, credit purchases could help developing sales only if the "product [was] in demand by the consumer."[94] According to this official, some people had tried to ease credit restrictions in scooters to start the market again, but this attempt failed. It was not solely credit that made consumers buy one item or another. Credit only made it easier to get what one wanted and to get it sooner. Instead of saving for years, credit enabled people to afford major purchases and enjoy the goods while they paid for them. The French credit system encouraged this development.

The growing use of consumer credit suggests perhaps a revolution in French mentalities, even if credit was still considered suspect at the beginning of the 1950s. This was illustrated in any case by credit practices, which, in spite of the speeches with a still negative outlook on credit, were more limited by the restrictive policies that public authorities pursued than by the borrowers' attitudes.

Notes

1. Henry Davezac, "Note sur les effets des mesures restrictives en matière de vente à crédit des appareils récepteurs de télévision," March 14, 1957, Archives Cetelem, 8-4-22.
2. Rosa-Maria Gelpi and François Julien-Labruyère, *Histoire du crédit à la consommation: doctrines et pratiques* (Paris, 1994), 23.
3. Ibid., 183.
4. Sean O'Connell, "Speculations on working class debt: Credit and paternalism in France, Germany and the UK," *Entreprises et histoire*, no. 59 (June 2010): 82.
5. Ibid.
6. Gelpi and Julien-Labruyère, *Histoire du crédit*, 184.
7. Hubert Balaguy, *Le crédit à la consommation en France* (Paris, 1996), 18.
8. "Une grande propagande 'Télévision,'" *Electro-Magazine*, no. 12 (September–October 1951): 10.
9. Balaguy, *Le crédit*, 19–20.
10. Information flowed in the opposite direction at the beginning of the century; see chapter 7 in this volume by Gunnar Trumbull.
11. Sandrine Bertaux, "Le crédit à la consommation à travers l'histoire d'un établissement financier, le CETELEM, 1953–1984" (MA thesis, Paris Diderot University, 1990), 27–33.
12. Ibid., 33.
13. It was 3% of Cetelem's turnover in 1966 and 19% in 1970; see Bertaux, "Le crédit à la consommation," 40. See also Balaguy, *Le crédit*, 43.
14. Simon Partner, *Assembled in Japan: Electrical Goods and the Making of the Japanese Consumer* (Berkeley, CA, 1999).
15. As early as 1924, Renault created the Diffusion Industrielle et Automobile pour le Crédit (DIAC) to offer consumer credit for cars; see Balaguy, *Le crédit*, 48.
16. Bertaux, "Le crédit à la consommation," 31.
17. "Rapport annuel de la SODETE," 1962, Archives Cetelem, 21-2-7.

18. "Projet de protocole d'accord entre la Société pour le Développement de la télévision et le CETELEM," 1953, Archives Cetelem, unclassified.

19. Bertaux, "Le crédit à la consommation," 4.

20. "Note de Jacques de Fouchier pour Messieurs Mathely et Mera," February 25, 1953, Archives Cetelem.

21. Ibid.

22. Jean Acquier, "Le crédit à la consommation dans les budgets familiaux," *Consommation* (October-December 1958): 7.

23. Commission de contrôle des banques, *Financement des ventes à crédit par les établissements financiers et les banques,* Archives Cetelem, 29-5-1; "Part du crédit dans le financement des téléviseurs," Position CETELEM, 1970–1975, Archives Cetelem, 29-5-1; "L'évolution des parts de marché du CETELEM," October 23, 1981, Archives Cetelem.

24. Figures from Olivier Marchand and Claude Thélot, *Le travail en France, 1800–2000* (Paris, 1997), 241; Jean Fourastié, *Prix de vente et prix de revient, Recherche sur l'évolution des prix en période de progrès technique,* 11th series (Paris, 1961), 198; France Philips archives, unclassified.

25. Marketing Cetelem, "Votre dossier brun pour 1975," p. 26, Archives Cetelem, 29-4-8.

26. Ibid.

27. "Barème financier télévision," October 1954, Archives Cetelem, unclassified.

28. "Enquête sur le crédit à la consommation," [late 1950s], p. 12, Archives du Ministère de l'Industrie, versement 19771521, article 126.

29. Cetelem, "Votre dossier brun pour 1975," Archives Cetelem, 29-4-8.

30. Retail prices exclusive of tax; statistics from Philips.

31. Catherine Gilles and Françoise Fauvin, "Du blocage des prix vers la déréglementation, 50 ans de prix à la consommation," *INSEE Première,* no. 483 (September 1996): 2.

32. "Document Cetelem," September 10, 1966, Archives Cetelem, 8-4-22.

33. Bertaux, "Le crédit à la consommation," 41.

34. "Dossier TV 1971," Archives Cetelem, 29-4-10.

35. "Evolution de l'activité CETELEM de 1954 à 1958," Archives Cetelem, 8-3-15.

36. "Dossier TV 1971," Archives Cetelem, 29-4-10.

37. Philippe Clément, "Temps, argent . . . et protection," in Philippe Heymann, ed., *De la 4CV à la vidéo, 1953–1983: ces trente années qui ont changé notre vie,* ed. Philippe Heymann (Paris, 1983), 151.

38. "La construction électrique: les raisons d'un mouvement ascensionnel," *Entreprise,* no. 40 (November 15, 1954): 26.

39. Michel Guillot, "Le crédit à la consommation dans les budgets familiaux," *Consommation,* no. 2 (1958): 50.

40. Ibid.

41. "La part du crédit dans le financement des téléviseurs," Archives Cetelem, 29-5-1.

42. Service des études et planifications, "Le crédit à l'équipement des particuliers," p. 12, Archives Cetelem, 27-3-13.
43. "Enquête sur le crédit à la consommation," p. 9, Archives du Ministère de l'Industrie, versement 19771521, article 126.
44. "Le marché du crédit," November 1962, p. 5, Archives Cetelem, 27-3-7.
45. "Enquête sur le crédit à la consommation," p. 9, Archives du Ministère de l'Industrie, versement 19771521, article 126.
46. "Evolution de l'activité CETELEM," February 1962, Archives Cetelem, 47-3-2.
47. Ibid.
48. Partner, *Assembled in Japan,* 169.
49. "Rapport annuel de la SODETE," 1956, Archives de PARIBAS, FIN 0752.
50. Christian Baudelot et al., "Les salaires de 1950 à 1975," *Economie et statistique,* no. 113 (July-August 1979): 16.
51. Bertaux, "Le crédit à la consommation," 61–62.
52. "Le marché du crédit," November 1962, p. 5, Archives Cetelem, 27-3-7.
53. Davezac, "Note sur les effets des mesures restrictives en matière de vente à crédit des appareils récepteurs de television."
54. See chapter 8 in this volume.
55. See chapter 7 in this volume.
56. "Enquête sur le crédit à la consommation," p. 3, Archives du Ministère de l'Industrie, versement 19771521, article 126.
57. Figures from Institut National de la statistique et des études économiques, *Annuaire statistique de la France* (Paris, 1960–79).
58. On this subject, see chapter 8 by Sabine Effosse.
59. Bertaux, "Le crédit à la consommation," 17.
60. Archives Cetelem, 8-4-22.
61. "Note relative aux modalités d'intervention du CETELEM," March 30, 1954, and "Note sur les conditions de crédit," April 5, 1954, Archives Cetelem, 27-2-1.
62. Acquier, "Le crédit à la consommation," 28.
63. Commission permanente de l'électronique, Commissariat général du Plan d'équipement et de la productivité, *Situation de l'électronique en France* (Paris, 1962), 21.
64. *Guide de l'acheteur à crédit,* 1968, Archives Cetelem, 47-3-2.
65. Balaguy, *Le crédit,* 103.
66. Claire Andrieu, "A la recherche de la politique du crédit, 1946–1973," *Revue historique* 271, no. 2 (1984): 391.
67. "Avis adopté au Conseil économique et social sur le crédit à la consommation," February 1983. Archives Cetelem, 27-3-3.
68. See Jean Pierre Krafft, Economic and Social Council, 1961, Archives Cetelem, 27-3-7.
69. Ibid.
70. *Compte-rendu de la visite de M. Ibar, représentant la maison Sonora,* December 15, 1953. Archives Cetelem, unclassified.

71. Bertaux, "Le crédit à la consommation," 32.
72. Acquier, "Le crédit à la consommation dans les budgets familiaux," 34.
73. Ibid.
74. Krafft, Economic and Social Council, 1961, Archives Cetelem, 27-3-7.
75. Acquier, "Le crédit à la consommation dans les budgets familiaux," 34. Cetelem likewise tried to collaborate with manufacturers. From 1953, they wanted to obtain "in precise cases" a contribution to advertising costs and "to assure good personal contacts with the main manufacturers"; see "Testament CETELEM," November 30, 1953, Archives Cetelem, unclassified. When the company tried to establish hire purchase by following the English example, they also looked for manufacturers to collaborate with; see "Réunion du mardi 8 janvier concernant la CLEF," Archives Cetelem, unclassified.
76. Ibid.
77. On Schufa, see chapter 6 by Larry Frohman in this volume.
78. "Testament CETELEM," November 30, 1953, Archives Cetelem, unclassified.
79. Bertaux, "Le crédit à la consommation," 44.
80. See "Monsieur Frontard nous ouvre les portes de Radio Fiduciaire," *Phil à Phil* (June–July 1955): 4.
81. "Le marché du crédit," November 1962, p. 3, Archives Cetelem, 27-3-7.
82. "Pour accroître l'expansion, la France doit user plus largement des achats à crédit," *Entreprise,* no. 233 (February 20, 1960): 54–57.
83. Sabine Effosse also observes this phenomenon in chapter 8 of this volume.
84. Paul Henry Chombart de Lauwe, *La vie quotidienne des familles ouvrières* (1956; Paris, 1977), 95.
85. Ibid.
86. Gérard Noiriel, *Les ouvriers dans la société française, XIXe-XXe siècle* (Paris, 1986), 209.
87. Ibid., 224.
88. Olivier Schwartz, *Le monde privé des ouvriers: hommes et femmes du Nord* (Paris, 1990), 114.
89. Ibid., 118.
90. See Edgar Morin, *La métamorphose de Plozévet: commune en France* (Paris, 1967), 96.
91. Laurence Wylie, *Village in the Vaucluse,* 3rd ed. (Cambridge, MA, 1974), 347.
92. See chapter 10 in this volume.
93. Figures from Institut National de la statistique et des études économiques, *Annuaire statistique de la France* (Paris, 1971).
94. "Enquête sur le crédit à la consommation," p. 9, Archives du Ministère de l'Industrie, versement 19771521, article 126.

CHAPTER 2

Moral or Modern Marketing? *Sparkassen* and Consumer Credit in West Germany*

Rebecca Belvederesi-Kochs

The Sparkassen-Finanzgruppe is the biggest consumer financial services provider in Germany today. Its workforce numbers more than 250,000 employees. In 2009, the 431 savings banks or *Sparkassen* (singular: *Sparkasse*) that comprise this financial group offered an extensive branch network with more than 14,000 district offices. During fiscal year 2009, they dealt in consumer loans amounting to €59.5 billion.[1] Their consumer credit business is highly developed. Compared to the overall volume of retail credit offered by all other financial groups in Germany, the involvement of the Sparkassen is much higher in this business line. In 2009, for example, the powerful Deutsche Bank only granted consumer loans totaling €13.6 billion.[2]

These figures suggest that consumer loans comprise an essential part of day-to-day Sparkasse business, but this situation is not a matter of course. In historical perspective, the current practices of the Sparkassen in the consumer credit business are surprising, as are their attendant marketing efforts, because the attitude of these savings banks toward consumer credit was still ambivalent, in many ways even negative, in the middle of the twentieth century. Sparkassen and especially their umbrella association, the German Savings and Giro Association (GSGA), focused much more on fostering savings. They justified this business strategy with their public mandate to promote savings, which derived from their social commitment as nonprofit institutions under public law.[3]

Due to this strategy, any active promotion of consumer loans long remained more of an exception that proved the rule. After World War II, retail banking was still strongly affected by managerial faith in the utility and necessity of thriftiness.[4] Thus, a specific set of beliefs dominated the savings banks' organizational culture at mid-century.[5] It was influenced by the original Sparkasse business model, rooted in the late eighteenth century, when the first savings bank on German territory was founded by the Hamburgische Patriotische Gesellschaft in 1778. The goal of this pioneering institution in the savings business was to educate low-income earners about thrift and show them the benefits of private savings. Self-help principles motivated the early founders to establish savings banks.[6] Sparkassen were supposed to strengthen the self-reliance of the "lower classes" and enable them to learn to organize their lives in a sustainable manner. Considering this approach, the accumulation of capital qua private savings seemed an apt instrument to encourage members of the working classes to integrate themselves into the emerging capitalist civil society. This intellectual concept was of eminent social importance at a time when public or corporate insurance companies did not yet exist.

The close connection between the Sparkassen and savings is indicated by the corporate name, which derives from the German word *sparen,* to save. Even though the focus was initially on personal savings, Sparkassen entered the personal loan market as early as the nineteenth century.[7] Many of their charters foresaw granting private loans to the poor, because that, too, was part of the charitable business conception. In case of genuine need, the poor should be able to borrow money without falling prey to usurers. The option to grant personal loans was a complementary strategy to prevent an excess of pauperism caused by private debt. However, the deposit business had a stronger influence on the institution's self-image, and thrift educational approaches became a long-lasting constant in the policy of Sparkassen, which was reflected in the joint advertising campaigns of the GSGA.

Considering the epoch-spanning predominance of a thrift mentality, this essay analyzes the external and intraorganizational reasons behind why the Sparkassen argued for a low-key consumer credit policy after World War II and how this policy affected their marketing guidelines. In order to understand the interplay of product and marketing strategies, the original corporate mission of the Sparkassen and their development under National Socialism will be briefly discussed. The latter needs to be emphasized, in particular, because it was formative for the early postwar period. After this excursion into the earlier history of the Sparkassen, three periods of their postwar consumer credit business and marketing efforts are presented in detail.

The first period started in 1948, when the Sparkassen began to offer personal loans again. A few years later, the "purchase loan" *(Kaufkredit)* was introduced. Even though this offer enlarged the existing range of these banks' financial services, it was not reflective of the still limited intraorganizational significance of consumer loans after the war, particularly inside the GSGA. Until the late 1950s, normative "basic assumptions," as Edward Schein calls them, still dominated organizational thought and practices, influencing decision making.[8] This circumstance was reflected in "moral" marketing strategies and advertising campaigns, which warned the public to economize and save. In this first phase, the promotion of consumer credit was a marginal phenomenon in Sparkasse marketing.

The internal relevance of this financial product would change during the late 1950s when competition from commercial retail banks rose. In consequence, people had easier access to credit in the second period. In 1961, the Sparkassen introduced the acquisition loan *(Anschaffungsdarlehen)* as the first flexible, cash-paid consumer loan in West Germany. Subsequently, marketing strategies and advertising campaigns began to downplay the distinction between the lending and deposit business of the savings banks. Nonetheless, their promotion of consumer credit remained small in comparison to their thrift advertising.

A real breakthrough came in the second half of the 1960s, caused largely by institutional and legal changes, as well as by personnel changes within the GSGA's management. By 1968, the consumer credit business attained a new level through the introduction of overdraft loans for checking accounts. By now, the Sparkassen had adopted "modern marketing management" and were promoting consumer loans as aggressively as other financial businesses.[9] Although the Sparkassen simplified access to credit during this third period, their portfolio of credit services also diversified because of growing customer demand.

The Initial Position after World War II

Three trends lay behind the difficult relationship between the Sparkassen and consumer credit. First, the original mandate of the Sparkassen caused intensive concentration on the savings business. The public interest was to be served by giving poorer people the opportunity to accumulate private capital with the aim of preventing pauperism and strengthening social freedom.[10] In the long run, the mission of thrift education was regarded as an appropriate instrument to influence people's ability and motivation to save. This educational approach was cultivated in private circles and societies where the savings idea predominantly matured.[11] Drawing on the philosophy of public utility, the initiators of Sparkassen viewed education as a central issue. Their underlying self-help concepts and self-made-man mentality stood in the context of an emerging civil society, creating a new system of "bourgeois" values in which thrift and moderation played an important role in order to improve the economic situation of the masses and protect personal vested rights.[12]

Thus, a self-image as a savings institution accompanied the Sparkassen since their early inception and made the deposit business historically a priority of their retail banking. Traditionally, their concept of social responsibility was interpreted as a duty to thrift education. The internal records, even into the postwar era, show that Sparkasse managers believed they had a mission to educate the population. In the 1950s, they declared it a self-imposed obligation to support and strengthen what they held up as a "German" savings culture.[13] The latter was closely linked to the commonsense conception of German cultural identity, in which secondary virtues like punctuality, thriftiness, orderliness, and steadiness played an important role.

A second historically relevant context was the Nazi era and its impact on the entire Sparkasse organization. At the peak of the Great Depression in Germany, during the summer of 1931, several banks collapsed and the functionality of the capital market was in danger. In order to stabilize the financial system, the state's involvement in the German credit sector grew, and major incorporated banks were partially socialized. Regulatory measures aimed to decrease the instability of the credit market. In the same year, the crises also affected the Sparkassen and their liquidity. Liquidity was at risk, because local authorities had direct access to the institutes, which by law had to provide them with credit. This dependency, however, put the efficiency and functionality of the German savings bank system to the test during the crisis. Consequently, the autonomy of the Sparkassen was expanded and the Weimar government put them under public law in November 1931.[14] After the Nazi seizure of power in 1933, however, the regulation of the German credit sector grew further and was reorganized to comport with the ideological aims of the Nazi regime.[15]

For the Sparkassen, this development meant organizational changes, as higher management positions were filled with sympathizers—or at least fellow travelers—of the Nazi regime. Due to this staffing policy, resistance to the regime's policies, especially in the umbrella association, remained quite low. The Sparkasse leadership also hoped that the Nazis and their centralized approach to economic policy could cope with the Great Depression.[16] In the end, voluntary subordination was the result of economic and social circumstances. During that era, the Sparkassen served "the Führer," meaning they promoted the virtue of thrift as a patriotic duty and contributed to nationalistic thrift propaganda.[17] To save now meant to serve the interests of the *Volk,* the racially defined national community. The original interpretation of a savings culture as the backbone of civil society vanished and, with it, its "bourgeois" connotations and individualistic implications. In 1933, Sparkassen created the advertising motto "first save—then buy," which was supposed to encourage people to be thrifty and motivate them to a moderate way of consumption.[18]

To professionalize Sparkasse marketing with the intention of fulfilling the regime's need for capital, an autonomous advertising division was created in 1935, the Deutscher Sparkassenverlag.[19] It was responsible for the joint advertising of the Sparkassen and introduced systematic methods, as well as efficient planning systems. Accordingly, deposit marketing was expanded once more, and the Sparkassenverlag was partially responsible for a savings boom, which began in 1936 as the German economy started to recover. Mirroring this concentration on the deposit business, lending for private needs was largely proscribed for Sparkassen. Although some specialized consumer lending institutions remained active, hoarding money and financing consumption through credit were widely regarded as patriotic treachery.[20] This mind-set partially outlived the Nazi period, even if the policy considerations behind them did not, and the Sparkassen stuck to ingrained patterns regarding the consumer credit business even after 1945.

A third factor that negatively influenced the savings banks' attitudes toward consumer loans in postwar Germany can be found in the difficult economic conditions during reconstruction. After the war, the capital market was out of kilter. Severe postwar inflation necessitated a currency reform in June 1948, which entailed a dramatic devaluation of deposits.[21] The resulting loss of private savings angered people who had trusted in the stability of savings banks and saved at them for years. This situation greatly damaged the image of the Sparkassen, which customers regarded as abettors of the "currency injustice" because of their dominant market position in retail banking.[22] Their market share accounted for about 70 percent of private deposit banking immediately before the currency stabilization.[23]

In order to regain customer confidence and counteract widespread suspicion of savings,[24] the Sparkassen had to restore savers' trust. Confidence in the reliability of financial institutions had to be reconstructed by systematic public relations.[25] However, restoring trust was a very difficult task, as this was the second currency reform within a generation for many Germans. "Contrary to its later reputation, public confidence in the new currency was not very high, which is another reason why people did not save. Instead money was used for consumption."[26] The urgency to rebuild a savings culture was enhanced by a tremendous demand for investment capital in postwar

Germany. Reconstruction—rebuilding infrastructure and the economy—was capital-intensive, which also put the Sparkassen under pressure to foster savings.[27]

In line with their traditional stance, the German savings institutions promoted thriftiness as an ethical standard because they were "convinced of the thrift idea's rightness."[28] In contrast to Nazi savings propaganda, however, especially the GSGA reconnected to the "bourgeois" tradition by framing its advertising messages within a broader set of liberal civic virtues. Both the internal rhetoric of the Sparkassen and the messages they conveyed to the public portrayed thrift as a necessary element of modern capitalistic-democratic societies, a message that comported with broader West German discourses at the time.[29] The virtue of thrift was closely connected to the values of West Germany's liberal social market economy, because an "egoistical" act like saving was thought to boost economic growth and social progress. Federal President Theodor Heuss underscored this point on World Thrift Day in 1952: "By thinking of himself, the saver helps others."[30]

First Phase: "First Save, then Drive"

During the 1950s, the Sparkassen practiced what I term "moral marketing," which reflected their organizational culture. Because of their public mandate, they understood themselves as "moral institutions," a term originally used by the German poet Friedrich Schiller in reference to the pedagogical influence of the theater. Schiller had declared that actors on stage would be able to teach the audience essential virtues and values.[31] The management of the GSGA used this paradigm, insofar as the umbrella association published booklets and other marketing materials in which Sparkassen appeared as "moral institutions" with the mission to morally educate the German population.[32] Sparkassen had to communicate the necessity of savings and thriftiness to the public. Their social commitment became manifest in moral marketing strategies that corresponded with their corporate values and self-perception.

Accordingly, thrift was regarded and promoted as a character trait that boosted individual, social, and economic progress.[33] Marketing stressed that savings provided personal security, while keeping people grounded during economic downturns. Corresponding to this message, Sparkassen and especially the GSGA declared that personal financial reserves created economic independence for everyone. In this context, thrift was even treated as a precondition of personal freedom—much in contrast, it should be noted, to the ads for easy cash loans since the 1990s that Silke Meyer discusses in chapter 10 of this volume.[34] For postwar Sparkassen, this general marketing focus on thrift education was instead combined with negative attitudes toward consumer credit and a distinctive lack of advertisements for consumer loans.[35] This was insofar surprising as personal loans had long been a central part of their traditional business. The role of the Sparkassen had also been to provide cities, local enterprises, and the "common people" with access to credit.

After World War II, however, a confluence of the several factors discussed above prevented any extraordinary activity within the consumer credit sector. Instead, reluctant decision making predominated within the GSGA, hindering Sparkassen from venturing into this market unreservedly. This conservative strategy was certainly fostered by personnel continuities in management. Most of the managers in the GSGA had been socialized during the Great Depression and Nazi era, when capital investment had been directed to industry and the state, while private consumption had needed to be self-financed. Their generation had grown up in an economy of scarcity, in which thrift was a necessary virtue. The internal records of the central advertising committee testify to the internalization of this thrift logic in the 1950s.[36] There was a genuine trust in the utility and moral correctness of "saving ahead" *(vorsparen)* for consumer goods purchases. Marketing, advertising, and publicity touted regular saving as the only way to finance personal dreams.[37] They idealized thrift as a guiding principle for happiness. A popular Sparkasse slogan emerged in this context: "First save, then drive."[38] This catchphrase underlined once more the intellectual impact of the Nazi era for postwar Sparkasse history, because it derived directly from National Socialist thrift propaganda, which had launched the slogan "first save, then buy" in 1933.[39]

The aversion of Sparkassen to consumer credit corresponded in many respects to overall public opinion. In postwar society, conspicuous consumption and buying on credit were perceived as indecorous. A representative 1955 survey found that a majority of interviewees still felt obliged to the idea of thriftiness. Although a certain pent-up demand for consumer loans existed after the war, 77 percent of respondents still refused even hire-purchase offers and stated that they had not paid any installments in the last month, while 57 percent assertively supported the virtue of saving.[40]

Although Sparkassen did not overtly market consumer loans, they nonetheless had a leading position in the consumer credit business.[41] Because of this paradoxical situation, they can even be described as "reluctant leaders" in postwar West Germany's consumer credit sector (next to specialized installment finance institutions). Already in 1948, the Sparkassen offered personal loans up to DM 600, but access to this form of credit was hindered by autocratic complexity and restrictions. The Sparkassen rigorously tested for economic and occupational need in every individual case, and usually it was difficult to obtain this kind of credit for personal consumption. In 1952, the Sparkassen introduced the purchase loan as a form of installment credit, but it was similarly overburdened with administrative barriers. These problems, along with anticipated social stigmatization, kept away many clients in need of money. Furthermore, purchase loans were intended only for durable consumer goods—household items such as refrigerators and other major electric appliances, for example. They were also meant for small-scale entrepreneurs who needed capital investment for a concrete purchase. Before a loan was approved, customers had to save 20 to 30 percent of the product's price. After that, the sum of money was not transferred to their personal account, but was booked directly to the merchant. The products bought with this loan served as security.[42]

Even though the purchase loan enlarged the Sparkasse portfolio of loan products, the GSGA still openly dismissed it as demoralizing for society. According to the organization's president, Fritz Butschkau, who headed it from 1953 to 1967, Sparkassen were supposed to focus on their educational duty and prevent overconsumption. Butschkau admonished member institutes on various occasions to remember their public responsibility, including their social mandate for thrift education. At the same time, he equated consumerism with social conformism. In his opinion, borrowing would lead to personal bondage, whereas savings symbolized freedom. In this context, he referred to the German adage, "borrowing brings sorrow" *(Borgen bringt Sorgen).*[43]

In sum, negative attitudes to installment buying remained the norm among Sparkassen during their first decades of postwar business.[44] How much this circumstance affected their advertising during this time is reflected in the fact that today there are no documented posters that promoted purchase loans. The seemingly complete absence of that business segment from Sparkasse marketing evidences how restrictive their consumer credit policy actually was. In contrast to the rhetoric of the GSGA, however, the consumer credit business actually became a successful sector for Sparkassen during this time. For example, the Sparkasse market share of installment loans was a little over 20 percent in 1956. Their strongest competitors were specialized installment banks, which had similarly reemerged since the late 1940s in order to fill pent-up demand. These specialized banks boomed above all during the early 1950s, when the volume and number of installment loans they granted increased quickly. From 1951 to 1957, their market share remained higher than that of all other financial institutions combined, including the Sparkassen.[45] Yet, compared to other major full-service banks in West Germany, the quantitative engagement of the Sparkassen in the personal loans sector was above average. Their credit volume grew from DM 83.7 million in 1951 to DM 581.1 million in 1957.[46] Even if these figures evidenced economic success, however, internal resistance still remained blatant as late as the second half of the 1950s. Aside from Willy Krämer, who was a driving force in the Sparkasse organization and an early supporter of consumer financing in the GSGA,[47] skepticism and discomfort prevailed:

> The purchase loan business is . . . more dangerous for the customer himself. Upon thorough examination of the purchase credit agreements, one can recognize more and more clearly that things are purchased that would not even be an option for the household for cash-only transactions . . . Simply the fact that one does not need to spend any money at the moment tempts one again and again to buy more than necessary and to buy things that one could definitely do without.[48]

Second Phase: "When Money Is Concerned . . . Sparkasse"

Although the Sparkasse consumer credit business had gained momentum by mid-century, doubt remained within the organization about whether this lending activity comported with the public mandate of these savings banks. Questions also persisted about the implications of consumer lending for thrift education. At the beginning of the 1960s, however, this negative perception of consumer credit began to dissipate because of changes outside the Sparkassen and the GSGA, namely, in sociological determinants and competitive parameters.

First of all, the Federal Republic's general socioeconomic upward trend influenced the decision making of the Sparkassen, because it directly affected the demand for credit and the supply of savings. The "extraordinary" economic development of West Germany since the so-called Korea boom in the early 1950s was important. Contemporaries termed it the *Wirtschaftswunder* or economic miracle, referring to the boom of the West German and other West European postwar economies with increasing employment rates and rising wage levels.[49] Due to growth in real wages, the purchasing power of the average household rose. Living standards in West Germany improved in an unexpected way, at least from the perspective of contemporary witnesses, who could not have imagined such potential for growth immediately after the war had ended. A new spending mentality took hold, and more affluent consumption patterns emerged.[50] The rise of new personal needs and wants had worried Sparkassen in the 1950s; however, in retrospect, there was little cause for alarm, because the savings rate boomed as well. People saved more and bought more at the same time.

In addition to the expanding rates of savings, which indicated that the savers' trust had not been as negatively affected as the Sparkassen and the GSGA had feared, another trend strengthened the business development of the savings banks: the reorganization of wage payment methods at the end of the 1950s.[51] Since then, weekly payments in cash were a thing of the past, because companies now preferred to pay wages with monthly direct deposits. In consequence, the number of checking accounts grew rapidly.

These economic changes helped make even low-income earners increasingly "bankable." Therefore, private commercial banks discovered a new potential clientele in what had long been the target group of the Sparkassen, and they began retail banking in 1958 by offering financial services to the "average" person.[52] Thus, competition in the German credit sector rose, and banks started to offer attractive services to private households in the lower-income groups. In the same year, economic minister Ludwig Erhard called on financial institutions to offer consumer loans to stimulate further economic growth.[53] His focus on the consumer goods industry derived from the notion that the success of the West German social market economy could only be guaranteed by individual consumption, which he declared to be a fundamental right of every citizen. In Erhard's opinion, high average consumption was the motor of prosperity.[54]

Once the bank regulatory authorities adopted this idea and changed the underlying legal conditions, the "small loan" *(Kleinkredit)* was introduced by both savings and commercial banks. The "big three" commercial banks—Deutsche Bank, Dresdner Bank, and Commerzbank—launched such loans in May 1959. Deutsche Bank called this important product innovation the "small personal loan" *(Persönlicher Kleinkredit)* and opted for an extensive marketing campaign. So did Commerzbank, which coined the slogan "Consumer Loans for Everyone" in order to capture public attention.[55] Compared to the marketing activity of the Sparkassen, the competitors' involvement was higher in this business line, because internal objections still existed within the GSGA. Overcoming the internalized thrift mentality of its management's value system was not easy. Established organizational modes of thinking and acting persisted and hampered a forward-looking strategy. Despite the internal skepticism regarding the promotion of consumer loans, however, the Sparkassen had the strongest market position, which arose from their dominant position in the savings business. Thus, with regard to market share, their broad customer base was a competitive advantage. In June 1960, the Sparkassen were responsible for 44.8 percent of the country's volume in consumer loans, whereas other banks held 37.6 percent and credit unions 17.4 percent. The Sparkassen held 608,399 such "small loans" at this time, and the amount on them outstanding was DM 483.8 million. The growth of this segment was noteworthy, because—in total credit volume—this new personal loan quickly achieved higher demand than the older purchase loan, which accounted for DM 420.8 million in June 1960.[56]

In retrospect, the launch of personal loans was a significant step in the development of the German consumer credit business, which in turn provoked changes in Sparkasse credit policy. The maximum available credit sum for personal loans rose from DM 600 to DM 2,000. This increase matched the general rise in household prosperity, but a relatively short loan period of six to twenty-four months (at most) still showed the limits of the savings banks' flexibility. Another advancement in the Sparkasse consumer loans business was achieved in 1961 with the introduction of the acquisition loan.[57] The idea of offering a more flexible form of consumer loan with cash paid directly to the consumer was first realized by the District Savings Bank of Cologne and its president, Willy Krämer, who spearheaded the consumer credit movement inside the national organization. This consumer loan, which was a customer-friendly modification of the so-called small loan, became part of the regular Sparkasse credit portfolio shortly after Krämer implemented it.

All in all, the Sparkassen had a first-mover advantage in this lucrative market. The introduction of the acquisition loan quickly paid off, soon becoming the most successful form of installment credit, outperforming other kinds of consumer loans. For this reason, other banks followed the example and launched competing products the following year. Already in 1965, the Sparkassen made acquisition loans for some DM 751 million. This was quite high compared to the volume of small loans, which accounted for DM 698 million in the same business year.[58]

The advantages of this consumer loan consisted of higher credit sums determined on a case-by-case basis, as well as variable loan periods, so that the process of borrowing became more individualized and responsive to the differentiation of customer demands. Even though acquisition loans were supposed to be used for durable goods, they were not limited to specific items, which strengthened the autonomy of borrowers; it was an important step in the monetary emancipation of the private household. However, acquisition loans did not completely replace the existing portfolio, but rather complemented the small loans by filling a market niche, insofar as at least DM 2,000 had to be borrowed.

The pioneering efforts of the Sparkassen with their acquisition loans showed that these banks were trying to anticipate shifting market conditions, mapping out a new strategy in order to hold their position as market leader in consumer lending. At first, they accepted the rising demand for credit services reluctantly. Nevertheless, they diversified their credit services efficiently and successfully. The volume of consumer loans held by the Sparkassen grew throughout the decade, for example, from DM 2.22 billion in 1963 to DM 3.17 billion in 1967.[59] Ultimately, a combination of external pressures and material success brought about a slowly changing mind-set within the organization.

Competition did not just arise within the banking sector, however. Since the mid-1950s, credit brokers had capitalized on consumers' sense of shame when borrowing money outside the family. For this reason, brokers intervened by offering anonymity in the process of borrowing in return for higher interest rates. This trend, as well, pushed the Sparkassen to invent a creative, less bureaucratic, and more flexible form of consumer credit, like the acquisition loan. In order to fulfill their public mandate, they felt obligated to prevent uncontrolled borrowing and overindebtedness. Expanding their credit portfolio could be portrayed as part of the institution's social mission, because the banks were offering responsible financial products tailored to their customers' needs at reasonable interest rates.[60]

Consumer loan advertising still remained underrepresented in comparison to the various thrift-marketing campaigns during the early 1960s, although Sparkasse marketing moralized less than before. Internal and external Sparkasse communications gradually changed. This trend was exemplified by the slogan "When money is concerned . . . Sparkasse," which is still in use today.[61] It was created in 1963 to underline the institutions' full-service approach, emphasizing their entire range of business activities. The gradual shift in marketing is evident in contemporary billboards, posters, and other advertising matter, which explicitly promoted consumer loans since the mid-1960s. However, a radical rupture of the intraorganizational thought and belief system was not yet observable. Until 1966–67, decision making was in many respects still influenced by the traditional Sparkasse mentality and its focus on thrift education.

Third Phase: "Grandpa's Sparkasse Is Dead"

Ludwig Poullain, president of the GSGA, asserted in a 1969 speech, "Grandpa's Sparkasse is dead."[62] He was characterizing the corporate transition that had just changed the product policy and marketing strategy of the Sparkassen. At that time, the operational business was already pervaded by modern marketing management. In this case understood as an integrated management system driven by market developments, modern management includes much more than established methods to increase sales, because it determines corporate direction and goal setting.[63] This shift in management philosophy was, of course, closely connected to the socioeconomic development of the time, giving rise to a pluralization of cultural values and lifestyles, which in turn advanced the rise of systematic marketing in Germany.

As a result of the new approach to management, the Sparkassen developed into market-oriented financial service providers. Their self-perception as moral institutions grew obsolete. This transition in corporate culture was caused by the interplay of internal and external factors. In 1966–67, leading positions in the GSGA and the Sparkassenverlag were occupied by a new generation of managers, who broke with the conservative interpretation of a public mandate and proved open-minded toward modern marketing management.[64] In addition, the West German credit sector was partially liberalized in 1967. Essential laws were revised to remove many restrictions, especially those concerning interest rates and marketing.[65] One milestone for German credit institutions was that they were now permitted to do comparative advertising, as long as they avoided using superlatives and did not present misleading information. As a consequence, competition in retail banking rose and encouraged further customer and market orientation. These legal changes complemented the transformation in Sparkasse leadership in facilitating fundamental organizational change.

The introduction of modern marketing management was a key moment in the history of consumer credit supply and access. The GSGA modernized the interpretation of their members' public mandate. Now that these banks were supposed to make the whole range of financial services available to the population, both the deposit and lending businesses achieved equal status in Sparkasse policies.[66] These banks now behaved even more proactively in the consumer credit business and were able to secure first-mover advantages, which were important in many respects.

A prime example was the launch of automatic overdraft loans for qualifying checking accounts *(Dispositionskredit)* in 1968. In this special case, the Sparkassen tried to "reverse the initiative" in the lending business, because in former times clients had needed to apply officially for a loan.[67] The procedure was simplified in a customer-friendly manner. According to the changing initiative of the Sparkassen, checking account clients who had a regular income deposited to their accounts received lines of overdraft credit as a matter of course, without any special application. Customers could interpret this credit line as a "mark of confidence" in them.[68] The amount of credit depended on income level. The growing importance of professional marketing could also be seen in the new financial product's name, which the GSGA chose in response to knowledge gained from market research. The term Dispositionskredit suggested that funds were at the disposition of the consumer. A possible alternative, *Überziehungskredit,* more literally conformed to the English word "overdraft," but this was rejected as too negative in connotation.[69]

In other words, the process of decision making was increasingly affected by the customers' perceived frame of reference. This shift was reflected in Sparkasse advertising, too, as this form of credit was often portrayed as suitable for an individualistic, modern, uncomplicated way of everyday borrowing. This way of discussing consumer credit became increasingly prominent during the last quarter of the twentieth century, as other contributions in this volume suggest.[70]

The success of this marketing strategy convinced the Sparkassen to extend their lead in the consumer lending business even further. In 1969, they launched the so-called all-purpose mortgage *(Allzweckhypothek),* a long-term product with individually negotiated terms of up to fifteen years.[71] Then, two years later, the credit portfolio was supplemented by a medium-term loan in the tradition of the acquisition loan. By calling it a "self-service loan" *(Selbstbedienungsdarlehen),* advertisements suggested that it was the most modern and flexible mode of financing consumer needs.[72] By the mid-1970s, the Sparkassen offered and promoted a wide range of consumer loans.

However, this broad array of credit services also caused confusion among customers who were irritated about the seemingly endless variety of choices. At the same time, the market share of the Sparkassen in private lending edged downward. In 1968, they were the undisputed market leader with 35.5 percent of all private loans. In 1975, they were still the market leader, but with a downward drift. Now, their relative market share was at about 32.8 percent. In addition, a structural shift in credit demand occurred. From the end of the 1960s to the middle of the 1970s, long-term loans gained roughly 5 percent, whereas short- and medium-term loans lost ground.[73]

As a consequence, the GSGA commissioned further market research. The resultant study found that those surveyed wanted more clarity and transparency in the consumer credit business. Especially product names were perceived as inconsistent and confusing. Therefore, a new credit concept with new terms needed to be devised to meet the customers' desire for "relevance, simplicity, shortness, and integrity."[74] The GSGA umbrella association consequently created the "all-purpose credit program" *(Allzweckkreditprogramm)* in 1976, which summed up the entire range of services and presented it for the first time in a uniform manner.[75] Inventing this "credit program" was a matter of rearranging the existing order of credit products. It was clearly much more of a marketing-based solution, which corresponded to the image of a modern full-service financial institution, rather than a genuine product innovation. The credit program was presented as a hierarchy of loan products organized according to credit terms and volumes, with overdraft loans on top, consumer loans in the middle, and mortgages on the bottom. This marketing strategy resulted in the improved market performance of the Sparkassen in the following decade. They regained their former strength in the consumer credit business, holding a market share of 40.2 percent in the private lending business in 1984. The absolute value of Sparkasse consumer loans that year amounted to DM 61 billion.[76]

During the period analyzed, the level of borrowing in the Sparkassen increased steadily, and it is still increasing today. Over the long term, consumer loans expanded dramatically in the Federal Republic. Recent studies, adjusted for inflation, show that, in the late 1950s, West German financial institutions dealt in consumer loans of about €1.8 billion. By the late 1970s, the volume had already reached about €60 billion; and in 2009, consumer loans of about €228 billion circulated in Germany.[77] Even though these absolute numbers evince a rising supply of, demand for, and access to credit, the annual rate of growth in the credit market has regressed since the late 1970s. During recessions, like the first oil crisis of 1973, this rate even declined due to negative economic expectations. Such findings suggest that German consumer behavior in private lending is proactive. This conclusion is drawn in Sparkasse literature, too. It acknowledges that, in the midst of an economic crisis, debtors try to avoid further borrowing and attempt to pay back their consumer loans faster than they do during a booming period.[78]

Besides the rising level of private debt, savings ratios developed extremely positively, which was caused by expanding average incomes and rising living standards. Therefore, the German savings rate has multiplied since mid-century. Today, it is about 11 percent, which is significantly different than the U.S. savings rate, which has shrunk dramatically since the early 1980s with a first-time, twenty-first-century negative growth in 2005.[79] In light of these facts, it is clear that saving and lending alike belong to everyday life in Germany nowadays—and the public mandate of the Sparkassen still ensures that private clients get both the opportunity to save and access to credit.

Conclusion

Explaining the shifts in the consumer credit products and marketing policies of the Sparkassen after World War II is not an easy undertaking, especially if the banks' internal perceptions of consumer credit are related to their actual market performance. In this context, the periodization proposed in this essay provides the basis for systematic analysis, even though the actual complexity of this phenomenon is considerably reduced. In reality, progressive and conservative moments often overlapped or worked against one another.

Therefore, the actual extent of internal frictions regarding consumer credit has just been sketched schematically. Nonetheless, three broad phases can be identified.

The first one, in the decade after the 1948 currency reform, was characterized by hesitant decision making and restrictive activity in the consumer credit business. During that period, the Sparkassen positioned themselves as reluctant leaders in this business segment. Instead of promoting consumer loans, they concentrated on fostering savings, an emphasis that was rooted in their conservative interpretation of their public mandate. The promotion of thrift and "moral marketing" prevailed, because the Sparkassen still understood themselves as "moral institutions." In the second phase, however, new credit forms were launched and competition in retail banking rose. The Sparkassen tried to react sufficiently to changing social and market conditions. Although internal skepticism and resistance were still detectable, the Sparkasse portfolio of consumer loans was expanded and consumer credit access was much easier than before. In addition, product offerings became more flexible and, in the mid-1960s, consumer credit advertising started to spread. Yet a real breakthrough can only be observed following the generational and conceptual change in management in the late 1960s. With the implementation of modern marketing management, the Sparkassen assumed the initiative in the consumer credit business, chose aggressive marketing strategies, and procured important first-mover advantages. According to their new self-image as "modern" financial service providers, their range of credit services was tailored to the specific needs of their customers.

That the former self-perception of the Sparkassen as "moral institutions" had vanished became not only obvious in consumer credit advertising. The most visible sign of the far-reaching organizational change was the redesign of the traditional logo, commissioned by the GSGA in the early 1970s. Otl Aicher, a famous contemporary designer who also revised the visual image of Dresdner Bank, created a new, modernized corporate design. He eliminated the previous logo's analogy to a classic piggy bank and abolished its coin slot, which represented the former internal emphasis of the banks on private savings accumulation. In its place was a bold red "S," slightly wider than it was tall, with a big red dot above it. If the dot still symbolized a coin dropping into a piggy bank, the direct link to savings was no longer obvious in the abstract logo. What remained was the association of the Sparkasse with money, whether for savings or credit or both. Thus, the Sparkasse logo redesign may be interpreted as a symbolic act through which the corporate transformation was completed; it showed that "Grandpa's Sparkasse" really was a thing of the past.

Parallel to the outlined trend in the Sparkassen, the strong sociocultural affinity for thriftiness and other "German" secondary virtues such as frugality, order, duty, and punctuality faded among German consumers because of the pluralization of lifestyles, which was to a certain extent induced by the so-called Americanization of advertising. Nowadays, it is not unusual to allow oneself to fulfill some personal dreams and consumer wishes by means of credit, while saving for economically difficult times. Hence, it could be argued that the complex interaction of changing credit supply and demand led Germans finally to get over their traditional economic moral values by learning to integrate saving *and* borrowing into their common money-management practices.

Notes

*I would like to thank the Wissenschaftsföderung der Sparkassen-Finanzgruppe, especially Dr. Thorsten Wehber, for giving me unrestricted access to the internal minutes and records of the Deutsche Sparkassen- und Giroverband (German Savings and Giro Association) in this organization's archive, the Sparkassenhistorisches Dokumentationszentrum, located in Bonn Germany. I refer to this institution below as the GSGA archive.

1. Finanzgruppe Deutscher Sparkassen- und Giroverband, *Der Finanzbericht* (Berlin, 2009), 27, http://www.dsgv.de/_download_gallery/Publikationen/Finanzbericht2009_D.pdf.

2. Deutsche Bank, "Konsumentenkreditengagement," *Geschäftsbericht 2009,* http://geschaeftsbericht.deutsche-bank.de/2009/gb/risikobericht/kreditrisiko/klassifizierungdeskreditrisikoengagements/konsumentenkredite.html.

3. Rebecca Belvederesi-Kochs, "Von der 'moralischen Anstalt' zum vertriebsorientierten Finanzdienstleister: Der unternehmenskulturelle Wandel des Deutschen Sparkassen- und Giroverbands im Spiegel seiner Marketingstrategie," *Zeitschrift für Unternehmensgeschichte* 53, no. 2 (2008): 192–215.

4. Rebecca Belvederesi-Kochs, "'Von der Richtigkeit der Sparidee überzeugt': Selbstwahrnehmung und Werbestrategien der bundesdeutschen Sparkassenorganisation in den 1950er Jahren," in *Geld und Kapital—Jahrbuch der Gesellschaft für mitteleuropäische Banken- und Sparkassengeschichte,* ed. Ralf Ahrens (Stuttgart, 2008), 169–96.

5. On the concept of organizational culture, see Edgar H. Schein, "Organizational Culture and Leadership," in *Classics of Organization Theory,* ed. Jay Shafritz and J. Steven Ott, 5th ed. (Fort Worth, TX, 2001), 373–74.

6. Josef Wysocki, "Preface," in *History of European Savings Banks,* ed. Wissenschaftsförderung der Sparkassenorganisation e.V. (Stuttgart, 1996), 22.

7. Hans-Joachim Möhle, "Sparkassenkleindarlehen oder Kaufkredit" (PhD diss., University of Cologne, 1960).

8. Schein, "Organizational Culture and Leadership," 373–74.

9. Rudolf Zeiselmair, "Marketing: Initialzündung zu marktorientiertem Handeln: Zum Verständnis der Marketingaufgabe der Sparkassen," *Sparkassen-Werbedienst* 29, no. 4 (1971): 71–73.

10. Wolfram Fischer, "Gemeinsamkeiten in der sozioökonomischen Struktur der europäischen Länder als Voraussetzung der Sparkassenidee," *Zeitschrift für bayerische Sparkassengeschichte* 6 (1992): 33–43.

11. Klaus Tenfelde, "Vereinswesen und bürgerliche Gesellschaft im 19. Jahrhundert am Beispiel des Sparwesens," *Zeitschrift für bayerische Sparkassengeschichte* 1 (1987): 119–48.

12. Paul Münch, "Mangelökonomie und Sparsamkeit," *Zeitschrift für bayerische Sparkassengeschichte* 7 (1993): 7–12.

13. "Protokoll des Zentralen Werbeausschusses," May 25–26, 1948, GSGA archive, I.B/17/48; "Eine verlorengegangene Tugend," *Sparkassen-Werbedienst* 9, no. 9 (1951): 140; "Die Goldene Lebensregel: Sparsam sein!," *Sparkassen-Werbedienst* 13, no. 10 (1955): 184; Fritz Butschkau, "Sparwille zwischen Furcht und Hoffnung," *Deutscher Sparkassentag 1951,* ed. GSGA (Stuttgart, 1951), 40.

14. Jürgen Mura, *Entwicklungslinien der deutschen Sparkassengeschichte* (Stuttgart, 1994), 1:29–30; Günter Ashauer, *Von der Ersparungscasse zur Sparkassen-Finanzgruppe: Die deutsche Sparkassenorganisation in Geschichte und Gegenwart* (Stuttgart, 1991), 253.

15. Hans Pohl, "Die Sparkassen vom Ausgang des 19. Jahrhunderts bis zum Ende des Zweiten Weltkriegs," in *Wirtschafts- und Sozialgeschichte der deutschen Sparkassen im 20. Jahrhundert,* ed. Wissenschaftsförderung der Sparkassen-Finanzgruppe e.V. (Stuttgart, 2005), 201–5.

16. Annual Report of the GSGA, 1933, 3, GSGA archive; Rebecca Belvederesi and Paul Thomes, "Gesellschaftlicher Wandel und das Privatkundengeschäft der Sparkassen nach 1945," in *Sparzwang oder Kaufrausch? Spar- und Konsumverhalten im Wandel,* ed. Wissenschaftsförderung der Sparkassen Finanzgruppe e.V. (Stuttgart, 2007), 19–41.

17. Norbert Emmerich, "Die Sparkassenwerbung von 1924 bis 1925," in *Die Sparkassenwerbung—Historische Entwicklung und Zukunftsperspektiven,* ed. Wissenschaftsförderung der Sparkassenorganisation e.V. (Stuttgart, 1996), 34–64.

18. Hartmut Berghoff, "Enticement and Deprivation: The Regulation of Consumption in Pre-War Nazi Germany," in *The Politics of Consumption: Material Culture and Citizenship in Europe and America,* ed. Martin Daunton and Matthew Hilton (Oxford, 2001), 165–84.

19. "Stuttgart und der Deutsche Sparkassenverlag," in *50 Jahre Sparkassenwerbung,* ed. GSGA, special issue of *Sparkassen-Werbedienst* (1974): 38.

20. Paul Thomes, "Sparen und Sparsamkeit im Nationalsozialismus—Gedanken zur Pervertierung einer Institution," *Zeitschrift für bayerische Sparkassengeschichte* 10 (1996): 63–81.

21. Christoph Buchheim, "Die Währungsreform 1948 in Westdeutschland," *Vierteljahrshefte für Zeitgeschichte* 36 (1988): 198–231.

22. Fritz Butschkau, "Sparwille zwischen Furcht und Hoffnung: Bericht über die Lage der Sparkassen seit der Koreakrise," *Sparkasse* 68, no. 22 (1951): 339.

23. Günther Schulz, "Die Sparkassen vom Ende des Zweiten Weltkriegs bis zur Wiedervereinigung," in *Wirtschafts- und Sozialgeschichte der deutschen Sparkassen im 20. Jahrhundert,* ed. Wissenschaftsförderung der Sparkassen-Finanzgruppe e.V. (Stuttgart, 2005), 411.

24. Opinion research in the late 1940s and early 1950s revealed that the process of institutional saving had suffered huge losses in reputation. See Elisabeth Noelle and Erich P. Neumann, *Jahrbuch der öffentlichen Meinung 1947–1955* (Allensbach, 1956), 153.

25. "Werbung für die Werbung," *Sparkassen-Werbedienst* 8, no. 4 (1950): 59–61; Josef Hoffmann, "Sparkassenpolitik und Sparkassenwerbung unter veränderten Verhältnissen," in *Zentrale Werbetagung Stuttgart (12./13. Mai 1953): Referate und Berichte,* ed. Arbeitsgemeinschaft Deutscher Sparkassen- und Giroverbände (Stuttgart, 1953), 13.

26. Armin Grünbacher, *Reconstruction and Cold War in Germany: The Kreditanstalt für Wiederaufbau (1948–1961)* (Aldershot, 2004), 82.

27. For further information on the socioeconomic context of the reconstruction efforts, see Werner Abelshauser, *Deutsche Wirtschaftsgeschichte seit 1945* (Bonn, 2005).

28. "Mehr als die Pflicht tun!," *Sparkassen-Werbedienst* 9, no. 9 (1951): 140.

29. "Über die Notwendigkeit des Sparens," *Sparkasse* 73, no. 2 (1956): 357–58.

30. Theodor Heuss, "Sparsam sein, eine menschliche Haltung: Indem der Sparer an sich denkt, hilft er dem nächsten," *Sparkasse* 10, no. 21 (1952): 341–44.

31. Friedrich Schiller, "Die Schaubühne als eine moralische Anstalt betrachtet," in *Schillers Werke,* ed. Eduard von der Hellen (Stuttgart, 1867), 9:57–66.

32. Kurt von Heydenaber, *Sparkassenwerbung und Öffentlichkeitsarbeit—Einführung* (Stuttgart, 1981), 30.

33. Julius Heil, *Die Pflege des Spargedankens: Sparkassenwerbung und Sparwerbung* (Stuttgart, 1960).

34. Fritz Butschkau, "Sparen—ein Weg zur Freiheit," in *Im Dienste des Sparers: Reden und Aufsätze von Fritz Butschkau* (Stuttgart, 1967), 102–17.

35. This is indirectly documented in the book of Sparkasse posters by Friedrich Friedl, *Wer den Pfennig nicht ehrt . . . Plakate werben für das Sparen* (Stuttgart, 1992).

36. For example: "Protokoll des Zentralen Werbeausschusses," November 1950, GSGA archive, I.B/17/1950, 3.

37. "Von Generation zu Generation—sparsam sein!," *Sparkassen-Werbedienst* 14, no. 10 (1956): 252.

38. Protokoll des Zentralen Werbeausschusses, September 1953, GSGA archive, I.B/17/1953, 6.

39. Friedl, *Pfennig,* 76.

60   •   Rebecca Belvederesi-Kochs

40. Elisabeth Noelle and Erich P. Neumann, *Jahrbuch der öffentlichen Meinung 1957* (Allensbach, 1957), 229.
41. Willy Krämer, "Fünf Jahre Kaufkraft-Richtlinien," *Sparkasse* 15, no. 22 (1957): 349–52.
42. For more on the purchase credit, see Möhle, "Sparkassenkleindarlehen oder Kaufkredit," 63–99.
43. Butschkau, "Sparwille," 36–59; Butschkau, "Fünf Jahre Sparkassenarbeit bei fester Währung," in *Deutscher Sparkassentag 1954,* ed. GSGA (Stuttgart, 1954), 13–32; Butschkau, "Sparen in der vollbeschäftigten Wirtschaft," in *Deutscher Sparkassentag 1956,* ed. GSGA (Stuttgart, 1956), 35–49.
44. Borrowing was even described as a "drug" for the younger generation; see William H. Whyte Jr., " 'Verplantes' Einkommen—ein Rauschgift der jungen Generation," *Sparkasse* 73, no. 23 (1956): 366–68.
45. Ingo Ellgering and Peter Landsberg, *Das Allzweckkreditprogramm der Sparkassen: Kredite und Darlehen an private Haushalte* (Stuttgart, 1991), 19.
46. Britta Stücker, "Konsum auf Kredit in der Bundesrepublik," *Jahrbuch für Wirtschaftsgeschichte* 2 (2007): 70.
47. He was the director of the Cologne Sparkasse. See Willy Krämer, "Grünes Licht für Kleindarlehen? Ein Beitrag der Sparkassenpraxis zur Diskussion über das Bardarlehen," *Sparkasse* 75, no. 19 (1958): 307–9.
48. "Vom Sparkassenstandpunkt. Sorge um den Kaufkredit," *Sparkasse* 73, no. 5 (1956): 72.
49. Hans-Ulrich Wehler, *Deutsche Gesellschaftsgeschichte: 1949–1990,* (Munich, 2008), 5:49–59; Abelshauser, *Deutsche Wirtschaftsgeschichte,* 161.
50. Arne Andersen, *Der Traum vom guten Leben: Alltags- und Konsumgeschichte vom Wirtschaftswunder bis heute* (Frankfurt am Main, 1999)
51. Schulz, "Die Sparkassen vom Ende des Zweiten Weltkriegs bis zur Wiedervereinigung," 303–4.
52. Gerold Ambrosius, "Intensives Wachstum (1958–1965)," in *Geschichte der deutschen Kreditwirtschaft seit 1945,* ed. Hans Pohl (Frankfurt am Main, 1998), 149–202.
53. In October 1958, Erhard wrote a letter to banks stressing the positive effects of consumer credit on business. In this context, Erhard asked banks to deal in consumer loans. Willy Krämer, "Kredit für den Konsumenten: Standort und Bedeutung der Sparkassen auf dem Gebiete der Konsumentenfinanzierung," *Sparkasse* 76, no. 18 (1959): 315.
54. On the stimulativie economic consequences of consumer credit, see Friedrich A. Lutz, *Der Konsumentenkredit* (Cologne and Berlin, 1954): 79–97.
55. Hans Pohl, *Die Rheinischen Sparkassen: Entwicklung und Bedeutung für Wirtschaft und Gesellschaft von den Anfängen bis 1990* (Stuttgart, 2001), 261.
56. Ellgering and Landsberg, *Das Allzweckkreditprogramm,* 20.
57. Joachim Beier and Klaus-Dieter Jacob, *Der Konsumentenkredit in der Bundesrepublik Deutschland* (Frankfurt am Main, 1987), 42.

58. Ellgering and Landsberg, *Das Allzweckkreditprogramm*, 23.
59. Mura, *Entwicklungslinien*, 178.
60. Willy Krämer, "Der Konsumentenkredit auf neuen Wegen," *Sparkasse* 78, no. 23 (1961): 399–403.
61. Karl-Peter Ellerbrock, "Konsumentenkredit und 'Soziale Marktwirtschaft': Zum Wandel des Sparkassenbildes und des geschäftspolitischen Denkens in der Sparkassenorganisation zwischen Währungsreform und dem Beginn der 'Marketing-Ära' in den 1970er Jahren," in *Marketing: Historische Aspekte der Wettbewerbs- und Absatzpolitik,* ed. Christian Kleinschmidt and Florian Triebel (Iserlohn, 2004), 126.
62. Barbara Hillen, "Opas Sparkasse ist tot—oder wie ein Satz Karriere machte," *Sparkasse* 120, no. 3 (2002): 19.
63. Walter Freyer, *Tourismus-Marketing: Marktorientiertes Management im Mikro- und Makrobereich der Tourismuswirtschaft* (Munich, 2007), 40–41.
64. Belvederesi-Kochs, "Moralische Anstalt," 205–07.
65. Fritz Kulins, "Vom Sparer zum Universalkunden: Die privaten Haushalte und ihre Beziehung zur Kreditwirtschaft," in *Standortbestimmung: Entwicklungslinien der deutschen Kreditwirtschaft,* ed. GSGA (Stuttgart, 1984), 173–74.
66. Helmut Geiger, *Die deutsche Sparkassenorganisation* (Frankfurt am Main, 1992).
67. Mura, *Entwicklungslinien*, 186.
68. Ellgering and Landsberg, *Das Allzweckkreditprogramm*, 15.
69. The significance of the public image of the Sparkassen in the consumer credit market is described by Peter-Christian Rahn, "Marketingpolitik im Konsumentenkreditgeschäft der Universalbank. Konzeption und Stretegie für den Konsumentenkredit im Rahmen einer marktorientierten Gesamtkonzeption" (PhD diss., University of Hamburg, 1977), 370–71.
70. See esp. chapter 10 in this volume by Silke Meyer. For the United States, see chapter 9 by Jan Logemann.
71. Willy Krämer, "Allzweckhypotheken an Private," *Deutsche Sparkassenzeitung* (1969): 1; Hermann Kittel, *Marktstrategien im Hypothekarkreditgeschäft: Der Wettbewerb zwischen den Hypothekarkreditinstituten in der Wohnungsbaufinanzierung* (Berlin, 1974), 210–11; Ellgering and Landsberg, *Das Allzweckkreditprogramm,* 56.
72. Pohl, *Die Rheinischen Sparkassen*.
73. Ellgering and Landsberg, *Das Allzweckkreditprogramm*, 26.
74. Ibid., 34.
75. Willy Krämer, "Das Allzweckkreditprogramm der Sparkassen," *Sparkasse* 34, no. 11 (1976): 386–88.
76. Mura, *Entwicklungslinien*, 191.
77. Theophil Graband, "60 Jahre Bundesrepublik, 60 Jahre Konsumentenkredit—eine Bestandsaufnahme" (excerpt from *SCHUFA Kredit-Kompass 2010*), 136, http://www.schufa-kredit-kompass.de/de/studien/kreditkultur/60jahre.jsp.

78. Helmut Dorn, "Konsumentenkredit: Kredit mit 'sozialisiertem' Risiko," in *Konsumentenkredit im Blickpunkt,* ed. Klaus Goschler, special issue of *Schriftenreihe des Österreichischen Forschungsinstituts für Sparkassenwesen* 15, no. 4 (1975): 14–15.

79. Kathleen Camilli, "Household Wealth and the US Savings Rate," *Economics for Your Life* 1, no. 2 (2006): 1, http://www.camillieconomics.com/PDF/Economics %20for%20Your%20Life,%20Vol%201.2.pdf.

CHAPTER 3

Credit in a Nation of Savers: The Growth of Consumer Borrowing in Japan

Andrew Gordon

Japan has been famous for its high rates of savings for some time. In the past decade, the image of young Japanese in particular as profligate consumers, including young women condemned as "selfish" (*wagamama*) for their greed, has begun to spread as a counterweight.[1] I would resist such a moralistic judgment of either women or men, but I certainly agree that widespread enthusiasm for getting and spending—and the use of credit to support this—has been significant in Japan, not only recently, but for quite some time. Purchase of daily life goods on credit has roots in indigenous practices reaching back to the Tokugawa era. Since the early twentieth century, forms of credit associated with the modern West, most particularly America, have been culturally and economically important. And consumer credit played an important role in Japan's economic surge from the 1950s.

This role continues. Indeed, since the late 1980s, Japanese consumers on the whole (with some recent diminution) have borrowed in similar proportions to their American counterparts. As reported by the Japan Credit Association (JCA), drawing on government data from each country, outstanding per capita consumer debt in Japan surpassed American totals in 1989 when measured as a percentage of net disposable income. It remained greater for the next decade, standing between 20 and 25 percent compared to U.S. totals under or at 20 percent. The balance shifted in the past decade, as American debt relative to income rose to around 25 percent most years, and Japanese levels fell to 20 percent or less (figure 3.1). If the parallel boom in home equity loans in the United States is taken into account, the recent

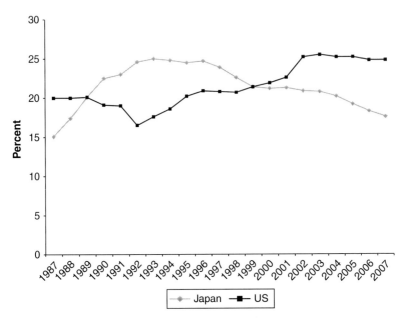

Figure 3.1 Consumer credit balance as proportion of disposable income, Japan and the United States, 1987–2007

Source: Nihon Kurejitto Kyōkai, *Nihon no shōhisha shinyō tōkei* (Tokyo, 2009), 78: U.S. data from Board of Governors of the Federal Reserve System and Department of Commerce, Bureau of Economic Analysis; Japanese data from Naikaku-fu, *Kokumin keizai keisan nenpō* (Tokyo, 1987–2007).

borrowing gap is greater than this. For my purposes, however, the key point is that the overall debt levels are in a comparable ballpark. Neither nation's consumers, by these measures, are vastly more debt-ridden than the other's. The notion of people in Japan as particularly averse to spending because they are obsessed with frugality and saving simply does not hold.[2]

My goal in this chapter is not to settle the matter of the gold, silver, or bronze medal winners in a consumer debt Olympics, and, in any case, the data are categorized in ways in each country that make precise comparison a treacherous matter. Rather, starting with the understanding that Japanese consumers borrow comparably to others relative to their income, I seek to describe and explain the historical generation of a structure of consumer borrowing in Japan that is distinctive in important ways in comparison to the U.S. and European cases. I will sketch the rise of consumer credit in Japan, focusing on a combination of indigenous and imported practices and goods across the twentieth century, and on the political and economic context of this borrowing. I argue that an early reliance on installment plans evolved into a pattern of credit card use marked to this day by a commitment to repayment through fixed installments as well as extremely high rates of monthly clearance. Of greatest interest, and most unusual, are two elements of the story: these practices have been shaped by a nearly accidental program of regulation—the regulation of credit, that is, for political reasons not linked directly to support for or opposition to borrowing itself; and they have endured to the present, long after the key regulations were lifted.

* * *

As historians are fond of noting, money-lending is one of the world's oldest professions.[3] In Japan, one finds literary reference to pawned clothing from at least the Heian era (900s c.e.).[4] Accounts of the origins of modern consumer credit typically point to diverse indigenous and foreign practices that emerged more or less simultaneously around the turn of the twentieth century. What principally defines them as modern is that borrowers were required to make regular installment payments linked to the new practice of monthly salaries or weekly wages for office or factory workers.

The most important indigenous installment sellers have been described with retrospective patriotic pride by some postwar commentators as a purely native source of modern consumer finance, more important than foreign sellers. But although both indigenous and imported credit practices were significant, it appears to me that, in the eyes of most commentators of the interwar era, credit was understood as something most essentially "modern" and "Western," even if the actual origins were mixed.

Indigenous providers of consumer credit in modern times emerged out of the lacquer industry, which had developed in the late Tokugawa era in central and southwestern Japan. Lacquerware in late Tokugawa times was sold to rural households on credit, improvising upon a traditional form of mutual credit provision called *mujin* or *kō*.[5] From the 1880s into the 1890s, the more successful sellers built regional networks and began to offer a range of goods, especially furniture and clothing, on monthly installments. Apprentice merchants split off from their masters, but retained the signature trademark of a kanji character in a circle (*maru*): Marui, Maruzen, Marukyo, Marutake, Maruichi, and so forth. These businesses evolved into "installment department stores" (*geppu hyakkaten*) from the late 1890s, selling household goods such as furniture, bedding, tatami, clothing, lacquerware, or ceramics. Customers included workers at the state-run Yahata iron works in Kyushu and seem to have generally been wage earners of limited means. The first such seller opened in Tokyo only in 1915, and a number of others immediately followed.[6] These businesses appear similar in customer base and products to

the so-called "borax stores" that spread in the United States from the 1880s or the German *Abzahlungshäuser* of the late nineteenth century.[7]

Foreign corporations provided the second source of modern installment credit. National Cash Register, the Tokyo office of the London *Times* in tandem with Maruzen booksellers selling the *Encyclopedia Britannica,* and the Singer Sewing Machine Company were among the most important. Of these, Singer was by far the leader in systematizing and spreading the practice of installment buying to a different sort of consumer than those who patronized installment department stores. Singer's clientele were middle- to upper-class urban families, wives and daughters in particular. In contrast to the native installment sellers, Singer and the other foreign sellers used more detailed contracts (some smaller clothing stores used no written contracts at all), their terms of repayment were considerably longer, and the cost of a typical good was higher.

A Singer machine, in fact, represented about two months' wages for an ordinary "salaryman" (this ratio held roughly constant from 1900 through the 1950s), making a purchase "on time" the only way for many to afford it. The company first offered machines on an installment plan in Japan in 1907. By 1918, Singer was importing 50,000 machines per year, a level it maintained with some fluctuation through the 1920s. Roughly 60 to 80 percent were sold on an installment plan.[8]

As elsewhere, installment selling was central to Singer's drive to create a new household market in Japan. The ease of the "modern" practice of installment purchase was a major selling point, but the company also framed its appeal in terms of progress for the individual and the nation. An early Singer leaflet from 1908 proclaimed, "Japan is the country of progress," and offered installment and cash prices for no less than nineteen different household models. A leaflet from about 1912 echoed the theme of installment credit as a progressive and modern "lifelong investment."[9]

Sellers and buyers were self-conscious in their view that they were engaged in a new, progressive, modern practice of American or British origin, something Japanese people should be proud to be doing. One marvelous early example of this consciousness is an article in the *Jiji* newspaper in 1902 that proudly announced the Maruzen bookstore (no relation to the Maruzen installment department store) was selling the *Encyclopedia Britannica* for a five-yen down payment and ten-yen monthly installments over a one- to three-year period, price depending on choice of binding:

> as this installment sales method is used especially in countries where individual credit is advanced, the fact that the Times corporation is using this method in Japan proves that it views Japanese and British people as equal and is giving

us sufficient trust. Therefore, if anyone somehow breaks the contract, this will wound the reputation of Japan and betray the hopes of the foreigners.[10]

The first organization in Japan to survey this emerging world of consumer credit in systematic fashion was the Tokyo Chamber of Commerce. Its pioneering 1929 study introduced readers to consumer credit in the United States and Britain and then examined the practices of Japanese retailers. It drew on state-of-the-art analyses, such as E. R. Seligman's important and just-published opus, *The Economics of Installment Selling* (1927), for the account of the American scene.[11]

The report noted that installment selling had been limited to a small number of products until the mid-1920s, when it expanded dramatically.[12] The "relatively organized present-day practice, which can be called installment sales," started with Singer. At about the same time, improvised practices of traditional credit emerged for household goods such as furniture, ceramics, lacquerware, and clothing (especially men's Western dress). Another new entrant was Nihon Gakki (Yamaha), selling pianos and organs from 1924. In addition to a scattering of other household appliances sold on credit, suburban homes were sold on several-year mortgages along the newly opened commuter railway lines as harbingers of the "modern, cultural" life.

The Chamber of Commerce thus explicitly divided consumer credit into two streams from about 1900 through the 1920s: the imported American practice and a modernized form of traditional credit practices centered on clothing, furniture, and dining ware. Other prewar surveys echoed these empirical judgments and this way of categorizing the phenomenon, but it was the American source of the imported practice that drew most attention. An academic article from 1933 based on a survey of 254 installment sellers in Osaka and Tokyo claimed the salaried urban life "was perfected" in the mid-1920s, a "cultured life" centered on "so-called 'American goods' " such as sewing machines and pianos. The author presented a supply-driven rationale for the sudden spread of payment plans: the largest number of installment sellers needed to find new customers because their output had increased due to greater manufacturing efficiency.[13] By 1934, according to another survey conducted by the city of Tokyo, roughly 10,000 of 130,000 retailers in greater Tokyo offered their goods on time. The survey estimated that 8 percent of all the city's retail sales were made through installment plans, which the survey authors considered a remarkably high number for a relatively new practice.[14]

It is also remarkable that none of these surveys made any effort to measure delinquency, default, or repossession; nor did they discuss such problems in any detail. I have found only one source from this era that mentioned at any length what one surely would expect to have been a major concern.

A best-selling book whose title might roughly translate as "Installment Selling for Dummies" was first published in 1930. In a chapter on installment selling of pianos, the author reported that only 7 to 8 percent of payments were made late, but that 15 to 20 percent of all pianos sold on time were repossessed before payments were completed.[15] These two data points do not mesh well. I suspect that some "purchasers" understood themselves to be renters and simply stopped payments and returned the good without necessarily falling behind on payments, for example, when a child lost interest in her or his lessons. In any case, neither this author nor other commentators saw delinquency or default as huge problems.

Overall, I am struck by the positive tone—and the calm view of problematic aspects—presented by this first generation to interpret the credit boom. Matsunami's guidebook for novices to installment selling grandly proclaimed that credit selling would "democratize mass access to commodities, spread human happiness more equally, and relieve troubling class struggles." The "unpropertied intellectual class" could, for example, afford a 100-yen phonograph on installment but not for cash. The practice thus "elevates the level of daily life." Also, installment purchase brought economic security to households by leading families to budget their expenses.[16]

Perhaps most noteworthy in its prescient and global perspective was the Tokyo Chamber of Commerce in 1929. The preface to its report stated:

> To recover from the long recession . . . along with urging the rationalization of management, the rationalization of daily life has come to be stressed in recent days. . . . [It] is necessary to reform the consumer economy, increase the efficiency of consumption, eliminate waste, lower the expense of daily life, and thus rationalize daily life. . . . The skillful operation of this [installment credit] system can make a major contribution to rationalization of both management and daily life. From the perspective of the consumer, installment purchases allow one to buy goods of considerable cost, which is far more economical [in the long run] than purchase of inexpensive shoddy goods with cash. . . . [This] allows one to level out expenditures over time. It is not only extremely useful in order to lead a disciplined life, planning a monthly budget of expenses; it also raises standards of living by allowing purchase of goods otherwise too expensive.[17]

Most striking in this passage is the appreciation of installment credit as a form of social discipline. Even Seligman's classic 1927 defense of consumer credit was arguably less explicit than these Tokyo authors (who read Seligman carefully) in stressing the centrality of the disciplining function of installment credit.[18] As the Chamber of Commerce authors recognized that the most vigorous and widespread installment credit system in the world was indeed that of the Americans, they found it strange that in the land of the most developed market for installment purchase, one seemed to find more opposition than support.[19] One thus finds in Japan an intriguing intertwining of "catch-up" and simultaneity. On one hand, American-style installment selling was imported to late-developing Japan several decades after it took off in the United States. Yet, by the late 1920s, Japanese observers were fully abreast of global trends, and were indeed precocious in their insight into the significance of the expanding practice at home and abroad.

Not all commentary on consumer credit was positive, to be sure. Even the "how to" promoter Matsunami asserted that installment credit could make buying too easy and overextend a consumer beyond his or her ability to pay.[20] The Tokyo Chamber of Commerce admitted that in Japan, as everywhere, the early days of installment selling had seen abuse in the selling of poor-quality goods at high prices and fraud in the sale of securities, so that installment selling came to have a poor reputation among the "ordinary masses." Many, it said, had come to see purchasing this way as shameful, or to see selling this way as below the dignity of high-class operations such as the major department stores. But the report ended on an upbeat note, pointing to progress in recent years: sellers offering good products on fair terms and middle-class families purchasing goods on time, including everything from radios, phonographs, and cameras to clothes, watches, jewelry, sewing machines, and even autos.[21]

In these and other popular assessments, in some contrast to the picture one takes away from Lendol Calder's account of the American scene (chapter 12), the scorn or sense of problem was directed not so much at the moral hazard to buyers, who might fall into hopeless debt or hedonistic abandon, as it was directed at the shadiness of sellers and the shoddiness of their products. Of course, the two perspectives cannot be neatly separated; a corrupt seller could snare an unsuspecting buyer in dangerous debt. Nonetheless, there seemed to have been some difference in the weight of criticism.

Consumer credit took on a new class and nationalistic dimension in the 1930s with the advent of a so-called "Japanese-style" and "populist" practice in installment sales, especially for sewing machines. By the late 1920s, a number of entrepreneurs, machinists, and disgruntled Singer salesmen had founded a handful of domestic sewing machine makers. The most successful was the Pine Company. Its first president, Ose Yosaku, believed Singer had alienated potential buyers and developed a reputation as arrogant because of stringent credit requirements and a tendency to avoid lower-income buyers. Ose set his sights on what he called the "plebian (*shomin*) class" with a modified installment plan that fit "the Japanese situation."

As Ose told the tale, he was inspired by the "smiling savings plan" offered by the Japan Real Estate Savings Bank, a popular small-loan plan for small businesses since 1916, whereby a saver made installment deposits to his savings account up to an agreed target. At this point, the saver qualified for a loan, to be repaid in monthly installments. This was a successful way to offer partially secured loans to small borrowers, as the borrower had already demonstrated the discipline to save on a regular basis.[22] In similar fashion, Ose offered customers who could not afford a down payment the chance to "reserve" their machines by paying in five yen a month for six months *before* taking possession. By that time, Pine had its down payment in hand, and the customer had the choice of paying cash in full, converting the remaining obligation to a series of ordinary installment payments, including interest, or continuing the layaway without taking the machine until fully paid. In the last case, the customer would be offered a discount against the cash price, in effect earning "interest" on the money deposited with Pine over the course of two years. Pine (later named Janome) touted the plan as especially suited to a family with young daughters. The parents could start paying at birth. When their youngster was ready to learn to sew, they would own the machine.

In the words of Shimada Taku, a key architect of Pine/Janome's marketing strategy, the company was cultivating "the bottom of the social pyramid," the "ordinary masses" such as "the wife in a back-alley tenement who carries her baby half-asleep on her back to go shopping." This creative financing strategy offered the maker a cash-flow advantage, for the prepayments essentially financed the subsequent installment credit. Prepaid orders allowed the company to calibrate production schedules to future demand. And a customer sufficiently disciplined to make regular prepayments—in essence a saver, not a spender—was likely to be able to continue to meet the installment obligations. But marketing rhetoric of "Japanese-style credit" notwithstanding, this was not a unique practice. Ford Motor Company, in 1923, had offered a poorly received layaway program that required customers to prepay the entire cost of the car. Chevrolet responded with a "6 percent purchase plan," which anticipated Janome's effort precisely.[23] It is not clear whether Pine executives were aware of this precedent.

In the late 1930s, the Japanese economy shifted to a war footing. Under such propaganda slogans as "luxury is the enemy," the state mounted vigorous savings campaigns, even prohibited women's permanents, and forced textile manufacturers to produce airplane parts. In the face of these stringent policies, the consumer economy—credit included—contracted and then virtually vanished between 1942 and 1945. But before this happened, the basic outlines of Japanese credit practice were in place. Most borrowing took place through installment credit, and a broad spectrum from the working through the middle class used such credit for purchase of the fruits of modern industrial civilization. The practice generated some anxiety, but on balance the contemporaneous assessments in the press and among official observers were positive or accepting.

* * *

After the war, almost as soon as the production of consumer goods resumed, consumer credit returned as well, both in the form of installment plans and, soon thereafter, in a creative new form that anticipated the credit card by some decades. Sewing machine producers were at the forefront of the revival of both consumer industries and installment sales. Singer was not able to reenter Japanese markets until the 1950s, and never regained its primacy, but the domestic producers built on both Singer's and their own prewar foundations. Industry publications mentioned installments prominently for the first time in late 1948; such credit was in great demand by individual families and schools. By 1950, sewing machine producers—together with makers of autos, bicycles, motorbikes, refrigerators, washing machines, and farm machines— echoed the prewar Chamber of Commerce as they spoke of installment sales as the key to "healthy" and "rational" growth.[24]

By the end of the 1950s, purchasing "on time" had become the method of choice for consumers seeking a wide range of "cultural" goods that defined the bright new consumer life of postwar and peacetime.[25] One 1959 survey enumerated the proportion of goods bought on monthly payments as follows: bicycles, 80 percent; televisions, 75 percent; automobiles, 70 percent; motorbikes, 68 percent; refrigerators, 66 percent; sewing machines, 60 percent; washing machines, 59 percent. According to a 1960–61 MITI survey of 6,200 retail sellers who offered a broader spectrum of goods that included clothing, from one-half to two-thirds of all sales at these stores were made on installment.[26]

In these same years, an important new form of consumer credit also came on the scene—a harbinger of the credit card called "ticket" or "coupon" sales. The ticket industry offered a form of credit midway between a small loan to be used at the consumer's discretion and an installment loan tied to the purchase of a particular good. As with a credit card company, the ticket company contracted on one hand with its member retail stores and on the other hand with consumers. The latter were given books of yen-denominated tickets to use in lieu of cash at member stores. Tickets denominated at 500 and 1,000 yen were typically sold in books of 10,000 or 20,000 yen. The installment payment obligations, ranging from three to twelve months, would commence at the moment a ticket was used to make a purchase. Ticket companies charged interest as part of the monthly installments at annualized rates of 1 to 9 percent, depending on the number of payments. They charged member stores from 5 to 10 percent of the value of the purchased goods.[27]

The retailers were divided into two distinct, competing sectors. On the one hand were the small neighborhood stores clustered in numerous shopping districts in all major cities. Most ticket companies were likewise small-scale, serving a limited number of local retail centers. Opposed to these small retailers were their archrivals, the department stores. The willingness of the latter to offer credit of any type, as well as to join hands with a handful of the largest ticket companies, were new postwar departures. With the exception of the slightly déclassé "installment department stores," the mainline emporiums such as Mitsukoshi had made cash-only selling a point of pride since the turn of the century.

Neighborhood stores and department stores alike jumped on the credit bandwagon in a small way in 1949 and 1950. Each retail segment presented its tactic as a defensive response to the other.[28] But the company that sparked the full-scale takeoff and the political contention in this industry was Nihon Shinpan (literally, Japan Credit Sales), to this day the largest consumer finance company. It was founded in July 1951 in partnership with the Tokyo outlets of four venerable department stores: Takashimaya, Matsuya, Shirokiya, and Keihin. The great majority of ticket associations linked to small retailers were founded in the following two years.

The practice spread rapidly. Three months after Nihon Shinpan began operations, the *Nihon mishin taimusu* (Japan Sewing Machine Times) reported that local merchants had started offering ticket sales in reaction to department stores doing likewise. The paper added a cautionary note that customers might buy useless goods with such credit (rather, one assumes, than sewing machines).[29] In March 1952, the *Asahi shinbun* headlined the contest of "Department Stores and Retailers Competing over Installments." It noted a surge of small-retail centered ticket groups and reported as well that Nihon Shinpan boasted 26,000 customer-members.[30]

This sort of ticket financing was not unique. It was in most respects quite similar to the popular systems of "check trading" in the United Kingdom, pioneered by the Provident Clothing and Supply Co. Ltd. in the late-nineteenth century (see chapter 4) and the "Königsberg system" introduced in that German city in 1926 by the Kundenkredit GmbH. Consumers in these systems would purchase checks on credit from Provident in the United Kingdom or from an installment bank in Germany, redeem these at participating local retailers, and repay the check company with interest over time.[31] These European programs were directed primarily at the working class and charged fairly high interest in view of the uncertainty of their customers' ability to repay the loans, whereas the Japanese ticket companies included a significant portion of middle-class and white-collar men and women among their customers. In addition and related to this difference, the most creative aspect of Japan's ticket industry, which I have not seen elsewhere, was the practice of contracting *collectively* with credit customers through workplaces or through community groups such as neighborhood associations.

Not until the late 1950s did any ticket company offer its product directly to individual consumers. Instead, a ticket company would reach agreement with a government office or a private firm to offer tickets to its employees, or it would arrange with a neighborhood association to offer tickets to its members. A company's welfare or general affairs section would issue the ticket books to employees and collect the subsequent payments via payroll deduction. Nihon Shinpan, for example, would collect the used tickets from the department stores on the fifteenth of each month. Shinpan staff stayed up all night to sort the tickets, write up invoices for each individual buyer, and deliver the tickets and invoices to the workplace (or neighborhood association office) the next day. At the company, tickets and invoices were stuffed into pay envelopes, deductions were taken on payday, and the proceeds were remitted to Nihon Shinpan. In most cases in the 1950s, companies did not charge the ticket vendors for their considerable effort in collecting and forwarding proceeds.[32]

This was a win-win situation for the credit companies and the customers. At a time when a credit-check industry scarcely existed, major finance companies were able to use employers to guarantee their loans and handle their paperwork (in the 1960s, Nihon Shinpan reported a loss ratio of just 0.1 percent of total credit volume).[33] Customers received relatively low-cost credit, usually less than a 10-percent annual rate, for use in purchasing a wide range of goods in local retail shops or department stores. This form of credit grew steadily through the 1950s, reaching a total of 6.6 billion yen ($18 million) in Tokyo in 1959. The six major finance companies that dealt mainly with department stores were growing at a particularly dramatic rate, up 93 percent in sales volume over the previous year.[34] As the 1960s began, well over half the consumer durables transforming daily life and driving economic growth were bought on time. The ticket companies offered a portion of this credit. Roughly fifteen years before the takeoff of bank cards in the United States (the parents of today's MasterCard and Visa), a creative system of credit tickets appeared to be evolving toward the credit card as we know it today. Observers, including state officials, worried some about inflation, default, and the socially erosive impact of "consumptive credit," but they recognized the benefits for industry of allowing credit to masses of customers. As in the interwar era, some understood the monthly payment as a form of social discipline, rather than as an invitation to excess and unsustainable debt.

Then, in 1959, against this background of support and modest concern, Japan's Ministry of International Trade and Industry (MITI) issued an administrative order to restrict the ability of the major "ticket" finance companies and department stores to offer consumer credit. This obscure order was arguably the most consequential decision in the history of Japan's postwar consumer credit.

This episode illustrates nicely the complicated contingencies of turning points in history, since the direct impetus for the order was a political struggle between large and small retailers stimulated only tangentially by worry about excess credit. The lines of political battle set local and national federations of small retailers and their allied ticket sellers against department stores and a handful of major ticket companies collectively known as the *shinpan*. The aggressive growth of the largest such finance company, Nihon Shinpan, was the proximate cause of the struggle. In 1956, it had expanded beyond its Tokyo-Yokohama base by opening Nagoya and Osaka branches. Federations of small-scale retailers, as well as 200 ticket companies nationwide with 10,000 member stores, launched a fierce lobbying campaign against this move. They heckled the Nihon Shinpan president as "Godzilla" when he visited Osaka. They complained that many members were on the verge of collapse. They wanted the government to limit the type and value of goods that department stores could offer on credit. They wanted to restrict the shinpan from issuing tickets that were valid nationwide. Nihon Shinpan and the department stores countered that the minimum purchase of 2,000 yen per item proposed in 1959 was too high: only 40 percent of their ticket sales exceeded that. A bit contradictorily, the large department stores also argued that the problem was exaggerated, because only 3 percent of their sales were through tickets. The practical struggle came to focus on what sort of regulation would be acceptable, and to whom. Nihon Shinpan said it would go bankrupt if tickets purchases were limited to a floor of 1,000 yen per item. The National Federation of Consumer Groups supported this position, claiming tickets were important to allow ordinary consumers to use department stores. But the consumer group did not oppose credit limits in principle. It could live with the prohibition of ticket purchases for less than 100 or 200 yen. And it agreed that ticket credit for purchase of perishables led to reckless spending and should be prohibited.[35]

After a year of intensive lobbying, the small stores won the battle. In October 1959, MITI sent 106 department stores and nineteen shinpan companies an "Order Concerning Self-Restraint by Department Stores." The ruling prohibited stores and credit companies from selling or financing installment goods priced below 500 yen per item nationwide, with a stricter floor of 1,000 yen in the six major cities. It prohibited department-store installment sales of any services, food, drink, plants, or pets. And it outlawed the use of tickets outside the prefecture of issue.[36] Quite simply, the small retailers had been granted a monopoly on installment credit for low-priced goods, and nationally or regionally portable consumer credit had been ruled illegal. An intense battle between large department stores and small retailers had been raging in Japan since the 1920s in other arenas as well.[37] It had now spilled over to restrain the spread of consumer credit.

Three years later, an Installment Sales Law—also drafted by MITI—took effect. It reinforced these administrative constraints. To further protect small businesses, the law stipulated that "if it is judged that a department store or manufacturer will cause great harm to the business of small-scale installment sellers, the relevant ministry can refuse to allow the former [to sell on installment]." And to prevent irresponsible use of "consumptive credit," the law mandated that the government, by administrative order, would designate a list of specified goods that could legally be sold on installment credit. The initial list of approved goods was issued in December 1961. It was quite extensive, allowing credit purchase of items such as toys and cosmetics, which were hardly in the class of "consumer durables." But it prohibited the category of what was called consumptive credit—food, drink, and tobacco—and ruled out credit for all services.[38]

A set of regulatory restraints was now in place. The 1959 order remained in force until 1992. Over these thirty-two years, the regulations reinforced customary practice and ideology to install an enduring system of consumer credit. This combination of regulation and habit accounts for key features of Japanese consumer credit as it expanded in volume from the 1960s onward. First, single-purchase transactions—one credit contract for the purchase of one item—dominated consumer credit into the 1980s. Most were so-called "installment" contracts and some (purchases made with just one or two payments) were defined as "non-installment" credit. Even through the mid-1990s, the combined total of these two categories was only slightly lower than total credit card volume (figure 3.2). To this day (data through 2007), these two categories are roughly the same as the volume of credit card purchases paid in installments or revolving fashion. Through 1992, regulations virtually guaranteed that the proportion of consumer credit provided through cards remained low. Only the finance companies (shinpan) were allowed to offer revolving or installment credit via cards (usually on installments). They replaced credit ticket books with credit cards in the mid-1960s (subject to the same regulations). Banks until 1992 were allowed to enter the consumer credit market only with convenience "credit cards" that had to be cleared

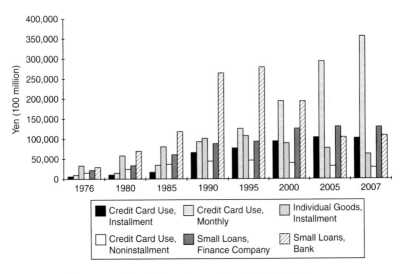

Figure 3.2 Consumer credit use in Japan by type of credit, 1976–2007

Source: Nihon Kurejitto Kyōkai, Nihon no shōhisha shinyō tōkei (Tokyo, 2009). (Data is in Table 3, pp. 32–33, entitled "Shinyō kyōyogaku sōkatsu jikeiretsu hyō: suikei.")

monthly by automatic deduction from a linked savings account. What is fascinating is that these behaviors, which were shaped by what is now a defunct regulatory system, have persisted to the present.

In broad outlines, the story unfolded as follows. In the wake of the MITI order of 1959, Nihon Shinpan closed its Osaka and Nagoya offices, set up a separate corporation to develop its business in Kansai, and saw total credit volume in 1960 fall to 1957–58 levels.[39] When one considers how quickly the economy was growing in these years, this was a dramatic setback.[40] But in 1963, Nihon Shinpan and other finance companies devised a clever tool to circumvent the 1959 order: so-called "shopping credit." On a purchase-by-purchase basis, any customer (not necessarily a pre-enrolled shinpan customer) who entered a member store anywhere in Japan could apply for credit from Nihon Shinpan and pay for that good on installments. Because there were no tickets or cards involved, MITI's 1959 order was not applicable; neither the regional restriction nor the price floor applied, and the ministry did not move to halt or regulate the practice. Although not as convenient as preapproved tickets or credit cards, this innovation sufficed to spark a second wave of growth for the company and its competitors. In sum, the 1959 order and the installment credit law channeled the expansion of consumer credit toward two practices: limited short-term (one- or two-payment) credit, often linked to salary bonuses, or single-good installment purchases.

At the same time, regulation guided the newly emerging bank cards down the path of least resistance: the "convenience" type of monthly cleared credit. All bank cards had to be linked to a savings account, from which payments were deducted in full each month. Although MITI had no legal basis for its action, because the Finance Ministry regulated banks, it nonetheless refused to allow banks to offer coupon, ticket, or shopping credit and to enter the long-term installment business dominated by the shinpan. Short-term monthly cleared credit, on the other hand, fell outside the scope of the 1959 order and 1962 law, and MITI made no claim against banks that offered it.

For its part, the Ministry of Finance maintained that longer-term card-based consumer credit—whether revolving or installment—amounted to unacceptable unsecured loans. As a result, from around 1970, when such bank credit cards began to spread widely, regulators and credit providers institutionalized and made customary the practice of monthly cleared credit cards. Card users came to see this as so "natural" that today most continue to use cards for convenience, not credit, even though the requirement to do so has long since vanished. The so-called 1959 Ordinance was revoked in 1992 as part of a compromise form of deregulation involving MITI, Ministry of Finance, shinpan, and major banks. The banks were allowed to issue revolving or installment credit via cards. In exchange for surrendering their monopoly on this instrument, the shinpan won access to the bank ATM network.

Since 1992, both banks and shinpan have been free to issue consumer credit via cards in three forms: monthly cleared credit; installment credit (typically ten payments); or revolving credit, whereby the consumer can decide the amount of the monthly repayment against an outstanding balance. The customer specifies which type of credit she or he wants at the point of purchase (rather than at the moment of payment, as in the United States). What is intriguing is that even fifteen or more years after the 1959 restrictions were lifted, the vast majority of consumers—indeed an increasing majority in the 2000s—have chosen, or simply accept as the "natural" default practice, the monthly clearing of outstanding balances. According to a survey of 1,455 credit card users in 2001, 71 percent reported making full payments monthly, 12 percent chose to make installment payments, 4 percent made payments linked to semiannual bonuses, and just 4 percent opted for payment on a revolving basis.[41] In 2007, 76 percent of credit card purchases were made with the obligation to clear monthly. This total included cash advances charged to credit cards and contracted for repayment in the next month's billing cycle. Of the 24 percent of credit card borrowing undertaken on an installment or revolving basis, about two-thirds took the form of cash advances.[42] This preponderance of "convenience" over "loan" users contrasts sharply to the American case; no more than 45 percent of U.S. consumers clear their balances monthly at present (2008 data).[43]

In sum, a large proportion of Japanese credit historically took the form of the installment purchase of durable consumer goods. This practice of one-off installment buying has decreased in the past two decades in both relative and absolute terms. In its place, one might say, what has increased dramatically has been credit card "borrowing," with the term placed in scare quotes to highlight the fact that most of this debt is repaid within the month; almost all of the remainder, as with the purchase of individual goods in times past, is repaid through fixed installments. Only a miniscule portion of borrowing has taken the form of card-based revolving credit. This historical outcome is an interesting social practice that is arguably worth praising, as well as explaining.

Borrowers in Japan may have taken on consumer debts at or close to American levels in the past two decades; but their forms of borrowing make them less likely to overextend themselves. Not only is their borrowing usually paid off monthly; in addition, credit cards—whoever the issuer might be—are typically tied to bank savings accounts from which payments are deducted. And Japanese borrowers have not been offered easy access to the sort of home equity loans that have proliferated so destructively in the United States in recent years. Perhaps for these reasons, it appears that the moral condemnation of consumer borrowing in Japan has been aimed less at foolish borrowers than at those unscrupulous or predatory lenders who provide black- or gray-market loans at high interest to consumers unable to access the relatively secure forms of credit under discussion here.

The Japanese practices detailed in this essay may well be closer to European than American ones. It is noteworthy that the institution of ticket finance, so important in Japan's postwar history of consumer credit, does not appear in the American story but is found both in the United Kingdom and on the European continent. Rosa-Maria Gelpi and François Julien-Labruyère argue that, beginning with Britain, credit in the late nineteenth and early twentieth centuries in Europe "aimed at cultured and well-to-do clientele who borrowed to improve their standard of living." This lending was structured as hire-purchase (installment) agreements with "practically no risk for lender or borrower."[44] And as was the case in Japan, European practices of lending appear to have been more closely regulated than those of the United States well into the late twentieth century.[45] On the other hand, the specific focus of regulation in Japan—aimed to protect small retailers as much as to curb credit per se—does not appear elsewhere.

These distinctive and persistent practices cannot be explained solely with reference to culture and custom, on the one hand, or politics and regulation, on the other. Culture is embedded in politics. One cannot explain a practice such as consumer credit in a zero-sum fashion in which either culture or regulation must be designated the independent causal factor. The regulations of the 1950s were shaped to some extent by anxieties and expectations concerning healthy and risky consumer behavior and economic development, but even more by the political power of small retail sellers. These regulations in turn shaped or reinforced consumer attitudes about which choices seemed obvious or natural. Consumer behavior was changing even in advance of deregulation: installment use of credit cards spiked up from the late 1980s. And even as regulations changed to allow other options, certain basic patterns such as the use of monthly cleared credit continued to be "natural" choices for many Japanese. Habit emerged as the hybrid product of crosscutting pressures.

Notes

1. See Peggy Orenstein, "Parasites in Pret-a-Porter," *New York Times Sunday Magazine*, July 1, 2001, 31.

2. The JCA data excludes home mortgages and home equity loans for consumers in both countries. Charles Horioka in chapter 11 of this volume shows that Japanese mortgage borrowing has been extraordinarily high in comparative terms among G7 nations relative to income, so inclusion of such data would actually raise the profile of Japanese borrowing relative to income or relative to other countries. Conversely, however, if one considers home equity loans as credit card borrowing in disguise, which they arguably have been in recent years in the United States, the recent levels of American consumer debt, excluding mortgages, outpace those in Japan by a more significant margin. I am indebted to Sheldon Garon for pointing this out to me.

3. Rosa-Maria Gelpi and François Julien-Labruyère, *The History of Consumer Credit: Doctrines and Practices,* trans. Mn Liam Gavin (New York, 1999), start their story with the Code of Hammurabi in 1792 B.C.E.

4. The *Kojien* dictionary (electronic version in Seiko Denshi Jisho) glosses "pawnshop" (*shichi*) with a literary reference from Taketori Monogatari (tenth century C.E.), considered Japan's oldest work of narrative fiction.

5. See *Geppu kenkyū*, series 4/1957–5/1958. Mujin or kō were revolving mutual credit funds, also described by Embree in Suyemura in the 1930s, where the funds' members met monthly, usually for a meal and drinks, and each contributed an agreed sum. The total was given to the winner of a lottery. Subsequent lotteries were limited to those who had not yet won. Community or peer pressure among people well known to each other served to insure against default. In the Ehime lacquer innovation, all members of a group received their goods upon an initial pooled payment, and periodic subsequent payments were collected from the entire group. Tetsuo Najita, *Ordinary Economies in Japan* (Berkeley, CA, 2009), 175–209, offers an important recent discussion.

6. Tokyo shōkōkaigisho, *Geppu hanbai seido* (Tokyo, 1929), 212–13.

7. Lendol Calder, *Financing the American Dream: A Cultural History of Consumer Credit* (Princeton, NJ, 1999), 56–57.

8. Janome kabushiki kaisha, *Janome mishin sōgyō 50 nen shi* (Tokyo, 1971) and Kuwahara Tetsuya, "Shoki takokuseki kigyō no tainichi toshi to minzoku kigyō," *Kokumin keizai zasshi* 185, no. 5 (February 2002): 50.

9. Singer sales leaflets, dated "Autumn 1908," and undated, approximately 1912, held in collection of Edo-Tokyo Museum; item numbers 91222544 and 93200196.

10. Cited in Fukushima Hachiro, "Geppu, wappu, kurejitto," *Gekkan Kurejitto*, no. 200 (1973): 20.

11. On Seligman, see Calder, *Financing the American Dream*, 237–48.

12. Tokyo shōkōkaigisho, *Geppu hanbai seido*, 227.

13. Hirai Yasutaro "Honpō ni okeru bunkatsu barai seido no genjō ni oite," *Kokumin keizai zasshi* 43, no. 2 (1933): 69–73, 81.

14. Tokyo shi, shiyakusho, kōgyōkyoku, shōgyōka, *Wappu hanbai ni kan suru chōsa* (Tokyo, 1935).

15. Matsunami Tadayuki, *Sugu ni yakudatsu geppu hanbai* (Tokyo, 1930), 193–200.

16. Ibid., 160 and 148, in that order for these two quotes.

17. Tokyo Chamber of Commerce, 1929, 1–2.

18. Calder, *Financing the American Dream*, 29–33.

19. Tokyo Chamber of Commerce, 1929, 181–88.

20. Matsunami, 1930, 149–50.

21. Tokyo Chamber of Commerce, 227.

22. *Janome mishin sōgyō 50 nen shi*, 194–200.

23. Calder, *Financing the American Dream*, 195–99.

24. *Nihon mishin taimusu*, no. 112, August 21, 1950, 1.

25. *Nihon mishin taimusu*, no. 249, August 21, 1953, 7.

26. Nihon mishin sangyô kyôkai, *Nihon mishin sangyô shi* (Tokyo, 1961), 9. Tsūsanshō (MITI), ed., *Wappu hanbai jittai chōsa* (Tokyo, 1962), 9. The MITI survey was limited to stores offering at least some goods on installment, so it exaggerates the proportional totals.

27. A useful description of the ticket business is offered by Takagi Kunio, "Chiketto hanbai no keitai," *Jurisuto* 382 (October 15, 1967): 68–69.

28. See "Ginza Ticket Incident," *Tokyo asahi shinbun*, April 10, 1950, 2.

29. *Nihon mishin taimusu*, no. 154, October 21, 1951, part 2 of series on installment selling.

30. *Tokyo asahi shinbun*, March 18, 1952, 2.

31. Sean O'Connell and Chris Reid, "Working-Class Consumer Credit in the UK, 1925–1960: The Role of the Check Trader," *Economic History Review* 57, no. 2 (2005), 378–405; Jan Logemann and Uwe Spiekermann, "The Myth of a Bygone Cash Economy: Consumer Lending in Germany from the Nineteenth Century to the Mid-Twentieth Century," *Entreprises et histoire* 59, no. 2 (2010): 12–27.

32. Nihon shinpan, *Za bunka: Nihon shinpan no 50 nen shi* (Tokyo, 1976), 1, and Takagi, "Chiketto hanbai no keitai," 68–69.
33. Takagi, "Chiketto hanbai no keitai," 69.
34. Tokyo shōkōkaigishō, *Tokyo ni okeru wappu hanbai no genjō to mondai* (Tokyo, 1960): 37.
35. Nihon shinpan, *Za bunka*, 3, and "Arguments over Department Store Installment," *Tokyo asahi shinbun*, November 4, 1958, 4.
36. *Tokyo asahi shinbun*, October 31, 1959, 1, and October 24, 1959, 4.
37. See Sheldon Garon and Mike Mochizuki, "Negotiating Social Contracts," in *Postwar Japan as History*, ed. Andrew Gordon (Berkeley, CA, 1993), 148–55.
38. Full text of the law and of all Diet deliberations on the bill can be found at the National Diet Library's website. The text of the law with discussion and detailed interpretation of each provision, plus the full list of specified goods, can be found in Shinada Seihei, *Wappu hanbai no hōritsu, kaikei, zeimu* (Tokyo, 1961), 63–218.
39. Nihon shinpan kabushiki geisha, *Nihon shinpan 35 nen no ayumi* (n.p., 1961), 135–36.
40. The spinning out of the Osaka and Nagoya operations as separate companies may account for part of the drop.
41. Nihon kurejitto sangyō kyōkai, *Kurejitto ni kansuru shōhisha chōsa* (Tokyo, 2001), 245.
42. Nihon kurejitto kyōkai, *Nihon no shōhisha shinyō tōkei* (Tokyo, 2009), 31–32, for data through 2007.
43. ComScore, September 2008, accessed January 13, 2010 at http://www.credit cards.com/credit-card-news/credit-card-industry-facts-personal-debt-statistics-1276.php#paymenttrends. A figure of 39% clearing monthly is reported for 2004 on http://www.cardratings.com/creditcardstatistics.html.
44. Gelpi and Julien-Labruyère, *The History of Consumer Credit*, 129.
45. Ibid., 129–46.

PART II

Borrowers and Credit Access

CHAPTER 4

The Business of Working-Class Credit: Subprime Markets in the United Kingdom since 1880

Sean O'Connell

Certain consumer credit businesses have historically been associated with distinct groups. This has been particularly true of working-class communities throughout the industrialized world since the late nineteenth century. This chapter uses a case study approach to explore a number of the themes around which this volume of essays is organized. Via an examination of the history of Provident Financial PLC, it provides examples of both transnational similarities in credit provision and details of how cultural and political patterns in individual countries led to sharply divergent historical pathways.

Provident is today associated with the United Kingdom's extensive subprime credit market, particularly that sector of it populated by low-income consumers. The term "subprime" is most commonly connected with developments in the United States during the 1990s, where the diminishing cost of computerized data storage and the emergence of sophisticated risk modeling led to many consumers, who had been previously categorized as too risky, being provided with high-cost credit products—even by "conservative creditors." These products included subprime credit cards, which attracted criticism due to their high charges.[1]

In the United Kingdom, Provident was one of the first companies to offer such a card, the Vanquis Visa, from 2003. The company, however, has 130 years experience dealing with customers who face difficulties securing credit from mainstream financial sources. For much of its history, Provident marketed products that preempted the subprime credit card in both the flexibility they offered less affluent consumers and in the high costs that were associated with them. Provident's story provides insights into the history of an important part of the United Kingdom's subprime sector. Unlike a number of defunct French and German finance companies that employed similarly bureaucratized and labor-intensive systems, Provident has survived and thrived in the modern credit market. Its ability to do so centered on a number of factors, including the approach to credit regulation adopted by UK governments, the comparatively high levels of financial exclusion in the United Kingdom, the limited success of British credit unions and other mutual bodies, and the continuing functionality (albeit a costly one) of doorstep collections for low-income consumers.

This chapter begins with a brief historical description of the context of working-class consumer credit in the United Kingdom in the years around Provident's creation. The origins of the company are then plotted, before the discussion turns to the company's relationships with retailers and consumers. The controversies that emerged from these relationships are explored, as are accusations that the system was exploitative. The next section discusses French and German companies that operated schemes not unlike the Provident system. However, these schemes died off in the second half of the twentieth century, whereas Provident retained its place among Britain's largest financial institutions. Two final sections examine this period. The first of these explains how Provident attempted to follow the increasingly affluent working-class consumer up the status hierarchy by offering new forms of credit and seeking to shake off its association with low-income consumers. The final section charts the company's successful and controversial engagement in the United Kingdom's extensive doorstep moneylending industry, which, having no European counterpart, demonstrates again that Provident provides a fascinating vehicle through which to explore the cultural, economic, and political shaping of consumer credit.

The Context: Working-Class Consumer Credit in the United Kingdom

As Paul Johnson has demonstrated, the extent and variety of consumer credit in late nineteenth- and early twentieth-century Britain reflected wide demand.[2] The most familiar consumer credit innovation of the period was hire purchase, which was associated with growing markets for consumer durables such as furniture, electric goods, and motor cars.[3] In the early twentieth century, the number of hire-purchase contracts rose by a factor of twenty.[4] By the late 1930s, hire purchase was believed to facilitate 3.5 percent of all retail sales.[5] The value of this business was then estimated at around £100 to £120 million, representing half of all credit sales.

Hire purchase had become the preferred option for credit retailers of furniture, pianos, and sewing machines in late Victorian Britain, while simultaneously raising concerns about high interest rates and high repossession rates. The latter was the case because—unlike in France, as Sabine Effosse explains in chapter 8—the retailer had a legal right to reclaim the merchandise if the purchaser fell behind with payments. Until the final payment was made, the goods were on "hire" to the buyer. Hire purchase was first used by the British working classes during the 1860s, when Singer marketed its sewing machines through the method. Many more working-class consumers became familiar with hire purchase during the Great War, when regular and remunerative employment in the war industries financed the phenomenon of the "munitions worker's piano." Recent work by Peter Scott has indicated that, in the 1930s, hire purchase facilitated new modes of working-class living that were related to an array of factors, such as rising home ownership among the best-paid workers, shrinking family sizes, and new modes of domesticated living.[6]

While what Scott calls modern working-class consumers were using hire purchase to shape new lifestyles, extensive use was also made of other modes of consumer credit for the purchase of nondurable goods. From the mid-nineteenth century, credit drapers—often labeled tallymen—sold clothing and drapery from door to door to urban working-class families. The weekly collection of payments was one factor that ensured goods bought in this way were costly. High prices and the use of the courts to pursue delinquent working-class debtors brought frequent controversy to the credit drapers. So did the fact that they did their business with working-class housewives, who, it was often assumed, had been duped or flattered into making ill-advised purchases. Although this was a highly gendered and negative stereotyping of the capabilities of many working-class wives, whose role included managing tight budgets, it was widely believed.[7]

Formed in 1880, the Provident Clothing and Supply Company claimed to have developed a fairer and thriftier form of working-class credit for the "respectable" working classes, who otherwise had to use credit drapers. Provident sold promissory notes, which it called checks, on installments to customers who utilized them to buy merchandise in the large number of stores where they were accepted in lieu of cash. By the late 1930s, Provident, the other smaller check traders, and the credit drapers were responsible for the extension of around £100 million in consumer credit per annum. By this point, Provident had reached its maximum market, serving around 1 million customers per annum.[8]

Also by the 1930s, it was clear that mail-order catalogs, offering clothing and other merchandise on credit, had unearthed a lucrative market. The introduction of parcel post in 1883 spurred on the development of several significant credit mail-order catalog companies. Unlike their North American counterparts, who competed with small, local retailers via price, UK mail-order catalog retailers such as Kays or Empire Stores attracted large numbers of customers by installment selling. By the 1930s, they were dispatching their catalogs to hundreds of thousands of agents, who earned small commissions for selling products. They also carried out informal credit vetting of customers recruited from their families, neighbors, and workmates. The zenith of credit mail order was reached between the 1950s and 1970s, when the sector was the fastest growing in British retail. In 1968, for example, mail order was responsible for 4 percent of all the United Kingdom's retail sales. More significantly, it accounted for 48 percent of all credit sales in the retail sector.[9]

The significant market shares taken by the mail-order companies, check traders, and tallymen indicated not only significant demand for working-class consumer credit, but also the continuing importance of traditional forms of credit based on the commercial penetration of preexisting social networks. The following case study of Provident allows greater explication of this phenomenon. It also demonstrates how the often deeply complex debates about the rights and wrongs, benefits and costs, of working-class consumer credit operated in the context of one major UK company, and it allows deeper reflection on a number of issues raised above.

The Origins of Provident

The Provident Clothing and Supply Company Limited emerged in 1880. Ironically, given its controversial history, founder Joshua V. Waddilove claimed to have commenced its activities because of the "dear" and "limited" merchandise bought by working-class housewives from tallymen (credit drapers).[10] Having first funded a charitable system to enable women to obtain goods from retailers who accepted his checks, a company was swiftly formed to take advantage of the demand that was unearthed.[11] Waddilove had been employed in the thriving Victorian insurance industry, where he witnessed significant numbers of working-class families paying small sums each week to collectors for what were termed "industrial insurance policies." Weekly doorstep collections and heavy overheads for bureaucracy, which ate up as much as one-third of payments, made these insurance policies expensive and subject to regular critiques by middle-class observers.[12] Despite this cost, their popularity was such that one-third of the population had one of these policies with the market leader, Prudential, by 1900.[13] The name "Prudential" was selected to stem accusations that the company promoted an unthrifty method of insurance, and the christening of Provident suggests a similar preemptive strike in anticipation of future criticism.

As credit drapers had discovered earlier, many Victorians viewed the extension of consumer credit with suspicion. In particular, those involved in credit deals with working-class consumers were disdained as "fringe capitalists."[14] The realities of working-class budgeting were frequently miscomprehended by those holding this attitude. These consumers were exhorted to embrace thrift and reject debt, not least by influential activists in the cooperative movement, who felt the latter "was at odds with the principles of cooperative idealism and respectable behaviour." One widely read cooperative activist opined that "the credit system of this country is only second in its demoralising influence to the drinking customs of the people." However, pressure from grassroots members who had to manage on incomes that were vulnerable to unemployment, underemployment, trade slumps, illness, and other factors militating against a steely commitment to thrift compelled cooperative stores to offer credit facilities. By 1911, 82 percent of them did so.[15]

As already indicated, Victorian and Edwardian negative sentiment toward working-class credit and the perils of indebtedness reached its zenith in discussion of credit drapers. Being among the heaviest users of the debtors' courts, credit drapers received extensive press coverage, which frequently portrayed them as irresponsible lenders and exploiters of feminine vanity and gullibility. While it is clear that there were devious characters among them, most credit drapers made money from establishing long-term relationships with customers that were based on a strong degree of trust and reciprocity. Like the insurance companies, they provided an expensive service that was nonetheless utilitarian for hard-pressed consumers with few alternatives.[16] Moreover, as credit draper Ron Barnes recalled, the fact that his transactions were played out in his customer's home ensured credit drapers were greeted with the "natural friendliness" that would have met other personal visitors.[17] This intimacy was highly advantageous, proving a more useful method of limiting bad debt than recourse to the courts. Provident drew upon this important factor in its own operations.

Provident's Modus Operandi

Although Provident's weekly visits to collect repayments echoed the credit drapery model, as did other aspects of its business, its approach to doorstep credit had important differences. This circumstance ensured that it attracted far less bad publicity for using the debtors' courts, while also assisting its rise to national prominence. Provident established a triangular credit relationship, placing itself between borrowers and retailers. It dispatched agents to identify customers who would buy its checks, which were then redeemed via weekly doorstep payments. For this service, customers paid a fee—or poundage charge—of 1 shilling (5 pence) for each 20 shillings (£1). This equated to an annual interest rate of 23.3 percent if repaid in the anticipated 20 weeks, although customers typically took 24 weeks to complete payments.[18] Once they acquired a check, customers were free to use it at any retailer accepting them.

Provident's success in persuading a great variety of shopkeepers to join its scheme was the key to its popularity and ensured that its customers prioritized their repayments to it over those to other creditors. In 1908, its checks could be used to procure merchandise ranging from "photographs to bassinettes and from barometers to artificial teeth." Three decades later, the brochure for Provident's customers in Wolverhampton included nineteen footwear stores, thirteen house furnishers, twenty-one clothing retailers, eleven opticians, nine purveyors of wireless sets, four jewelers and watchmakers, three wallpaper and paint shops, two secondhand furniture stores, two secondhand clothes shops, and one coal merchant.[19] To establish itself in a new locality, the company offered key retailers much lower than average rates for its service. While a department store might be charged 8 percent of the amount Provident's customers spent in the store, a hairdresser was asked to forfeit a hefty 20 percent.[20] In the 1930s, the company had agreements with 14,000 retailers—a figure that reached 20,000 by the 1960s and included several significant national retail chains.[21]

An Uneasy Relationship? Selling Provident to Retailers

Provident's arrangements with retailers were not secured without controversy. Shopkeepers opposed to the system claimed that Provident customers could be easily "spotted," that prices were raised to cover the discount the retailer had to pay Provident, or that "a special line of rubbish" was held in store for them.[22] In 1910, one female shopper provided evidence of such a tactic, informing a newspaper that when she produced a Provident check to pay for a jacket, she was asked for an additional 9 percent on the marked retail price.[23] The extent of these practices is unclear, but shopkeepers prioritized cash buyers over Provident check users, and the company advised its customers to "shop as little as possible" on Saturdays and to make purchases "around the middle of the week," when retailers would, they were instructed, "serve you far better."[24]

Despite Provident's instructions to its customers, many retailers and their representatives remained hostile to the check trade. In 1908, *Drapers Record* claimed the practice had caused "a decrease of legitimate profit-bearing turnover" and argued that "the retail trade must annihilate the [check] clubs or be itself destroyed."[25] Shopkeepers attempted to educate the public about Provident's hidden costs. In 1913, one group paraded a donkey through Bury town center, carrying a legend that labeled any check customer "an ass."[26] Twenty-five years later, the *Daily Express* reported that retailers' organizations had issued the public "with leaflets exposing the check system." The newspaper alleged that retailers and customers were being milked to enable check trading companies to make annual profits of up to 1,700 percent. It urged that these firms "be rigorously curtailed" and made subject to the 48 percent interest rate cap that had been applied to moneylending transactions in 1927.[27] The *Daily Express* had got its sums rather badly wrong. In 1934, for example, Provident's profit of £285,000 on a turnover of £5.7m was slightly less than 5 percent.[28] The charges imposed on retailers were significant, however, and it is important to ask why so many retailers were willing to accept Provident checks.

In 1915, *Credit Draper* debated this issue. It asked how, with fees up to 17.5 percent, Provident and other check traders had "managed to get reputable shopkeepers to fall into their trap."[29] One retailer who had succumbed to Provident's overtures claimed turnover rose only until other retailers also began to accept checks. Thereafter, he was left paying fees for what he dismissively dubbed Provident's "American business."[30] The allegedly Americanized and un-British nature of installment selling was a common theme in the early twentieth century, from the plebeian check trade through to much more affluent markets, such as that for motor cars.[31] But offering credit to the working classes always elicited the most heavily moralized discourse. Thus, another disillusioned shopkeeper, angered by waits of up to six months to be reimbursed by Provident for the checks presented in his shop, dismissed Waddilove's claim that his system facilitated working-class thrift: "The whole system is one of borrowing, not thrift, and any system that encourages the working classes to borrow must be demoralising."[32]

However, the enormous number of retailers who accepted Provident checks is evidence that many anticipated advantages from involvement in the scheme. Increased turnover was clearly one. Provident agents represented mobile advertisements for retailers whose details appeared on the shopping lists given customers. One retailer who had been converted to the system argued, in 1908, that far more misery had "been brought to homes by the packman [credit draper]." His view of the check trade was colored, no doubt, by the fact that his annual turnover had risen from £2,000 to £5,000. Another shop owner reasoned that check users "invariably spend more than their check," with additional cash purchases reducing the impact of the retailer's payment to Provident. Manufacturers also functioned as an ally in Provident's advance. One large footwear producer, for example, offered to stock a shop for a Manchester retailer, but only if he were to "open an account with the Provident."[33]

The issue of securing new types of customers for retailers lay at the heart of Provident's success. In effect, rather like modern-day subprime credit companies, the company developed a system that enabled it to operate in a market deemed too risky by regular retailers or banks. Melanie Tebbutt has argued that in early twentieth-century Britain a greater demand for consumer credit forced many reluctant retailers to adopt installment selling.[34] Provident lay at the heart of that process, because the company enabled retailers to avoid the costs and risks associated with financing credit independently. Retailers who joined the scheme did not have to assess credit risk, pursue nonpayers, or face the financial- or status-reducing costs of suing debtors in the courts. In short, it was Provident, not the retailer, that handled the economically and morally charged relationship with the customer, and it is that relationship to which this chapter now turns.

An Exploitative Relationship? Provident and Its Customers

Customer demand for Provident's service was evidenced by its startling growth. Provident agents followed a well-trodden path, pursuing credit drapers and insurance collectors into working-class districts; and, in turn, their track was taken by football pools collectors and mail-order catalog agents.[35] Thus, working-class households were accustomed to the weekly knock on the door from a variety of commercial callers. In 1920, one area of 3,500 residents in the port city of Hull was visited each week by as many as 100 insurance collectors.[36] Adopting a fieldwork organization that had served the industrial insurance companies so well, Provident amassed a small army of mainly part-time agents to seek out customers and, then, collect and monitor repayments. Agents were instructed to closely observe the rhythms of working-class life. Credit should be "kept low to the labourer with young children," because his disposable income would be limited, but it should be increased "in future when [the children] work." When the children left home, to set up their own households, their parents' "credit levels must be watched again and reduced," while the new home should be visited and the young adults "encouraged to take up credit."[37]

The agent also had a disciplinary function, similar to that noted by Paul Johnson for the industrial insurance collectors, whose weekly visits imposed the discipline of contract on working-class families by reminding them of "long-run goals" when "there was scarcely enough money to feed the family."[38] Waddilove used this argument himself, claiming that his system was a form of thrift. He maintained that although critical observers declared that "the working man ought to save his shilling a week himself" and acquire merchandise only when he had the funds to do so, it was "very difficult to keep the shilling untouched." The agent's visit, Waddilove argued, ensured that the shilling was kept as "payment for clothes and boots."[39]

Here we can see a leading promoter of credit reinventing ideas of thriftiness that anticipated Lendol Calder's argument in chapter 12 about the complex relationship between thrift and credit in modern consumer economies. The nature of that relationship differed between nations and among social groups in each national setting. Thus, the Provident model for credit rating differed markedly from that developed by Schufa in Germany (see chapter 6), being based on face-to-face local networks rather than the automated accumulation of data on consumer transactions. For example, one credit retailer reported in 1929 that Provident did not take on a customer without obtaining one reference from a shopkeeper and two local house-holders.[40] Thereafter, the company relied on the agent's skill in maintaining an effective and profitable relationship with the customer. Provident could also draw upon the fact that its checks offered access to numerous retailers to ensure that repayments to it had a higher priority than those to less utilitarian rivals.

The complicated financial interchange among customer, retailer, and Provident left check buyers with a vague notion of the system's full costs. For those managing tight budgets, the key issue was the size of the weekly repayment. If that sum could be met, there was, then, the prospect of paying something akin to cash prices. As one Belfast check buyer explained: "all you paid on these Provident checks was one shilling to the pound— five percent—so they weren't too bad, they weren't really extortive. But probably the shops who took the Provident checks were dearer to shop in than the shops that didn't."[41] From the perspective of many working-class customers with limited credit options, Provident stood out, and research indicates that it was their favored form of credit during the interwar period. One Newcastle woman recalled that "when the Provident came onto the scene it was ideal. That's how I brought up my family, with the help of the Provident."[42]

There were a number of reasons for this popularity. An extremely significant one is touched upon by Silke Meyer in chapter 10 for the German case. She explains the insights that anthropology can bring to our understanding of modern credit economies by viewing credit as a system of exchange and reciprocity. This perspective also informs the history of working-class credit in the United Kingdom. There, historians have explained how the employment of part-time agents deployed in their own communities enabled credit companies to embed themselves within established working-class social networks.

In doing so, they commercialized the trust that existed within those communities, while also utilizing the norm of respectability to ensure that bad debt levels were low. It was harder for a working-class woman to fall behind in payments to an agent whom she knew well than it was to ignore the letters of a distant corporation. Moreover, these close relationships ensured that Pierre Bourdieu's dictum that credit "creates obligations by creating people obliged to reciprocate" was central to the creation of long-term loyalty among customers of Provident and other credit companies, allowing them to capture elements of gifting within a commercial relationship.[43]

Customers also appreciated the fact that Provident checks represented a much more flexible form of credit than others on offer. This was reflected in the different uses that they made of checks. The more affluent of the company's customers used what were called "relay checks" (a series of checks granted one after another) to pay for higher-priced goods that normally were bought by hire purchase. Taking this route to the ownership of durable goods may have been viewed as offering security by many check users, who were aware of so-called hire-purchase "snatch backs." A great deal of press attention was focused on this repossession of merchandise due to late payment, and Avram Taylor has described the shame experienced by working-class consumers who had prized consumer goods removed from their homes in full view of neighbors during the 1930s.[44] Provident checks facilitated ownership of the merchandise and gave buyers a level of protection not available to hire purchasers.

Toward the other end of the working-class income spectrum, checks were acquired during passages of domestic crisis management. In such circumstances, Provident checks were often acquired to facilitate the purchase of items that were immediately pawned to raise cash.[45] Thus, the customer had only to raise the cash to pay for the first installment on the check, in order to realize a larger sum on the pawned item to deal with whatever pressing financial crisis was at hand. For similar reasons, a secondary market sprang up in the buying and selling of Provident checks. A court case in the port of West Hartlepool, in 1953, heard that several women were engaged in "wholesale illicit trading" in this respect, buying checks valued at £1 (20 shillings) for 15 shillings. They were then sold to more fortunate consumers for 16 shillings.[46] However, the majority of check users had more mundane reasons for their decision to employ the system, using it to meet family clothing requirements. Analysis of Provident's records demonstrate that demand for checks was greatest in the final quarter of each year, as customers readied themselves for Christmas.[47]

A further aspect of a Provident check's flexibility was its acceptance by so many retailers. Customers, therefore, did not have to engage in multiple requests for credit with a succession of retailers. Not only did this save time, but it also reduced the potential for publicly shaming rejections. Moreover, a check could be subdivided and spent in more than one store. In the view of one Scottish woman, this gave a Provident check more utility than the Cooperative movement's equivalent, the mutuality club voucher: "it was a big advantage . . . it was not a case of one shop. The Co-op gave you 20 weeks or 38 weeks but then you only had the Co-op, whereas the Provident gave you a selection of different shops . . . [Y]ou could spend it in Paisley and you could spend it in Glasgow, it was not as if you were constricted."[48] This viewpoint differed from one aired in a report by the Women's Group on Public Welfare in 1943. It was highly critical of "wrong spending" by consumers using checks, whereas it praised the mutuality clubs.[49] The Co-op's system levied similar fees for their doorstep collections as Provident, but purchases made contributed to the quarterly dividends earned by co-operative members. However, the Women's Group on Public Welfare was ignorant of the fact that only co-operative customers with healthy financial balances in their dividend accounts were granted credit, a factor that excluded large numbers of consumers.[50] Subsequent histories of working-class credit, which have acknowledged the cultural and economic context in which working-class families budgeted, have produced much richer understandings of their actions than that offered by either the Women's Group on Public Welfare or the civil servant who, in 1952, labeled check users as "the feckless and often stupid poor." Material factors such as family size, economic misfortune, or limited alternative credit channels had little place in his assessment.[51]

The size of Provident's customer base alone should have stifled such pejorative sentiments. By 1908, Provident's 85 branches employed 3,000 agents.[52] Two years later, it claimed to be the originator of "the best and most popular credit system ever devised," declaring itself a "real boon to the respectable working-class."[53] Annual collections, £1 million in 1910, rose to £5 million in 1925, at which point there were 616,000 customers. By the mid-1930s, and again in the 1950s, the company serviced over 1 million customers and their families.[54]

Provident in European Perspective

Our opinionated civil servant might have been given further food for thought had he taken a glance over the English Channel to France and Germany. In both countries, systems evolved that bore comparison with Provident checks. In France, Crépin coupons were the best known of these. Named after Jacques-François Crépin, they became a national institution under the direction of his successor, George Dufayel. They originated in the 1850s, when Crépin began selling photographic portraits on installment. Demand for this service led to the employment of travelers, who were also soon promoting the sale of furniture and clothing. Customers were granted a coupon, worth 100 francs, after an original 25 percent down payment, and they paid the remaining sum in weekly payments. Retailers met most of the system's costs, paying as much as 50 percent commission for the customers brought to their doors.[55] These high costs discredited the coupons and, in 1869, Dufayel reorganized the scheme. By 1904, it was claimed that the system had served 3.5 million customers. In Paris alone, there were 800 *abonneurs* (collectors), each responsible for two streets. They made inquiries with employers about potential customers' solvency, recorded other information on their reliability, collected repayments, and encouraged good payers to make further purchases. Four hundred shops accepted the coupons, paying 18 percent commission.

As was the case with Provident checks, questions were raised about the quality of merchandise sold to coupon customers and whether or not prices were inflated. Dufayel responded to critics by arguing that the system allowed workers to acquire the comforts of life without being exploited by usurers. The company also pointed out that it was sympathetic toward slow-paying customers, if they had been beset by matters such as disease, pregnancy, or prolonged unemployment.[56] This was an approach shared with Provident, which was compelled to present an empathetic persona when hearing of a customer's economic woes. In 1929, one Provident executive wrote that such cases "are normal trade risks, and the only course open is to encourage payment of a small amount from such sources as unemployment pay, until employment is once more obtained."[57] This approach was a further factor designed to elicit a sense of obligation and loyalty among customers.

Thus, like Provident, Dufayel's credit network "relied on local contacts, word of mouth, and face-to-face encounters."[58] On these foundations, Dufayel claimed—as Waddilove did—to have established the world's biggest consumer credit concern.[59] Dufayel's achievements forced other French retailers to form "an ambitious credit plan of their own." In 1904, more than fifty stores created the Economic Union of Saint-Denis, which offered an alternative to Crépin coupons. Several other such syndicates followed in its wake.[60]

Germany also developed a similar method of consumer credit, which has been described as "indigenous" and owing little to American credit models. This was the Königsberg system, named after the city in which it originated in 1926. Established by an installment bank (the Kundenkredit GmbH), it was most widely taken up by members of the industrial working class. Like the Provident system, customers avoided the daunting task of negotiating credit with numerous retailers. Instead, credit limits were arranged with the bank financing the scheme. Annual interest rates levied ranged from 35 to 53 percent, a level that one contemporary noted could be judged "unconscionable" in the German courts. Unlike Dufayel's business, the Königsberg scheme reemerged after 1948, but its history and demise have yet to be related fully.[61] As Rebecca Belvederesi-Kochs outlines in chapter 2, the Sparkassen (quasi-public savings banks) entered the installment lending market in 1952, and this development certainly provides one explanation for the death of the Königsberg system. In France, the view is that rising working-class living standards during *les trente glorieuses* increased spending power and created markets for more modern forms of consumer credit while also killing off demand for older forms. This process was assisted by the extension of banking services to 89 percent of the French population by 1980 and 100 percent by the 1990s.[62]

The Survival of Provident

In the United Kingdom, by contrast, Provident found a new lease on life in the final decades of the twentieth century. Initially, this appeared an unlikely outcome. Provident's market began to stagnate during the 1950s, and levels of new business fell persistently year on year by some 4 percent during the 1950s.[63] Many of its traditional customers were attracted to the increasing range of merchandise available in mail-order catalogs. By the early 1960s, mail-order companies produced colorful catalogs of up to 1,000 pages in length, which *The Times* described as "a riot of consumer goods" and "an index to the affluent society."[64]

Like Provident, the mail-order sector developed an agency system that tapped into working-class sociability and reciprocity. As many as 900,000 part-time agents were calling upon friends, neighbors, and workmates to show them their catalog by the 1960s.[65] Significantly, almost nine in ten agents were female and were stimulated predominantly by the opportunity the catalog provided to reinforce social relationships, or to establish fresh ones, rather than the modest sales commission that could be earned. This created a particularly effective sales force, whose connections with their customers ensured low levels of bad debt.[66] In this increasingly competitive environment, Provident was fortunate that many of its customers demonstrated significant levels of cultural inertia. Many continued to use the company when they might have been expected to utilize their rising earnings by accessing more modern forms of credit. Thus, there was a lag between economic and cultural change.[67]

The company responded to the changing economic climate by attempting to follow the path being taken by the new "affluent workers," who were the subject of so much postwar political and sociological discussion. In 1962,

Provident left the ownership of the Waddilove family and became a public company. A new management team, with experience in other fields of consumer credit, instigated a process of modernization. Richard Davenport, who had worked in hire purchase and rose to become Provident's chairman, was struck by the access it had to customer's homes via its 10,000 mostly female agents. He asked, "Who on earth else had that sort of lever?" and launched initiatives to exploit this relationship further and to remove the idea that Provident was a means through which "to buy coal and shoes."[68]

As part of its modernization, the company introduced vouchers of higher values than its traditional checks. Initially they were for sums of up to £100, but climbed to £200 by 1970. Collection charges for vouchers were as much as 15 percent of their value and were repaid over 40 to 100 weeks. The annual percentage rate (APR) levels of interest for these products were between 44 and 55 percent. This was lower than the rates for checks, for which customers, by the 1970s, also paid 15 percent of their value, but the shorter repayment periods meant they had APRs of up to 97 percent. The rise in collection charges for checks was the result of retailers negotiating down the commission they paid, as credit card and store card use took off and became more attractive to them.[69]

The introduction of vouchers was significant because they enabled consumers and retailers to circumvent the government's controls on hire-purchase and installment sales. In operation for most of the period between 1952 and 1982, so-called terms control stipulated minimum deposit payments and maximum repayment periods on installment sales.[70] The sale of vouchers, which could be used to pay for either deposits or for the full cost of consumer durables, was not covered by terms control. As a result, Provident was lifted out of an uncertain passage of trading by government policies that helped to associate the company with luxury rather than necessitous consumption.[71] The government described the use of vouchers as "a serious gap in credit controls at those times when it is needed," which had attracted "refugees from hire-purchase." By 1966, £25 million worth of business was being done by clothing and footwear retailers and department stores, offering their own checks and vouchers, including companies such as Great Universal Stores and Philips Electrical.[72] For Provident, vouchers opened the door to agreements with a number of major retailers such as British Home Stores, Foster Menswear, Halfords, Woolworth, Rumblelows Ltd., H. Samuel Ltd., John Collier, Burtons, Hepworths Ltd., Boots, W. H. Smith, and Debenhams.[73]

In the wake of this success, Provident made further plans to extend its financial services. Noting, in 1971, that half the UK population did not have a bank account, Provident purchased the People's Bank. The intention was to transform this moribund institution into a competitor to the government-backed Trustee Savings Bank. Its vision was to "move away from the Clothing and Supply image more and more into the People's Bank."[74] This initiative was deemed necessary, as the company was again losing younger and more affluent customers (typically those who were buying their own homes rather than renting) to credit and store card providers.[75] As a result, check and voucher sales declined by a third, in real terms, between 1971 and 1979.[76]

A survey of Provident's customers in this period is indicative of the solidly working-class nature of its business, with 92 percent of its turnover conducted with this group. Provident was particularly reliant on custom from families in the semi-skilled manual worker, unskilled worker, unemployed, and pensioner categories.[77] Heaviest users of the company were parents with young children, as indicated by the fact that children's clothing topped the list of items purchased by checks. A much greater proportion of check users lived in rented accommodation than the general population, with 71 percent of Provident customers residing in public housing estates.[78] Around half its customers held a bank account by the end of the 1970s, but hire purchase, bank loans, and retailers' credit were used by only 5, 7, and 7 percent, respectively.[79] In the final two decades of the century, it was from these groups—not the affluent working class—that Provident continued to obtain its core market. Moreover, this market was maintained through the transfer of its traditional techniques into the field of doorstep moneylending.

The Commercialization of Doorstep Moneylending

The Moneylenders Act of 1927 set a nominal interest rate that could be set for loans. This led to the stagnation of the legal moneylending sector; registered lenders fell from 9,173 in 1925, to 3,759 in 1930, and to 1,588 by 1949.[80] It did not, however, curtail the illegal moneylending market, which operated in working-class areas, often with female lenders providing small advances to their neighbors.[81] The authorities were not keen to investigate this market and, by the late 1950s, commercial moneylenders such as Neville Greenwood became aware that there was little official appetite to enforce the rate cap, so they began to experiment with doorstep lending.[82] They were joined by significant numbers of check traders or credit drapers who used their existing agents to market direct loans to customers.

Their experiments unearthed a significant demand. This was partly the result of the decline of pawnbroking; the number of pawnbrokers had dipped from 2,981 in 1935–36 to 402 in 1968.[83] Major redevelopment of inner-city neighborhoods, which often involved the demolition of the local pawnbroker's premises and the construction of new estates on city outskirts, was a major reason for this.[84] While a visit to the pawnbroker was increasingly impractical for any of the 3.5 million Britons living on council estates in the 1960s, moneylenders were willing to call to the homes of those who required a loan. Ironically, therefore, moneylender registrations climbed to 2,500 by the end of the swinging sixties.[85]

Noting this development, Provident began offering cash loans in 1972. Many of the company's customers quickly came to "prefer the cash scheme" rather than checks or vouchers.[86] *Credit Trader* explained that customers of the new moneylenders wanted "to shop at Marks & Spencer or C & A Modes, neither of whom accept checks, or buy a set of tyres with 30 percent off…all of which may be beyond their immediate needs." These customers wanted "cash, or, in the modern idiom, a personal loan."[87] By 1979, the value of personal loans issued by Provident was greater than that of its checks and vouchers, and moneylending was becoming its core activity.[88]

The rejuvenation of doorstep moneylending was given a further fillip by an increasingly liberalized approach to interest rates in the 1960s and 1970s. Financial journalists described how the courts began to view lending "money as comparable to the sale of a commodity" and upheld contracts with interest rates "as high as 120% on short-term advances."[89] Following the Crowther Committee's investigation of the United Kingdom's consumer credit market, the Consumer Credit Act of 1974 removed the 48 percent cap on consumer lending. Crowther's view was that the "first principle of social policy should be to treat the users of consumer credit as adults, who are fully capable of managing their own financial affairs, and not to restrict their freedom of access to it in order to protect the relatively small minority who get into difficulties."[90] The committee placed its faith on educating the public about interest rates and placing legal responsibilities on all lenders to display APRs prominently on all documentation. A safety net remained, with courts empowered to renegotiate agreements deemed extortionate. However, this measure proved of limited use. Only customers could make a legal complaint, not consumer bodies or other groups with greater knowledge of the legal intricacies. Very few cases reached the courts.[91] Crowther's support for consumer education, as opposed to a more paternalistic approach, reflected wider government policy during a period that witnessed a shift away from regulation in the belief that this would increase competition and consumer choice.[92] In 1981, an analysis of the cost of lending discovered that APRs for bank loans ranged from 20 to 23 percent, credit card rates were as high as 31 percent, hire-purchase rates were as much as 57 percent, whereas levels for Provident and other doorstep moneylenders were between 65 and 756 percent. The moneylenders claimed that this method of calculating costs did not compare like with like and that annual interest rates had a "distorting effect" when applied to short-term loans that were expensive to administer and collect.[93]

Despite the interest rates associated with their loans, Provident and other doorstep lenders had an estimated market of almost 3 million customers by the early 1990s.[94] A number of factors explain this development. The proportion of Britons living in poverty, or at its margins, rose from 22 to 28 percent between the late 1970s and early 1990s. An increase in unemployment levels was the most significant factor in this rise, but growing numbers in low-paid jobs and the reductions in some benefit levels also promoted this development.[95] A further factor was the rise in single-parent families (usually headed by women), whose numbers increased by 50 percent to 1.2 million during the 1980s.[96] These groups were to become a major component of the United Kingdom's subprime sector. It also included those excluded from mainstream credit due to their poor credit record or their history of bad debt, often as a result of the housing market crash of the early 1990s that resulted in mainstream financial providers engaging in "a flight to quality."[97]

The market for the UK's subprime sector included pawnbrokers, sale and buy-back outlets (like the Cash Converters chain), and rental purchase shops (such as Brighthouse, formerly Crazy George's), as well as the doorstep lenders.[98] The market for each of these products rose as the personal finance industry increasingly segmented the market through computerized risk assessment and credit scoring—a process that frequently sifted out council or housing association tenants.[99] As a result, large numbers of Britons remained without access to mainstream financial services. A study published in 2008 suggested the UK figure was 6 percent, compared with 3 percent for Germany and 2 percent for France.[100] Some even found it more difficult to access mail-order catalog credit, which was identified as the one form of credit that straddled mainstream and fringe credit markets. Between the 1970s and 1990s, traditional catalog agents dwindled in number, and average customers per agent had dropped to two or three, as the majority used their catalog for their own household only and were less willing to entrust their neighbors with credit.[101] This trend has been explained with recourse to the sociologist Philip Abrams's concept of "modern neighbourhoodism." The suggestion is that late twentieth-century communities did not "constrain their inhabitants into strongly bonded relationships with one another" and that the "diffuse trust and reciprocity of traditional neighbourhoods . . . collapsed in the face of new social patterns."[102]

It was in this climate that Provident abandoned its early 1970s plan to move upmarket and became as heavily associated with low-income consumers as it had ever been. This association proved highly profitable. In 1998, private investors were being advised to purchase shares in the company in order to "[b]uy on rising social inequality." With a market valuation of £1 billion, Provident's burgeoning share price left it knocking on the door of the United Kingdom's elite top 100 companies.[103]

Thus, a sector of the credit industry whose closest European counterparts had withered and died survived and thrived in the fertile soil offered by British legal and socioeconomic conditions. Unlike the French Dufayel system, Provident was not decimated by a German invasion in 1940. Thereafter, it was able to take advantage of cultural inertia among its traditional customers by devising new services that allowed it to tentatively engage with the affluent society. Then, once again, the company's fortunes reflected the ebbing nature of inequality in British society. When discussion of the affluent worker gave way to concerns about a developing underclass, Provident switched tack to utilize its traditional methods. Through the twists and turns of its history, it has also ridden on the back of UK government policies on consumer credit, first benefitting indirectly from controls on hire purchase before taking more direct advantage of a liberal approach to interest rates ceilings. In the final calculation, it was the absence of a ceiling that enabled lenders like Provident to continue their expensive form of face-to-face credit. This, rather than any cultural peculiarity of the British working classes, seems to offer the strongest explanation of why this area of the British consumer credit industry has persisted. Provident's loss of its more affluent customers to credit cards and store cards during the 1970s would also appear to support that view, as ultimately consumers chose the impulses of economic interests over culturally inherited forms of credit. The fact that Provident has, in the past decade, exported its lending model to new markets, including Poland, the Czech Republic, Mexico, and Hungary, also supports the view that British low-income consumers are not unique.[104]

British consumers have had to go without some of the more equitable financial options available to their European and North American counterparts. Credit unions, in particular, have had limited success in the United Kingdom. The scholars of Germany writing within this volume would no doubt agree that the Sparkassen promoted more equitable forms of lending than are associated with the United Kingdom's doorstep lenders. Indeed, if we compare the United Kingdom's record of financial inclusion with the rest of Europe, it is clear that the banks have failed to meet the financial requirements of the least affluent consumers.

In recent years, the UK government has resisted calls to impose a ceiling cap on doorstep lenders. The government accepted the view that any such cap would increase the scale of illegal moneylending, with all the potential for dubious lending and violence that might entail. This view was supported by controversial research carried out for the government, which claimed caps in France and Germany had produced illegal lending markets that were, respectively, three and two and a half times the illegal sector in the United Kingdom.[105] These findings have been hotly contested and labeled as "abominable research" by the European Coalition for Responsible Credit.[106] The UK government's perspective can certainly be critiqued as economically deterministic. It ignores, for example, the culturally specific aspects of consumer credit history and assumes that evasion of an interest ceiling is inevitable and that demand for credit is inelastic. It is oblivious to the claim that historians would make that each nation has its own particular history of credit that is infused with cultural, economic, and political contingencies. Jan Logemann has recently made a strong case for Germany in this respect.[107] This chapter has attempted to carry out a similar task in the case of the United Kingdom, where it is clear that the cultural and social history of UK credit merged with particular government policies to produce a very particular subprime credit market. The history of Provident lies very much at its center.

Notes

1. Donncha Marron, *Consumer Credit in the United States: A Sociological Perspective from the 19th Century to the Present* (New York, 2009), 134–35.
2. Paul Johnson, *Saving and Spending: The Working Class Economy 1870–1939* (Oxford, 1985), 144.
3. Sue Bowden and Paul Turner, "The Demand for Consumer Durables in the United Kingdom in the Interwar Period," *Journal of Economic History* 53, no. 2 (1993): 244–58.
4. John Hilton, *Rich Man, Poor Man* (London, 1944), 33.
5. The National Archive (UK), London: BT 64/3430, Hire Purchase and Consumer Goods (November 12, 1943).
6. Peter Scott, "Marketing Mass Home Ownership and the Creation of the Modern Working Class Consumer in Interwar Britain," *Business History* 50, no. 1 (2008): 4–25.
7. Margot Finn, "Working-Class Women and the Contest for Consumer Control in Victorian County Courts," *Past and Present* 161 (1998): 116–54.
8. Sean O'Connell and Chris Reid, "Working-Class Consumer Credit in the UK, 1925–1960: The Role of the Check Trader," *Economic History Review* 153, no. 2 (2005): 380.
9. Richard Coopey, Sean O'Connell, and Dilwyn Porter, *Mail Order Retailing in Britain: A Business and Social History* (Oxford, UK, 2005).
10. *Daily Mail,* April 17, 1908.
11. Provident Financial Group (PFG), Bradford: PFG/03/007: *Colonnade* (newspaper of the Provident Group), special issue, Provident's ninety years of service, 1970.

12. Timothy Albarn, "Senses of Belonging: The Politics of Working-Class Insurance in Britain, 1880–1914," *Journal of Modern History* 73, no. 3 (2001): 561–602.
13. Laurie Dennant, *A Sense of Security: 150 Years of Prudential* (Cambridge, UK, 1998), 107.
14. G. R. Rubin, "The County Courts and the Tally Trade, 1846–1914," in *Law, Economy and Society: Essays in the History of English Law, 1750–1914,* ed. G. R. Rubin and David Sugarman (Abingdon, 1984), 321–48.
15. Johnson, *Saving and Spending,* 126–33.
16. Rubin, "The County Courts and the Tally Trade." For an assessment of the credit drapers, see Sean O'Connell, *Credit and Community: Working-Class Debt in the UK since 1880* (Oxford, UK, 2009), 26–54.
17. Ron Barnes, *Coronation Cups and Jam Jars: A Portrait of an East End Family through Three Generations* (London, 1976), cited in Melanie Tebbutt, *Making Ends Meet: Pawnbroking and Working-Class Credit* (Leicester, 1983), 21.
18. Committee on Consumer Credit, *Report of the Committee* (London, 1971) 584; PFG: 01/067 Memorandum upon Miss Ellen Wilkinson's Hire Purchase Bill; National Archive: BT 250/37, National Check Traders Federation.
19. PFG/04/076: Wolverhampton Shopping Guide, 1935.
20. Economist Intelligence Unit, "Check Trading," *Retail Business* 71 (1964): 46.
21. PFG/01/067, Memorandum upon Miss Ellen Wilkinson's Hire Purchase Bill; Economist Intelligence Unit, "Check Trading," 45.
22. *Credit Draper,* April 25, 1915; *Daily Mail,* May 4, 1908.
23. *Penny Illustrated Paper,* October 15, 1910.
24. PFG/04/149: Slip advising customers not to shop on Saturdays, 1905.
25. *Drapers Record,* May 2 and 9, 1908.
26. *Daily Sketch,* December 1, 1913.
27. *Daily Express,* August 25 and 27, 1938.
28. PFG: 01/105, Shareholders' meeting minutes, April 23, 1934.
29. *Credit Draper,* April 25, 1915.
30. *Daily Mail,* May 4, 1908.
31. Sean O'Connell, *The Car in British Society: Class, Gender and Motoring 1896–1939* (Manchester, UK, 1998), 28.
32. *Daily Mail,* April 23, 1908.
33. *Daily Mail,* May 5, 1908.
34. Tebbutt, *Making Ends Meet,* 170.
35. The football pools were an enormously popular form of working-class gambling, with large financial prizes available to gamblers who could correctly predict the outcome of soccer matches. The largest company, Littlewoods, was launched in 1923, and it subsequently deployed its knowledge of working-class communities and their weekly disposable income to achieve equal success in mail-order retailing. Ten million people were speculating on the pools each week by 1939. Mark Clapson, *A Bit of a Flutter: Popular Gambling and English Society, c. 1823–1961* (Manchester, UK, 1992), 162.
36. Johnson, *Saving and Spending,* 31.

37. PFG/03/156: "Check and Credit Trading," typescript prepared for publication by H. Webb (1929), 63.
38. Johnson, *Saving and Spending*, 38–39.
39. *Daily Mail*, April 17, 1908.
40. Cited in Tebbutt, *Making Ends Meet*, 186.
41. Interview with Johnny (born 1930), April 15, 2001.
42. Avram Taylor, " 'Funny Money,' Hidden Charges and Repossession: Working-Class Experiences of Consumption in the Interwar Years," in *Cultures of Selling: Perspectives on Consumption and Society since 1700,* ed. John Benson and Laura Ugolini (Aldershot, 2006), 170.
43. See Margot Finn, *The Character of Credit: Personal Debt in English Culture, 1740–1914* (Cambridge, UK, 2003); O'Connell, *Credit and Community*; Avram Taylor, *Working Class Credit and Community since 1918* (Basingstoke, 2002).
44. Taylor, "Funny Money," 164.
45. Tebbutt, *Making Ends Meet*, 133.
46. *Daily Mirror,* March 6, 1953.
47. O'Connell and Reid, "Working-Class Consumer Credit," 388.
48. Interview with Mrs. A., cited in Adam Gibson, "Patterns of Demand for Working-Class Credit: The Case of Check Trading 1918–1970," unpublished undergraduate project (Glasgow, University of Glasgow, 1999).
49. Women's Group on Public Welfare, *Our Towns, Close-Up: A Study Made in 1939–42 with Certain Recommendations* (London, 1943), 10, appendix VII.
50. National Archives: BT 64/85, Orders prohibiting poundage charges by check traders. Representations by Newcastle and Tyneside chamber of traders.
51. NA: BT 258/172, Control of Check Trading Order 1948: evidence of contravention of Order by those trafficking in checks. Memo by Andrew, G. H., December 12, 1952.
52. *Daily Mail,* April 16, 1908.
53. PFG/04/076: Dublin Shopping Guide, 1910.
54. PFG/04/051: Summary of returns.
55. Theodore Zeldin, *History of French Passions,* vol. 2, *Intellect, Taste, and Anxiety* (Oxford, 1979), 628.
56. Charles Couture, "Des différentes combinaisons de ventes à crédit dans leurs rapports avec la petite epergne" (PhD diss., University of Paris, 1904), 66–79.
57. PFG/03/156: "Check and Credit Trade," typescript for publication by H. Webb (1929), 11.
58. Judith G. Coffin, "Consumption, Production, and Gender: The Sewing Machine in Nineteenth-Century France," in *Gender and Class in Modern Europe,* ed. Laura Levine Frader and Sonya Rose (Ithaca, NY, 1996), 119.
59. Zeldin, *History of French Passions,* 2: 628.
60. Lenard R. Berlanstein, *The Working People of Paris, 1871–1914* (Baltimore, MD, 1984), 49.

61. Jan Logemann, "Americanization through Credit? Consumer Credit in Germany, 1860s–1960s," *Business History Review* 85 (2011): 529–50; see also Jan Logemann, "Different Paths to Mass Consumption: Consumer Credit in the United States and West Germany during the 1950s and '60s," *Journal of Social History* 41, no. 3 (2008): 525–59.

62. Martina Avanza, Gilles Laferté, and Etienne Penissat, "O Crédito entre as Classes Populares Francesas: O Exemplo de Uma Loja em Lens," *Mana: Estudo de Antropologia Social* 12, no. 1 (2006): 7–38.

63. O'Connell and Reid, "Working-Class Consumer Credit," 387.

64. *The Times,* April 3, 1961.

65. Mass Observation Ltd./Economic Intelligence Unit, Retail Business Survey, "Mail Order," (November 1961), 16.

66. John Mann, "The Pattern of Mail Order," *British Journal of Marketing* 1 (1967): 26–28.

67. Johnson, *Saving and Spending,* 215.

68. *Investor's Review,* September 7, 1973.

69. Monopolies and Mergers Commission, *Trading Check Franchise and Financial Services: A Report into the Supply of Trading Checks in the United Kingdom* (London, 1981), 23–40.

70. For discussion of similar French controls on installment sales, see chapter 8 by Sabine Effosse in this volume. Both French and British government actions drew on the precedent set by the U.S. government's Regulation W in 1941.

71. National Archives: BT 250/14, Committee on Consumer Credit: Hire Purchase Controls: Note by Board of Trade and Treasury; Richard Berthoud and Eileen Kempson, *Credit and Debt: The PSI Report* (London, 1992), 44–45.

72. Committee on Consumer Credit, *Report,* 432; *Credit Trader,* May 2, 1970.

73. PFG/04/076, Provident shopping guide, Southampton-Hythe, 1974.

74. *Evening Standard,* May 20, 1972.

75. PFG/04/193: Provident Customer Survey, 1975.

76. Monopolies and Mergers Commission, *Trading Check Franchise,* 88.

77. Ibid., 59.

78. Ibid., 30, 50; PFG/04/193: Provident Customer Survey, 1975.

79. Monopolies and Mergers Commission, *Trading Check Franchise,* 58, 30.

80. National Archives: IR 40/3555 Registration of Moneylenders, 1929–1931; *The Times,* February 27, 1950.

81. For more on this, see Taylor, *Working Class Credit,* 46–67, and O'Connell, *Credit and Community,* 131–66.

82. Interview with Neville Greenwood, July 1, 2003.

83. *The Times,* February 17, 1950; National Archives: BT 250/38 National Pawnbrokers Association Inc. Oral Evidence to the Committee on Consumer Credit, March 20, 1970.

84. For a full discussion of the decline of pawnbroking, see Tebbutt, *Making Ends Meet.*

85. National Archives: BT250/34 National Association of Moneylenders (evidence to the Committee on Consumer Credit).
86. *Shields Gazette,* April 5, 1974.
87. *Credit Trader,* May 2, 1970.
88. Monopolies and Mergers Commission, *Trading Check Franchise,* 90.
89. *The Times,* March 10, 1971.
90. Committee on Consumer Credit, *Report,* 153.
91. *Financial Times,* September 16, 1991.
92. Matthew Hilton, *Consumerism in Twentieth-Century Britain: The Search for a Historical Movement* (Cambridge, UK, 2003), 292.
93. Monopolies and Mergers Commission, *Trading Check Franchise,* 91–93.
94. Karen Rowlingson, *Moneylenders and Their Customers* (London, 1994), 4.
95. Janet Ford, *Consuming Credit: Debt and Poverty in the UK* (London, 1991), 7; David Vincent, *Poor Citizens: The State and the Poor in Twentieth-Century Britain* (Harlow, 1991), 202–4.
96. Berthoud and Kempson, *Credit and Debt,* 182.
97. Janet Ford and Karen Rowlingson, "Low-Income Households and Credit: Exclusion, Preference and Inclusion," *Environment and Planning* 28 (1996): 1346.
98. Sharon Collard and Elaine Kempson, *Affordable Credit: The Way Forward* (Bristol, 2005), 1.
99. Ford, *Consuming Credit,* 74–75.
100. European Commission, *Financial Services Provision and Prevention of Exclusion* (Brussels, 2008), Table 4.
101. Monopolies and Mergers Commission, *The Littlewoods Organisation PLC* (London, 1997), 121.
102. Taylor, *Working Class Credit,* 43.
103. *New Statesman,* August 16, 1996; *Money Observer,* June 1998.
104. *Independent,* July 24, 2003.
105. Department of Trade and Industry, *The Effect of Interest Rate Controls in Other Countries* (London, 2004), 40–41.
106. European Coalition for Responsible Credit, *Newsletter* 13 (July 2009), 9.
107. Logemann, "Americanization"; Logemann, "Different Paths."

CHAPTER 5

American Women's Struggle to End Credit Discrimination in the Twentieth Century

Lawrence Bowdish

Creditors control access to consumer credit in two main ways. First, a lender can discriminate against a potential borrower if his or her income or other economic characteristics are not sufficient to secure the desired credit. Economists sometimes call this "rational discrimination." For example, a creditor might view someone who is unemployed or who has never received a loan before as not creditworthy, because his or her ability to repay is suspect.[1] The second type of credit discrimination is more ambiguous and is based on a number of what credit activists and legislative leaders call "invidious distinctions." In such cases, a borrower suffers discrimination for reasons that have no direct bearing on his or her ability to repay.[2] Until the mid-1970s in the United States, this type of discrimination plagued women who tried to secure credit on their own. These distinctions not only harmed the credit status of women, but also negatively impacted their economic rights and hindered the already flailing 1970s U.S. economy. Difficult to quantify, this type of gendered discrimination became the grounds for the struggle that American women pursued against an entrenched credit industry.

This chapter analyzes the widespread credit discrimination against women in the United States and how they fought back in the 1960s and 1970s. Banks and other creditors, including student loan companies, credit card companies, and department stores, did not believe that women were good credit risks, even though the creditors did not have any quantitative evidence to justify this belief and were unwilling to open their own ledgers to permit necessary statistical analyses. Many creditors in the United States practiced invidious distinctions against women by requiring their husbands to cosign on loans, by discounting their income, or by requiring a so-called baby letter, that is, an affidavit that the female applicant would not have a child over the course of a loan.

Discriminatory credit practices kept millions of women in the postwar era away from the consumer credit market and prevented them from enjoying their full economic citizenship—what historian Alice Kessler-Harris describes as an individual's ability to exercise one's economic rights and participate in the economic aspects of one's society, such as work, property ownership, and investments.[3] In mid-twentieth-century American society, consumerism and economic well-being became more dependent on an individual's ability to procure credit in an increasingly systematic credit market through banks and other large lenders. Because of those changes, a discriminatory credit market could economically harm every unmarried woman who wished to leverage her future income. For any woman, student loans, credit cards, department store cards, mortgages, car loans, insurance policies, and utility hookups could be limited just because of her gender and marital status. Attempts to secure these types of credit often ran up against the increasingly embattled social ideal that women should rely on men in the economic realm.

Until recently, the issues of women and credit have not been the topic of much historical research. This lack of attention stems from the fact that credit history only became popular after the study of "second wave" feminist history slowed in the early 1990s. During that more recent period, women's historians focused on microlevel studies of women left on the fringes of the broader feminist movement, and popular culture embraced the emergence of a "third wave" of women's activists.[4] Therefore, as credit history grew in the 1990s, it missed the main thrust of second wave history and the women who fit within it.[5]

Telling Their Stories

The most compelling part of this history comes in the stories that women told to banks, creditors, and legislators in an attempt to correct the problems they faced when trying to secure credit. Out of the thousands of these stories that remain in the historical record, it would be impossible to claim that a small representative sampling might show all of those credit problems. However, the following three can introduce some of the more prominent issues that women faced when they tried to secure credit in their own names.

Speaking to the National Organization of Women on February 20, 1973, one woman reported:

> I have been employed as a teacher and guidance counselor for 8 years in Philadelphia. My salary is near $14,000. I have no children. I had been a depositor [with] checking and savings accounts since 1965. [My bank] would not give me a $2,000 loan so I could get a car. Consequently, I took the bus to work and to and from the university [a four-hour round trip] for a year when I had to drop my classes.[6]

The never-married Ms. Deal made a decent wage by the standards of early 1970s Philadelphia, yet she could not get a loan equivalent to two months' salary to purchase a new car. She had these problems even though banks in the United States generally used cars as collateral and every state had a requirement to hold automobile insurance. Clearly, she had sufficient income to purchase a car worth only two months of her salary, but she was still in an economic position that left her vulnerable to patriarchal lending decisions that kept women from securing credit. Single women were especially unable to secure needed financing if they could not, or would not, solicit a man's support on a credit application.

Responding in 1972 to a questionnaire from the Ohio Governor's Task Force on Credit for Women, another woman told her credit story:

> Upon [my] husband's notice to cancel my credit cards, I was told I was responsible for his debts and if [I] didn't pay for them, they would take away the house deeded to me in the divorce decree. I could not, however, keep my husband from using the cards... It went on for 2 years [before she was removed from their joint credit cards] while we were separated but not divorced. In which time my husband ran up $15,000 in debts. [Her monthly income was $200 to $400.][7]

Ms. Corgan's bitter divorce was the direct cause of her heart-wrenching situation and severe credit problems. After she and her husband had separated, but before their divorce was finalized, Corgan's husband maliciously ran up the balance on their jointly held credit cards. Their divorce decree gave her both the deed to the house, which represented a majority of the couple's assets, *and* responsibility for the jointly held debt, primarily the mortgage and installment debt on those joint credit cards. She was unable to take out a second mortgage on the home because no bank would give her a loan due to the financial troubles in her marriage and her subsequent separation. As an added complication, if Corgan decided to sell the house, she would have to split its sale price with her ex-husband as per the divorce agreement. To make matters even worse, she left a well-paying clerical position because of continued sexual harassment from her boss. She suffered from general problems that many divorced women faced. Creditors often did not count alimony as dependable income, and since many credit bureaus only gave married couples credit in the husband's name, they did not keep any credit information on married women or just gave them their ex-husband's credit rating. In Corgan's case, this shared credit rating and history, which persisted through their separation, impacted her well into her post-married life.

Finally, Nancy Pierce Leeth, a professional office manager who worked for the National Women's Political Caucus in Ohio, went to a public proceeding in 1974 to tell the stories of a few women who failed to secure credit and could not come to the meeting themselves. Her own story, however, proved to be the most eloquent, if not the most powerful. As a professional, single woman, Leeth tried to find a mortgage to purchase a home she could easily afford on her salary. The banker admitted as much and knew that she had the capacity to repay the mortgage in a timely fashion, but he still required that Leeth submit a document commonly referred to as a "baby letter." These letters, from a doctor stating that the woman was practicing birth control or would otherwise not get pregnant, were a common practice across the country and were required for many Federal Housing Authority (FHA) and Veteran's Administration (VA) loans in the postwar period. Leeth quipped, "some people needed a lawyer, or a realtor to get a house—I needed a gynecologist."[8]

These examples illustrate why equal economic citizenship was a central issue for women's advocates in the middle of the twentieth century. They are representative of the thousands of women who tried to secure credit and whose experiences may seem unfathomable today but which were common just a few decades ago. Whether they were divorced, married, or single, women encountered a considerable number of problems when they tried to use their future income to access a line of credit through mortgages, credit cards, or other types of bank loans.

With rare exceptions, like that of Leeth, there is no reason to assume that these women had defined themselves as feminists before these instances of credit discrimination made them activists. Unlike issues of discrimination in society and culture that primarily attracted women who considered themselves liberal or radical, the issue of economic discrimination, including credit, attracted women from across the political spectrum. The addition of a wider range of women to those already grappling with other concerns of the women's rights movement helped to broaden the opposition to credit discrimination beyond the standard coalition that addressed most other feminist issues of the 1960s and 1970s.

In the 1970s, the success of fights for equal credit access largely depended on the compelling nature of anecdotal evidence, like the stories here, not on data. Indeed, few statistics are available to evaluate lending practices at the broader demographic levels. The analyses that consider this type of discrimination do not agree on whether credit discrimination existed, nor are those analyses complete enough to draw any succinct conclusions. Banks were unwilling to volunteer the information required to construct an evidentiary base of data, because they did not want to divulge details of their lending processes or subject themselves to further regulation, not even if those numbers could exonerate them of discrimination charges.

Most women who suffered discrimination did so because of men, whether as a result of problems associated with their current or former husbands or because of male creditors' discriminatory views about women's earning potential and economic management skills. Often, these women cited sufficient income and the need for economic equality as ways to explain why they deserved credit. Occasionally, they pulled from the rhetoric of the Women's Liberation Movement and claimed that they should enjoy the same economic and consumer rights as men. In other cases, politically conservative women argued that equal access to credit was important to the new market economy in the 1960s and 1970s. Significantly, women who raised the issue did not, by and large, base their complaints about credit discrimination on economic hardship or need. Rather, equal access to credit offered a path for women across the political spectrum to gain full participation in the consumer's republic. Indeed, most of the women's advocates of equal credit access operated under the assumption that credit discrimination was a civil rights issue. These women realized that American society was changing into one where consumption was important to their identities as full American citizens.[9]

Discovering a Problem

Discrimination against women in the credit market began once women made considerable strides out of home-based work and into the industrial-era labor market.[10] Before World War I, employers hired younger unmarried women who were not planning to be lifelong career workers.[11] Mobilization during World War I stepped up demand for labor, giving more women the opportunity to enter the workforce. However, these women mostly stayed within the established boundaries of so-called women's work and the burgeoning service industry.[12]

An increasing number of women in the workforce meant more economically independent women, including those who held jobs before marriage and the small number who opted not to get married. These women, like all wage earners, sometimes required credit to cover immediate shortfalls or long-term larger purchases. Like women in Austria who were customers of major pawnbrokers such as Wagner and Berger, American women turned to smaller local pawnbrokers and department store revolving credit in the early part of the twentieth century.[13] Once the formal credit market had developed in the United States, by the middle of the twentieth century, women found themselves excluded from new forms of consumer credit by banks and other creditors.

When servicemen returned from World War II, there were concerns about how the labor market would reabsorb them. Previously nontraditional workers, including women, filled the early 1940s workforce, and many of them were expected to give up their jobs to the returning GIs. Although many working women did go back to their prewar lives in the home, others chose not to return to domesticity, because they experienced and preferred greater independence or their new wages were too important to their family's well-being or upward mobility.[14] Limitations in advancement and job availability, commonly referred to as the "glass ceiling," created vast differences in the pay rates between men and women. Banks and other creditors used these discrepancies against women to severely limit their credit access.

The postwar American credit market continued to make it difficult for women to secure credit. In most cases, banks still operated under the assumption that women did not have complete agency over their own incomes because of community property laws or the demands of having a family. Therefore, creditors required men to cover women by cosigning on loans, even when it did not make any economic sense. Women who borrowed and repaid money under these conditions did not build their own credit histories, so they experienced problems if they ever sought credit in their own names. Women also experienced credit discrimination because of childbearing decisions and other life choices, including remaining single, which placed them outside societal norms that expected them to get married and raise families. Patriarchal tradition in the capital markets and long-standing stereotypes about the participation of women in the economy worked to keep capital out of reach for many women.

In 1968, Congress passed the Consumer Credit Protection Act (CCPA), which "assure[d] a meaningful disclosure of credit terms so that the consumer will be able to compare more readily the various credit terms available to him and avoid the uninformed use of credit."[15] By supporting the "informed use of credit" and making it easier for consumers—assumed to be males in the legislation—to find "meaningful disclosure of credit terms," Congress established precedence for federal regulations through legislation and Federal Reserve rules on how creditors managed their businesses. Aside from its provisions to require credit card companies and other creditors to be more forthright with their policies, the CCPA also established the National Commission on Consumer Finance (NCCF). This body was to investigate current credit conditions, determine when discrimination occurred, and find how credit practices—either open or secretive—might hurt consumers, whether as individuals or groups.

In December 1972, the NCCF released its report, *Consumer Credit in the United States.* It supported the theoretical goals of the CCPA and claimed that credit discrimination was harmful to the economy at large. If a creditor denied a loan to a consumer for a noneconomic reason, essentially anything other than income or wealth, then the competitiveness of the market should produce another lending agent willing to make that loan.[16] However, while the NCCF report recognized that women might experience obstacles to securing credit, it did not recommend new policies or legislation, such as the CCPA, to correct this type of problem. Although women had come forward with examples of discrimination, the NCCF did not find any systematic discrimination against them in the limited data they had acquired.

Even though the NCCF report did not recommend new policies, the finding that women encountered credit discrimination encouraged many lending institutions, primarily FHA and VA lenders, to phase out their discriminatory behaviors. However, advocates for equal credit access remained committed to ensuring that women could get the credit they deserved. Many of them remained convinced that legislation, not reliance on changing the will of creditors through a social movement, was the best way to secure that access.

Even without damning statistical evidence, emerging problems in women's access to credit were impossible to ignore. As more and more women realized that they were not alone in their negative experiences in the late 1960s and early 1970s, they joined their voices and created a chorus against credit discrimination. Working women fought against the discounting of their incomes; married women argued against requirements for their husbands to cover them; and higher-income women demanded greater access to consumer, business, and housing credit. Within women's groups and on their own, these women turned to state and federal legislatures to show that their problems were common enough to merit broad legislative action to outlaw credit discrimination.

State-Level Efforts and the Ohio Credit Task Force

Before the U.S. Congress considered national legislation in 1974 that made legislative efforts at the state level obsolete, twenty states enacted equal credit laws.[17] Concurrently with the federal debate over legislation in 1974, nine more states introduced bills in their legislatures to guarantee equal access to credit for women. The experience of one of those nine states, Ohio, can shed light on all of the state-level attempts for three reasons. First, because Ohio started its process relatively late, advocates and legislators there were able to learn from the experiences of advocates in other states. For example, some language in Ohio's state law mirrored the language of other state credit laws, and Ohio borrowed the idea of soliciting letters from aggrieved citizens and holding meetings with those citizens and banking representatives. Second, Ohio had a number of women from different economic and political backgrounds who both were affected by and publicly advocated against discrimination. This variety of personal experiences permits broad analysis of why different groups of women might have issues with credit availability. Third, creditors in Ohio put forward a cohesive defense against further financial legislation. Therefore, at least in Ohio, one could see a clear fight against extending legal protection to women trying to secure credit.[18]

Most of Ohio's efforts to learn about the problems of credit discrimination occurred under the auspices of the Ohio Credit Task Force, also known as the Governor's Task Force on Women and Credit, appointed by Governor John J. Gilligan to investigate credit discrimination against women.[19] The organization collected over seventy questionnaires during 1973, including the one from Ms. Corgan quoted above.[20] These standardized forms asked the aggrieved female responders a number of questions that included the length of their employment, the sources of their income, and their marital status. Another section allowed these women to provide details about the problems they encountered in the credit market. While in some instances these qualitative sections were terse and straightforward, some women attached multiple legal-sized sheets to expand their testimony.

A majority of the respondents had applied for credit cards, either directly through national credit card companies or locally through banks. Most of the others had applied for retail credit, and some had applied for auto loans and mortgages. The types of credit that these women had applied for and the reasons that creditors had given for denying the applications were typical.

The most common reason creditors offered was the requirement that husbands sign the credit applications, which was primarily a problem when women were applying for credit cards. Women often saw this requirement as discriminatory, because they were never required to sign credit applications for their husbands.[21] One woman repeatedly refused charge cards sent in her husband's name for a Sears account she maintained, arguing that it was her card for her use. Another woman married a graduate student, so she wanted cards in her name because his credit was weak and his income low. At least one woman specifically asked for a credit card in her maiden name because she knew married and divorced women who had experienced credit access problems and discrimination.[22] At least some of these women understood that if a credit card was in her husband's name, only his file in the credit bureau would benefit from earning good credit.

Sometimes the justifications that creditors offered for denying credit to women made no economic sense. One woman included a statement from an auto insurance company that refused to issue a policy to any single woman. A bank refused to give a credit card to a single woman who had seven other credit accounts and an income over $17,000—the average household income in central Ohio in the early 1970s hovered around $10,000 to $11,000—because she had a "lack of credit experience." Some credit card issuers refused women because they did not have a "high enough" net worth or because they had part-time employment, obstacles that men rarely encountered when they applied for credit.[23]

Although most problems concerning credit centered on installment credit, barriers to mortgage credit created a bigger ordeal for many women. These women suffered economic discrimination when they applied for mortgages, since their income was discounted. Banks would not count women's total incomes, because they believed these incomes were unstable as a result of their family responsibilities and supposedly lower dedication to their work. Discounting a wife's income on a mortgage became more important in the 1970s as homeownership and interest rates increased, because many married couples required both incomes to secure a home as housing prices and the cost of mortgages increased. Discrimination against women, particularly married women who saw their incomes discounted, made mortgages even more expensive.

After compiling these stories and testimonies, the Ohio Credit Task Force held public hearings in the summer of 1974. Over 250 mostly white working- and middle-class women, credit industry officials, and government representatives attended hearings in Columbus, Toledo, Cincinnati, and Cleveland.[24] The women's statements fit the general pattern of the statements from the Ohio Credit Task Force questionnaires. Many of them were divorced or widowed, and their inability to find a man to cosign loans or vouch for their credibility was the main problem they encountered when trying to secure credit. Overall, these women were in their late thirties to middle forties and had incomes of around $10,000 a year, which was squarely in the median range for the early 1970s. In other words, they were average credit-seeking people who had experienced many more credit access problems than men with comparable criteria.[25]

Married women had problems different from those experienced by single women. One married woman applied for a small business loan to open an antique store, but the bank denied her application. The loan officer who had worked on her application suggested to her, "Well honey, what makes you think you know anything about business?"[26] Another married woman, Mrs. Staley, could not get a student loan to attend graduate school from either private sources or the university itself. The university told her that, for loans, the school ranked her fourth priority behind single men (first), married men (second), and single women (third).[27] Another issue involved a married woman who unsuccessfully attempted to take out a life insurance policy as the primary wage earner of her household. The insurer's policy did not allow it to insure working women if they were a family's primary source of income.[28]

Testimony in the Ohio Task Force Hearings from individuals representing creditors, banks, and other parts of the financial services industry expressed different concerns. In general, creditors were worried that new regulations would circumscribe their lending practices. By claiming there was no discrimination in their institutions, these creditors hoped to influence the task force against new credit laws. Most of them asserted that if discrimination—such as requiring male signatures or discounting women's incomes—might occasionally occur, it never happened in the offices they managed. Almost all of the creditors also complained about the level of regulation that they had been forced to endure, especially since passage of the CCPA. They expected still more unnecessary regulations if an equal credit statute passed.[29]

Richard Wade, the president of First State Bank, gave the broadest defense of creditor practices. He bracketed his entire testimony by reminding the panel that credit was a "privilege, not a right" facilitated by the credit industry. He argued that bank lenders were interested in the individual borrower and that women who had positive lending characteristics would get the credit they deserved. Further, he averred that the real problem was that most women credit seekers did not "know what to ask."[30] Wade's last claim amounted to an admission by the credit industry that they knew there was a discrepancy between how women understood credit and what their actual credit rights were. By advocating financial literacy among women, these bankers, on some level, understood that women had been disadvantaged in the credit market in the 1960s and 1970s, but these same bankers were largely unwilling to undertake any significant reforms.[31]

Each of the credit industry's representatives took pains to explain why its current practices were good, even if women had occasional problems securing credit. One of the most eloquent of the credit representatives, Dan Shackleford of State Savings Company, explained that the reason why many creditors required husbands to cosign on all loans was that "if he [the husband] doesn't sign it, he knows something we don't."[32] This terse statement showed how banks valued information and wanted to be able to make better lending decisions with full disclosure. In the mid-1970s, when credit was tighter because of higher interest rates, creditors wanted to know even more about a debtor's ability to repay.

Admittedly, the creditors did not have many advocates in these hearings. Most people attending them were hostile to the creditors' position, because they saw themselves as victims of discrimination. The commissioners of the hearings were largely community leaders with little banking or regulatory experience, and they made their sympathies toward the victims clear. However, having little knowledge of the particular mechanics of bank lending and banking legislation, the commissioners were largely unable to bring the creditors to task. This information asymmetry played to the creditors' advantage; Ohio was not among those states that passed equal credit legislation before 1974. No equal credit legislation made it through the Ohio Legislature before the U.S. Senate passed federal legislation.

Although twenty states passed state-level legislation to end credit discrimination against women and ethnic or racial minorities, and although more states considered such action in 1972 and 1973, the main goal of many advocates of equal credit access was legislation at the federal level. Credit access proponents wanted a federal law, because the federal government had greater regulatory strength and because creditors would not be able to hide discrimination by chartering in a state with lax discriminatory laws. In addition, federal legislation would solve the problem in states like Ohio, where efforts to pass state-level legislation had stalled. As credit and women's activists had hoped, the quick acceptance of federal credit legislation in 1974, the Equal Credit Opportunity Act (ECOA), rendered many of these state actions obsolete.

Federal Legislation and the Equal Credit Opportunity Act

After making their cases to rights organizations and to their state-level legislators, women sought to convince national legislators and creditors that the sole factors of gender and marital status did not make them bad credit risks. Advocates for equal credit access before the ECOA's passage in 1974 believed that current federal legislation on the issue of equal credit availability, which then consisted of a few points in the CCPA, was insufficient in both its scope and enforcement. Many argued that these unsatisfactory regulations required a "reappraisal" that culminated in a new, powerful, overarching policy that clearly outlawed invidious distinctions in the credit market.[33] This policy took shape in the ECOA.

The development of and debates over the ECOA began primarily by looking at state-level actions. In the process, the proponents of legislation ran into the old problems of having insufficient statistical evidence to prove routine discrimination. The 1972 report from the National Commission on Consumer Finance found issues in credit applications that were discriminatory, such as requiring women to reapply at marriage or get a husband's signature, but the commission did not find that women were systematically denied credit. It decided not to suggest new legislation, moreover, because it questioned the ability of regulators to measure success or bring charges against offending creditors.[34]

The supporters of equal credit access legislation, both on the state and federal level, believed that forcing a woman to reapply for credit after she married was an invidious distinction, especially when placed in the context of the era, when women were achieving greater economic equality. A quotation from a mortgage-lending case study conducted in Hartford, Connecticut in 1974 illustrated the problem:

> Whether because discrimination in mortgage lending is prohibited by both Connecticut and federal law or for other reasons, lenders in Hartford do not generally admit that they reject applicants on the basis of the race or national origin . . . (discrimination there is "subtle") . . . [D]iscrimination on the basis of sex is a different matter. Here, the major problem is not that mortgage procedures or criteria *permit* opportunities for decisions on the basis of discrimination. Rather, traditional mortgage lending criteria followed by Hartford mortgage lenders virtually *require* sex discrimination.[35]

Sex discrimination was "required" in the Hartford mortgage lending offices, because a patriarchal tradition with no statistical validity forced female applicants to navigate difficult obstacles when they applied for credit and then offered them worse terms on that credit. Aside from almost all lenders requiring spousal permission, only 22 percent of Hartford lenders counted 100 percent of the wife's income when making a decision about a joint proposal. A similar percentage did not count any of a woman's income. The authors of the case study suggested that one of the main problems was the lack of women in decision-making roles at the lending institutions. Even though women and minorities both experienced problems when securing credit, there were fewer female than African-American loan officers in Hartford in the early 1970s.[36] The discrimination was clear to activists, but problems in measurement, confusion over consideration of the protection of other demographic factors, and a well-organized credit industry that loathed regulating such a subjective part of the process worked against the act's proponents.

Republican Senator William "Bill" Brock of Tennessee sponsored the ECOA after his office's efforts to find the stories of victimized women in the credit market in the early 1970s. It was the first federal attempt to legislate against gender discrimination in the credit market.[37] Senator Brock became passionate about the issue after his participation in a CCPA hearing in 1972, where he was moved by numerous letters from his constituency and by testimony in the hearing to help stop credit discrimination. Emily Card, one of Brock's legislative assistants who helped push Brock in this direction, drafted the bill that would become the ECOA and built a substantial case based largely on the same public support evidenced by the thousands of letters received by national organizations, state legislatures, and Brock's office.

Although there was a mix of "bottom-up" qualitative evidence and "top-down" quantitative data, the majority of the support for legislating against credit discrimination was qualitative.[38] Nonetheless, the two types of evidence led to a bill balanced enough to pass the Senate. Looking at how the ECOA sailed through that body, one might assume that a bill that attacked discrimination against such a wide group of people had little problem gaining legislative and general support. While this might be true, the qualitative and anecdotal evidence presented a relatively weak analytical and statistical argument that left holes for detractors in the credit industry. Credit granters made profits by exploiting a serious information asymmetry that made their business both profitable and defensible against attacks on that asymmetry. If individuals seeking loans knew the mechanics and regulations that went into loan decisions, or if they had more power to manipulate them, the industry believed it would become less profitable, because the grounds for negotiations would be more even.[39]

Though creditors had strong reasons for maintaining their secrecy, there was increasing suspicion that their secret systems, because of mounting qualitative evidence, were propagating invidious distinctions against women creditors. The reasons for supporting a law were powerful enough that supporters of women's rights had little problem securing Senator Brock's effort to gain unanimous passage of the ECOA in the Senate in 1973, including its original beginning: "It shall be unlawful for any creditor to discriminate against any applicant, with respect to any aspect of a credit transaction on the basis of race, color, religion, national origin, sex or marital status, or age."[40]

Instead of serving as a culmination of women's credit rights, however, the ECOA was the start of a new phase in the struggle for those rights. The following year, the ECOA took some hits in the House Subcommittee on Consumer Affairs of the Committee on Banking and Currency, where the punitive points of the law were weakened and the non-gender-based demographic factors eliminated.[41] By the time the Federal Reserve wrote the rules for the ECOA and President Ford signed it in 1976, those other demographic factors returned, but creditors retained some protection even with the weakened punitive measures.

The legislative debate showed how the women's and economic regulatory movements in the 1970s interacted with the broader political system, but the debate was also notable for its clear emphasis of social values. If society attached importance to credit and access to it, then legislators and creditors had to find some balance between the efficiency of capital and how equitably creditors distributed access to it, a process that had just begun with the equal rights legislation instituted in the late 1960s. The future of that balance depended on Congress's passage of the ECOA and the dialogue that would open.[42] The ECOA showed how these two debates about social values and economic opportunity arose and entwined as they moved from the private sphere of the individual and firm into the public sphere of the legislature and society.

Studies about the effectiveness of the ECOA in the late 1970s and early 1980s showed positive and negative consequences. On one hand, the regulations of the ECOA were good tactics to convince creditors to give women fair access to credit, even if few cases concerning credit access for women ever made it to the courts. Others argued that the ECOA proved to be pointless because discrimination did not exist, or that discrimination was quickly going away because of a change to a consumer-based economy where creditors could not afford to turn down good credit risks. Others complained that the ECOA did not have sufficient power to keep discrimination from occurring, because there were few lawsuits as a result of the construction of the act's regulations, and consumer literacy about women's rights remained abysmally low.[43]

Conclusion

Women in the United States in the 1960s and 1970s pursued and protected their economic, consumer, and credit rights by joining together in a broad coalition that pressured state legislatures and then Congress to act. Banks and credit card companies increasingly controlled credit access in the United States after the 1950s, just as that access to credit was becoming more important to economic citizenship. Women's activists realized this importance and sought to protect women's economic rights. Proponents of equal rights first established that there was a problem in securing equal access to credit by offering anecdotal evidence. Later, they employed that evidence to secure state and federal legislation.

As the postwar economies around the world changed to take advantage of increased credit availability, women in the United States realized that they needed to be able to claim their fair share of the consumer economy. By ensuring that creditors' decisions would be based on appropriate criteria such as income and debt load, but not biology, women's activists made sure that they would not be left behind in the new world of consumption.

Forty years after women started to fight against credit discrimination, a consumerist society and consumer credit have changed the environment in which women fought for equal credit access. The increasing ease with which anyone, regardless of economic status, could secure credit in the past twenty years has completely overshadowed any credit issues specific to women. For most of the 1990s and 2000s, many creditors wanted to extend credit to whomever they could, and women made up too many potential customers to discriminate against or ignore for noneconomic reasons.

On the other hand, women did not necessarily have access to "good" credit, that is, credit on the most advantageous terms possible. As consumer credit became more prominent in the second half of the twentieth century, changes in the credit industry created more options for lower quality credit. While some of these types of credit, such as pawnshops and loan sharking, are much older than most other credit instruments, new industries, such as payday advance loan centers, sprang up in the late twentieth century to take advantage of the increased demand for consumer credit. Because many single and divorced women were unable to secure higher quality credit, they suffered disproportionally in the late 2000s mortgage crisis. The Consumer Federation of America found that women had been 32 percent more likely to receive subprime loans than men in the past decade.[44]

It is unknown if the problems that women suffer in the American economy today are the result of invidious distinctions or rational discrimination. Thirty-five years ago, proponents of equal credit access for women were able to convince policy makers and most creditors that they suffered from invidious distinctions. Four more decades of unequal treatment, though, might change some of those conclusions. Women's pay equity has been slow to improve, and this lack of equal pay limits the creditworthiness of women.

As the story of women in the recent subprime mortgage market attests, the improving status of women in today's credit market does not mean that they experience no problems in the credit market. Like in the 1970s, the only real chance to eliminate that discrimination is to educate debtors and consumers. The nascent Consumer Finance Protection Agency is working toward educating consumers and creditors about their credit rights. If debtors, women included, become more aware of their rights and the paths they can take to ensure them, they will be better able to secure the credit they deserve.

Notes

1. For a discussion on the differences between these types of discrimination, see Charles W. Calomiris, Charles M. Kahn, and Stanley D. Longhofer, "Housing-Finance Intervention and Private Incentives: Helping Minorities and the Poor," *Federal Credit Allocation: Theory, Evidence, and History,* special issue of *Journal of Money, Credit and Banking* 26, no. 3, pt. 2 (August 1994): 652–56.

2. "Invidious distinction" was terminology developed during the civil rights era to describe the types of discrimination that legislation could prevent; it was used both by civil rights activists and Congress. This usage differs from the "invidious distinction" outlined in Thorstein Veblen, *The Theory of the Leisure Class: An Economic Study of Institutions* (New York, 1912), 4–6, whose author uses the term to describe how consumption patterns play a role in distinguishing the working class from the leisure class.

3. For more on the issues surrounding economic citizenship that women experienced in the twentieth century, see Alice Kessler-Harris, *In Pursuit of Equity: Women, Men, and the Quest for Economic Citizenship in 20th-Century America* (New York, 2001).

4. There is much on the history of women in the twentieth-century United States, and many people who study that history find the wave metaphor useful. Very briefly, the first wave, near the start of the twentieth century, aimed to secure basic political and economic rights for women, such as voting and property ownership. The second wave, from the late 1960s to sometime in the 1980s, aimed to erase many of the differences between men and women—this was the time that the Equal Rights Amendment gained the most traction, for example. The third wave, starting in the late 1980s or early 1990s, aimed to celebrate women's differences and diversity, while ensuring their equality to men. For more on the historiography of the women's movement during the second two movements and the wave metaphor that describes it, see Linda K. Kerber, "Separate Spheres, Female Worlds, Woman's Place: The Rhetoric of Women's History," *Journal of American History* 75, no. 1 (June 1988): 9–39; Linda K. Kerber, Alice Kessler-Harris, and Kathryn Kish Sklar, "Introduction," in *U.S. History as Women's History: New Feminist Essays,* ed. Kerber, Kessler-Harris, and Sklar (Chapel Hill, NC, 1995); and Sara Evans, *Tidal Wave: How Women Changed America at Century's End* (New York, 2003).

5. For more on credit history, see Donncha Marron, *Consumer Credit in the United States: A Sociological Perspective from the 19th Century to the Present* (New York: 2009); Lendol Calder, *Financing the American Dream: A Cultural History of Consumer Credit* (Princeton, NJ, 2001); Louis Hyman, *Debtor Nation: The History of America in Red Ink* (Princeton, NJ, 2011). Note the more recent publication dates compared to the women's history above.

6. Emily Card Papers, Newcomb College Archives, New Orleans, LA. The names of women who participated in hearings or wrote letters in a nonprofessional capacity have been changed in this article to protect their privacy.

7. Ohio Governor's Task Force on Women and Credit (1972), Ohio Historical Society, Columbus, OH (hereafter referred to as OHS), State Archive, box 312, folder 2.

8. Governor's Task Force on Women and Credit State OHS, State Archive, box 312, folder 1. For more on baby letters, see Ira M. Millstein, *Report of the National Commission on Consumer Finance: Consumer Credit in the United States* (Washington, D.C., 1972). Credit legislation in the 1960s did not explicitly outlaw baby letters, but the main government lenders, the FHA and the VA, removed them from practice on their own in the early1970s following the NCCF report. Independent banks, though, continued to require these until the mid-1970s.

9. See Lizabeth Cohen, *A Consumers' Republic: The Politics of Mass Consumption in Postwar America* (New York, 2003).

10. For the economic impact of these demographic changes at the macro level, see Jeremy Atack and Peter Passell, *A New Economic View of American History*, 2nd ed. (New York, 1994). For the impact on workers, especially women workers, see Susan Porter Benson, *Counter Cultures: Saleswomen, Managers, and Customers in American Department Stores* (Urbana, IL, 1986); Roy Rosenzweig, *Eight Hours for What We Will: Workers and Leisure in an Industrial City* (New York, 1983).

11. For the former, see Nan Enstad, *Ladies of Labor, Girls of Adventure* (New York, 1999); and Kathy Peiss, *Cheap Amusements: Working Women and Leisure in Turn-of-the-Century New York* (Philadelphia, PA, 1986). For the latter, see Maurine W. Greenwald, *Women, War, and Work: The Impact of World War I on Women Workers in the United States* (New York, 1990).

12. Greenwald, *Women, War, and Work.*

13. See chapter 12 in this volume by Lendol Calder.

14. Joanne Meyerowitz, *Not June Cleaver: Women and Gender in Postwar America, 1945–1960* (Philadelphia, PA, 1994).

15. Consumer Credit Protection Act, United States Code 15, §§1601–13 (1972).

16. Millstein, *Report of the National Commission on Consumer Finance.* The report, however, did not address the question of how competitive the market was in the 1970s. With a stagnating economy and soaring interest rates, it was not necessarily likely that another creditor would always have been available to grant credit.

17. California, Colorado, Connecticut, Florida, Illinois, Indiana, Kentucky, Maine, Maryland, Massachusetts, Minnesota, New Jersey, New York, Rhode Island,

Tennessee, Texas, Vermont, Washington, and Wisconsin all passed some form of equal credit legislation before federal legislation passed in 1974.

18. Lawrence Bowdish, "Invidious Distinctions: Credit Discrimination against Women, 1960s-Present" (PhD diss., Ohio State University, 2010).

19. Ohio Governor's Task Force on Women and Credit, OHS, State Archive, box 312, folders 1–3; Diane Poulton, *She Supports Her Children, and Can't Get a Loan or Buy a Car or even a House: Final Report of the Governor's Task Force on Credit for Women* (Columbus, OH, 1974).

20. The commission put out one-eighth-page advertisements in the front section of the major Ohio newspapers (*Columbus Dispatch, Cincinnati Enquirer, Cleveland Plan Dealer, Toledo Blade,* and *Akron Beacon Journal*) asking women who had experienced discrimination to send them their information. They also asked women's groups to direct complaints to the commission. Poulton, *She Supports Her Children,* 1–4.

21. This was particularly true in community property states, where husbands were held responsible for the debts accrued by the couple before legal reforms, including the ones mentioned in this chapter, in the 1970s. Since creditors had very limited legal recourse against wives in that situation, they required husbands to sign off on those applications.

22. Poulton, *She Supports Her Children.*

23. Ohio Governor's Task Force on Women and Credit, OHS, State Archive, box 312–1, folder 1.

24. Ohio Governor's Task Force on Women and Credit, OHS, State Archive, box 312–1.

25. One widow inherited a successful gas station from her deceased husband. Even though she had worked at the gas station for over twenty years while he was still alive, the bank would not offer her the same line of credit to keep the business running. Another woman wanted to open a bookstore. She needed a male cosigner and had to get her ex-husband to do it, even though he was a student with no income. Another widow had her credit card revoked when her husband died. She was only able to reestablish the card when she reminded the credit card company that she had a good job and her deceased husband had been a successful banker and a state politician with considerable influence. *Proceedings of the Governor's Task Force for Credit for Women* (Columbus, OH, 1974), 2 and 31 (July 29, 1974).

26. Ibid., 170.

27. Ibid., 38.

28. Ibid., 45. Discrimination in insurance policies is even more convoluted than in more standard credit policies, but actuarial science gives the fight against this type of credit discrimination a different tint. Often, economic and actuarial statistics are sufficient by themselves to justify (or not) specific insurance costs for women in relation to men.

Unlike the middle-class women who dominated the discussion, a few of the women who spoke up during the hearings were on welfare or advocating for women who were. Obviously, the economic position of women in this last group was more precarious than that of other affected women. Creditors refused to accept welfare as income, severely hampering the ability of welfare recipients to secure credit based on their state-ordered income. Instead of being able to budget long-term, without installment credit these women had to budget month to month, which left them without any flexibility in their spending.

29. Much civil rights legislation, including the CCPA, required creditors and credit bureaus to maintain records and to make them available upon the request of government regulators or individual customers.

30. *Proceedings of the Governor's Task Force for Credit for Women,* 11–30 (July 30, 1974). A few other representatives agreed with him. Robert Fickline, Director of Consumer Credit at Ohio National Bank, claimed that "education" was the biggest problem facing women in the credit market.

31. In fact, in the mid-1970s, a number of banks realized how they were missing out on a huge part of the market and started offering more services to women looking to learn more about credit.

32. *Proceedings of the Governor's Task Force for Credit for Women,* 62.

33. Barbara A. Curran, *Legislative Controls as a Response to Consumer-Credit Problems,* 8 B.C.L. Rev. 409 (1967), http://lawdigitalcommons.bc.edu/bclr/vol8/iss3/2.

34. Millstein, *Report of the National Commission on Consumer Finance,* 152–53.

35. *Mortgage Money: Who Gets It? A Case Study in Mortgage Lending Discrimination in Hartford, Connecticut,* by Arthur S. Flemming, chairman, U.S. Commission on Civil Rights. Washington, D.C., Government Printing Office, 1974, 18, original emphasis.

36. Ibid., 20–23. For a discussion on how collecting information on minorities and women is more costly for banks because of this underrepresentation, see Calomiris, Kahn, and Longhofer, "Housing-Finance Intervention."

37. During the Senate process, gender and marital status were the only demographic groups represented in the bill.

38. The statistics in those reports were either inconclusive or they showed discrimination against women in certain circumstances that was insufficient to require a reworking of the credit system on just those findings.

39. For more on information asymmetry in lending decisions, see Kam Hon Chu, "Free Banking and Information Asymmetry," *Journal of Money, Credit and Banking* 31, no. 4 (November 1999): 748–62.

40. 15 U.S.C. §1691.

41. Leonor Sullivan, *Hearings before the Subcommittee on Consumer Affairs of the Committee on Banking and Currency on H.R. 14856 and H.R. 14908* (Washington, D.C., 1974).

42. For a discussion of government policy on women's rights and social values, see Cynthia Harrison, "Women, Gender, Values, and Public Policy," in *Democracy, Social Values, and Public Policy,* ed. Milton M. Carrow, Robert Paul Churchill, and Joseph J. Cordes (Westport, CT, 1998): 147–62.

43. Perhaps the most striking proof that credit literacy among women remained low was a June 1977 survey conducted by the Women's Year Project through the New Jersey Division of Civil Rights. That survey found that only half of the female respondents could correctly answer at least *three* out of sixteen questions about equal credit rights, laws, and opportunities. Joan Cook, "Credit: Confusion Persists," *New York Times,* June 19, 1977.
44. "Field Guide to Women Homebuyers," National Association of Realtors, http://www.realtor.org/library/library/fg212.

CHAPTER 6

Virtually Creditworthy: Privacy, the Right to Information, and Consumer Credit Reporting in West Germany, 1950–1985

Larry Frohman

Risk, Surveillance, and Consumer Credit

Modern societies are information societies. They depend on the collection by bureaucratic organizations of vast quantities of information on the productive, reproductive, and consumptive activities of the population in order to manage large-scale social processes. Indeed, it is difficult to envision how a modern society could exist without the capacity to gather such information and then apply it for strategic decision making.

One of the most important domains of information collection and use in modern society is the consumer credit reporting field. Since the 1920s, consumer credit reporting in Germany has been dominated by a single organization: Schufa, the Protective Society for General Credit Assurance.[1] As such, Schufa has been the largest and most sophisticated collector of personal information in the private sector. In 1977, the company held records on 22 million people, that is, on virtually every (male) head of household and 80 percent of all economically active individuals in a population of 60 million; and in 1976, it issued over 21 million credit reports.[2] In this essay, I use the development of Schufa's credit reporting system as a vehicle for analyzing the role of information collection and exchange in modern society, the impact of such surveillance on our understanding of privacy, and the politics of personal information in West Germany as they played out in the consumer credit sector from the 1950s through the mid-1980s.

The 1950s were a paternalistic era, although this search for new binding norms represented less a restoration of the world of yesterday than a creative, conservative response to the challenges of modernity. Just as the Adenauer government claimed the right to guide the media,[3] and just as the churches reasserted their role as the guardians of public morality, so, too, did business claim the right to manage the personal information of consumers in the name of the public good, which it understood in terms of the minimization of fraud, excess consumer indebtedness, and the overall cost of credit to the national economy. In the late 1960s, however, a number of factors converged to raise public awareness of the privacy implications of consumer credit reporting: the continued expansion of consumer credit and the development of new means of financing such purchases; sensationalist exposés on the abuse of personal credit information at home and abroad[4] and the transnational flow of ideas emanating from American discussions—culminating in the Fair Credit Reporting Act (1970)—on discrimination and privacy protection in the credit sector; a broad, pan-Atlantic unease with new computer and communication technologies; and the formation of an active consumer protection movement. In turn, all of these developments were refracted through the political tensions of the time, which heightened German public sensibility about the ways in which personal information could be used—and abused—by both the public and private sectors. This new awareness of the political implications of control over personal information led to the passage of the 1976–77 Federal Privacy Protection Law (*Bundesdatenschutzgesetz,* BDSG), which provided the legal framework for the collection and dissemination of consumer credit information in Germany.

The development of both Schufa's credit reporting system and German privacy legislation needs to be understood as much sociologically as historically. Credit transactions are, by their very nature, risky, and credit reporting systems represent an institutionalized means for transforming uncertainty into the calculable probability of repayment, thus enabling the establishment of an efficiently functioning credit market in which the interest rate charged is proportional to the degree of risk associated with the transaction.[5] But the contingency of the future means that this task of transforming uncertainty into probability can never be completed, and every disappointment leads not to the abandonment of the quest, but to its renewal with increasingly sophisticated informational tools.[6]

In stable, geographically bounded societies, lenders and sellers normally possess a great deal of information about credit customers, and in such communities there are effective means of sanctioning those who fail to live up to their financial obligations.[7] However, the geographical scope of such knowledge is limited, and both the quality of information and the effectiveness of sanctions are progressively attenuated by that set of social processes known as modernization, as are the reciprocal obligations that Silke Meyer identifies as the social foundation of credit in chapter 10. The network of doorstep credit agents that Sean O'Connell describes in chapter 4 represents an intermediate stage in this process, one in which the Provident agents instrumentalized existing social networks without truly belonging to them. The founding of Schufa represented the decisive step in the modernization, bureaucratization, and professionalization of consumer credit reporting, and it is entirely appropriate that the first exposition of Schufa's inner workings should have appeared in a journal devoted to the rationalization and "organization" of business processes.[8]

In the years after World War II, the disembedding of markets for goods and money from bounded communities and the growing integration of smaller towns and rural communities into regional and national markets, combined with rising affluence and the transition to a consumer society, generated new flows of information. Producers engaged market research firms to investigate the desires of consumers, whose purchasing habits were becoming more labile and whose preferences these producers hoped to link in a more integral manner to their own production decisions. Consumers themselves began to demand more information about technologically sophisticated products bought from merchants with whom they did not have relationships built on familiarity and trust. Mass advertising sought to communicate information about the proliferating number of consumer goods on the market while shaping the tastes and preferences of potential purchasers. And, most relevant to the matter at hand, merchants and lenders began to demand more information about the financial history and habits of the increasingly affluent, increasingly mobile consumers seeking to make credit purchases in an increasingly anonymous national market. In fact, just as mail-order firms were keenly interested in providing distant, anonymous customers with more information on products with which these persons lacked direct experience or access, these companies were also among the biggest users and generators of credit data in Germany during these years.[9] For the sociologist Helmut Schelsky, these channels through which knowledge about consumers, producers, and products was exchanged satisfied a fundamental human need for information, a need which, Schelsky argued, had been created by the loss of immediate, prereflective knowledge as individuals learned to live through those abstract social institutions of the modern industrial world that Schelsky's mentor, Hans Freyer, called "secondary systems." In fact, the 1950s discussion of the status and function of public opinion and of what Jürgen Habermas later called the "structural transformation of the public sphere" was really a debate about the nature of these information flows, the extent to which they served instrumental or manipulative, rather than critical or communicative ends, their impact on the autonomous subject, and the proper means of governing them.[10]

Ultimately, credit reporting achieved a critical mass in the 1950s and 1960s not only because of the rising standard of living, but also because merchants hoped to compensate for increasing social and geographical distance through the intensified collection and analysis of information on their customers—and thereby to recreate in a more abstract form something akin to the personal trust and communal capacity for sanction that had existed in more traditional societies. But the kind of surveillance undertaken by Schufa and other credit reporting agencies did not generally involve the direct observation of one person by another, and its master metaphor was less the omniscient, omnipotent Big Brother of Orwell's *1984* or the overseer in Bentham's Panopticon than the anonymous, perhaps even well-intentioned bureaucrat. Here, I use surveillance to mean the systematic collection—by an organization—of personal information on the individual members of a population with whom it regularly comes into contact. Almost by definition, such surveillance is undertaken on a mass, rather than an individualized, basis, and, in the case of credit reporting, the information collected is either provided by consumers as part of the credit application process or generated by member firms as part of their everyday record-keeping. The ability to collect, analyze, and use this information as the basis for both strategic decision making and the reflexive monitoring of the organization itself enables surveillance systems to generate administrative power, and, building on Anthony Giddens, one can usefully conceive of the credit sector as a kind of social or economic space produced through control over the information deemed relevant to credit decisions.[11]

The purpose of credit reporting systems is less to uncover some hidden truth about consumers than to construct knowledge about them that can then be used as the basis for strategic credit decisions. In an essay that has become a standard point of reference in recent work on surveillance, Kevin Haggerty and Richard Ericson have described—drawing on Gilles Deleuze and Félix Guattari, rather than Foucault—how modern electronic surveillance systems enframe, fix, and appropriate discrete elements of the fluid unity of individual experience by overlaying upon it a schema or set of categories designed to isolate and catalog the facets of this whole that are deemed relevant to those who collect and control this information—in this case, consumer financial behavior. The descriptive characteristics resulting from this process can then be reassembled to form an infinite number of virtual subjects or "data doubles," depending on the specific needs of the moment.[12] However, since the representations produced by these credit surveillance systems reflect the strategic interests and definitional power of these organizations, they have the potential to alienate consumers from their identities, exert a pervasive normalizing effect, and at the same time serve as the basis for self-governance by the consuming subject.[13]

In view of the rapid pace of innovation in the domain of surveillance technologies, the growing market for personal information, and the proliferation of surveillance systems, which increasingly come together in contingent "assemblages" for individual acts of opportunistic surveillance, there is no intrinsic limit to the number of virtual identities that can be constructed for any given person. In such a situation, Haggerty and Ericson suggest, privacy is now "less a line in the sand beyond which transgression is not permitted, than a shifting space of negotiations where privacy is traded for products, better services or special deals."[14] But the fact that such an infinitude of virtual identities is theoretically possible does not mean that all will actually come to pass. Rather, I would suggest that privacy must be understood not only as a negotiation of what one person will get in exchange for the disclosure of personal information, but also as a negotiation of how particular domains of knowledge can be enframed by surveillance systems, what kinds of information can be collected, and under what conditions they can be exchanged and combined to construct financial identities that then become the object of strategic decision making and social control. In the remainder of this essay, I attempt to describe the process through which these issues were negotiated in the credit domain in postwar West Germany.

"In a Few Years, It Will be Unimaginable to Offer Credit in West Germany without Consulting Schufa"

Historically, the development of consumer credit reporting systems has been slowed or blocked by two major obstacles. The first was the problem of overcoming the reluctance of merchants and financial institutions to share their highly valued and closely held customer information. The second was the need to devise an information system capable of collecting, integrating, and ensuring the timely dissemination of all relevant information on potential credit customers. These two issues are discussed in this and the following section, respectively.[15]

Widespread credit sales and systematic consumer credit reporting developed in tandem; neither emerged in Germany until the mid-1920s; and their joined history is closely linked to the changing involvement of banks in the field.[16] Although the stabilization of the currency in 1924 unleashed a wave of installment purchases, merchants generally lacked both the capital to finance these sales and the expertise to evaluate the creditworthiness of the individual consumer, whereas commercial credit reporting agencies did not possess the information needed to make informed decisions concerning the creditworthiness of a clientele comprised of the laboring classes and the middling estates, both old and new. The solutions to these two problems proved to be interrelated, however, because the need for additional capital brought banks—with their focus on fiscal discipline and their greater experience with commercial credit rating—into the field of installment selling for the first time, something that they had theretofore shunned. This involvement of the banks, the decision by the Hermann Tietz department store to abandon its strict cash-only policy, and the decision by the Berlin municipal utility business to enter the installment sales business in order to expand the market for electricity all combined in the spring of 1927 to provide the impetus for the founding of a consumer credit reporting agency in Berlin.[17] In turn, success of the Berlin Schufa led to the establishment of similar organizations in other cities, which from 1931 were loosely linked in a national organization.

After the 1948 currency reform, installment sales in Germany experienced a second postwar boom. That same year, the individual Schufas resumed their activity, and in 1952 the thirteen regional Schufa organizations came together to form a national organization, the Bundes-Schufa, to coordinate the exchange of information among the regional agencies. The postwar consumption surge was, however, accompanied by an equally large surge in wage garnishments. This increase was widely attributed to predatory practices on the part of merchants who used installment sales to entice improvident workers (and their spouses) into making purchases that they could neither afford nor resist. This attack on installment sales was reinforced by the influential liberal economist Wilhelm Röpke, who damned installment sales as a form of "premature consumption" *(Borgkauf)* that was diminishing the country's economic substance while undermining the "savings discipline" that he regarded as the moral foundation of bourgeois society.

The ensuing culture war pitted the installment sales banks against the savings banks, which were the protectors of the traditional financial morality championed by Röpke, and in chapter 2, Rebecca Belvederesi-Kochs relates how this culture war played out within the savings banks themselves as they sought to modernize their operations in the postwar decades. However, it proved much easier to determine the causes of the spike in garnishments than to end the culture wars spawned by the transition to a more affluent consumer society. A 1953 study by the German Chamber of Commerce and Industry exonerated installment sales from the charges made against them by showing that most garnishments were related to either family support payments or the purchase of everyday consumer necessities, rather than ill-considered outlays for expensive consumer durables or luxury items by consumers who could not govern their passions. But the study also showed that garnishment rates for workers who had borrowed from installment sales banks or other credit institutes that relied on Schufa reports were far lower than for those who had been able to make their purchases without undergoing a prior credit check.[18] These findings led the Economics Ministry and a number of important business groups to endorse Schufa as the best way to combat excess consumer debt and the problems that it created,[19] while the merchants and installment financing organizations that controlled Schufa concluded that the sharply reduced credit losses resulting from the Schufa system meant that no company that wished to do business on a credit basis would long be able to resist the competitive pressure to join the organization. "In a few years," they prophesied, "it will be unimaginable to offer credit in West Germany without consulting Schufa."[20]

Between 1950 and 1963, the number of installment banks belonging to Schufa rose from 71 to 235.[21] Beginning in the late 1950s, however, commercial and savings banks were being drawn more deeply into the consumer credit business, a field from which they had traditionally shied away. On the one hand, they began to offer unsecured personal loans to the increasingly affluent working and middle classes, who were opening larger numbers of checking accounts in response to the growing use of electronic salary payments by employers; these personal loans were more convenient than traditional installment sales loans, which had been approved on a case-by-case basis for specific purchases.[22] On the other hand, banks were also drawn more deeply into the consumer credit field by the development of new forms of credit. First, the growing reliance on electronic funds transfers in the 1960s meant that, to retain the loyalty of wage earners, banks had to be willing to offer overdraft credit privileges to these customers, whose creditworthiness thus became an issue for the banks for the first time. Second, the Eurocheck system also involved credit risk, because the issuing banks were committed to redeeming all properly written checks regardless of the balance available in the cardholder's account. The introduction of credit cards beginning in the late 1960s accelerated these trends.[23] By the end of the decade, savings and commercial banks had begun to eclipse the importance of traditional installment sales banks in the consumer credit field. As a result, more and more banks joined Schufa, so that by the time the Bundestag began considering privacy legislation at the beginning of the 1970s, it was virtually impossible to open a checking account without the financial institution first obtaining a credit report from Schufa. The only major financial institution that did not belong to Schufa was the Postbank. Although approximately 30,000 financial institutions, mail-order firms, department stores, and other retailers belonged to Schufa, the actual decisions to grant or refuse credit were ultimately made by individual merchants and lenders, so that the Schufa system can be better characterized as totalizing, yet decentralized, rather than panoptic.

In postwar France, the involvement of commercial banks in the consumer credit field served to block the development of a private consumer credit reporting agency, while the relative informational self-sufficiency of these institutions, and the correspondingly reduced need to exchange consumer information, diminished the fervor with which these banks opposed privacy legislation.[24] By contrast, the involvement of banks in Germany seems to have had the opposite effect. In its early years, credit reporting there had been largely limited to blacklists maintained by individual trade associations. In 1926, the leading commercial credit agencies had already pooled their available information to establish a consumer credit reporting firm. However, this firm was unable to convince the merchants and financial institutions with which it did business to share information on their customers. The attendant disproportion between the quality of the credit information that the company provided and the cost of its reports led to the rapid collapse of the venture.

In Germany, the highly developed corporatist structures of the banking sector and the willingness of the state to act as a bridge among these groups— as evidenced in the Economics Ministry's de facto blessing of Schufa at the 1953 conference—played a crucial role in overcoming the competitive pressures that threatened to fragment any systematic credit reporting system. This helped Schufa become an effective quasi-public provider of an important collective good. One can only speculate that this dynamic also played an important role in the founding of Schufa, whose early years are only sparsely documented due to the loss of so many papers in World War II. On the other side of the Rhine, however, the relative underdevelopment of consumer credit sales and the absence of such coordination diminished both the incentive to establish a private nationwide system of consumer credit reporting and the capacity to do so. Today, the only nationwide credit registry in France is a public registry of negative information maintained by the Bank of France, and the limited availability of consumer credit information has combined with restrictive privacy legislation to give consumer credit surveillance a very different shape than in Germany.

Total Credit Information Awareness

Installment purchasing, like social insurance and the other risk-based strategies for managing the social problems of the industrial world, was predicated on the emergence of a population of regularly employed wage-earning "workers" capable of governing themselves by thinking in a providential manner about the future. It is this optimistic view of the self-governing subject that has underlain the belief that past financial behavior represents the most accurate predictor of future repayment for consumers without substantial property.

Schufa's mission has always been twofold: to protect member firms from credit risk and to protect consumers from excessive indebtedness, though the latter goal has generally been little more than a means for achieving the former. Schufa's ultimate goal has been to bring light and legibility to the dark, messy domain of consumer financial morality, and its basic strategy for achieving this goal has been to leverage the information generated by each of its individual member firms by acting as a clearinghouse to make this information available to all other members. In contrast to much pre-1970 credit reporting in the United States, Schufa has always reported only "objective" information (though into the 1980s, it also reported steps that had been taken by lenders to recover outstanding debts without noting whether these debts had been disputed by the purchaser or confirmed by the courts). Although detailed investigative reports might have permitted their users to form a more textured picture of the applicant, such information would have defied standardization and easy communication. In fact, the flow of information through the Schufa system was facilitated by the development of a set of standardized codes for describing the entire spectrum of financially relevant behaviors.[25]

Schufa's most important innovation was the development of an organizational technology for collecting this information, classifying it, ensuring that it was associated with the proper physical person, and then making it available in a timely, controlled manner and in a usable form to those lenders and merchants who were ultimately responsible for making credit decisions. This technology was a self-acting mechanism in which the initial act of inquiring into the creditworthiness of a prospective customer automatically set in motion the process by which information was exchanged and a credit dossier—which represented the virtual credit or financial identity of the individual—was established. In response to an initial inquiry from a merchant or a financial institution, Schufa recorded the fact and the purpose of the inquiry, while the agreement that member firms signed with Schufa required them to promptly report either the amount and terms of the credit granted (up to DM 20,000; after 1970, DM 30,000) or the fact that the application was refused; if neither of these actions was reported, the record of the inquiry was deleted after two months. Member firms were also obligated to report any failure to adhere to the terms of the credit agreement (including early repayment of the debt), and the absence of negative reports was taken to mean that the borrower was continuing to pay on time.

This automatism was embodied in a special office or paperwork management technology that was designed by the founders of the organization and that, in computerized form, continues to lie at the heart of the company. The core of the Schufa system was its archive, which was continuously fed more and more information on more and more individuals from more and more sources, so that the information on the credit-seeking population became continuously more systematic, comprehensive, and finely grained. This member-provided information was also supplemented by public record information, such as bankruptcy declarations, garnishment proceedings, and arrest warrants. The information collected in this manner was operationalized by means of index cards, which ensured that every piece of incoming information was assigned to the proper person, that no person had more than one such "master" card, and that, therefore, all relevant information would be systematically revealed to the gaze of the Schufa employee as he or she responded to a credit inquiry and added new information to the card. However, all of this information would have been for naught if the individual had been able to escape from his or her credit history simply by moving to a different town. To police the geographical boundaries and internal comprehensiveness of its surveillance system, Schufa maintained a tracking system that flagged any debtor who tried to escape obligations by moving to a new location without notifying creditors and who then attempted to apply for credit in a new place of residence under his or her real name and date of birth.

The temporal dimension of the Schufa system was just as important as the spatial one because the creditworthiness of a prospective customer was constantly changing. The speed with which information was collected, classified, and reported mattered because of the fear that "notorious swindlers" would attempt to defraud the system by rapidly making credit purchases beyond their means from a number of different merchants. This was one of the reasons why the mere act of making a credit inquiry became one of the items included on the credit report itself. In the 1920s, inquires had been made by messengers sent to the Schufa office by member organizations, though Schufa also made use of such modern technologies as pneumatic tubes, and direct phone connections were maintained to some of the larger member firms. In addition, even after the credit report was issued, Schufa continued to surveil the consumer through a system of follow-up reports. These reports, which contained any newly reported negative information on the borrower, were automatically sent by Schufa to every member firm with whom the customer still had an open contract at the time that this negative information was received in the hope that such information would enable the merchant or lender to reevaluate his initial determination of creditworthiness and take whatever actions were necessary to protect his financial interests. Conversely, loans remained in the Schufa system as long as the borrower owed money, and Schufa retained—for three additional years—a record of both repaid loans and any negative information that had been reported.

By the end of the 1960s, Schufa's surveillance capacity had to be rated rather high.[26] As noted above, Schufa held credit records on virtually every head of household. Moreover, the increasing desirability of consumer credit during the economic miracle, combined with the continued growth in the number of member firms, created many points of contact between the Schufa system and the consuming population. Each new encounter with each of these contact points offered Schufa the opportunity to expand the amount of relevant data that it held on the individual, to reassemble and reevaluate this information, and to appropriately sanction poor risks by denying them access to credit or taking steps to recover outstanding debts. Especially crucial here were the extensive branch networks of the major regional banks, which ensured that virtually anyone in regular employ in a large firm was brought into the system via a payroll deposit account. In theory at least, new information was recorded on the person's master record card at the moment when he or she applied for a loan, and this information could be disseminated with equal rapidity to those responsible for actually making credit decisions. On the other hand, there was always the possibility that incoming information would be attached to the wrong person or that an outgoing credit report would confuse one individual with another person who had similar or identical personal information. Nor was there any system for ensuring that public record information was up to date. But the greatest weakness remained the division of the country into regional Schufa organizations. Since a single manual file containing more than 20 million records would have been completely unworkable before the advent of the computer, there was no better alternative to regional decentralization—with all of the inefficiencies and loopholes this entailed. This was one reason why Schufa had such high hopes that the introduction of a national identity numbering system and the creation of a computerized network linking the nation's local population registries would substantially enhance the efficiency of its own system.

Competing Rights and the Redefinition of Privacy in the Computer Age

There had, of course, been critics of credit reporting since the establishment of the first commercial credit reporting agencies.[27] However, credit privacy did not become an issue of widespread public concern until the late 1960s.

Although automation promised immense efficiency gains, it also raised new questions as the principle of the unrestricted exchange of personal credit information was confronted by an expanded conception of individual liberties and growing concerns about personal privacy. This section will examine the conflict between the competing rights to information and privacy as they were mediated through the new conception of informational privacy.

In the 1950s and 1960s, privacy was understood in terms of different "spheres" enjoying varying degrees of protection according to their relative intimacy and sensitivity. Although the country's Constitutional Court recognized the existence of an "inviolable private domain for the development of the individual personality" *(unantastbarer Bereich privater Lebensgestaltung)*,[28] jurists found it nearly impossible to develop a coherent account of the nature and scope of this private sphere. This debate remained unresolved when, in the second half of the 1960s, the underlying problematic was transformed by the spread of computer databases and the development of a new conception of "informational privacy," which emphasized less the intrinsic secrecy or sensitivity of information than the context within which this information was collected and the individual's right to control these flows of personal information.

One of the most systematic early analyses of the problem of personal privacy in the computer age came from Ulrich Seidel.[29] Drawing on the work of the American legal scholar Alan Westin,[30] Seidel argued for a fundamental rethinking of the concept of privacy and for a much more expansive individual right to control the collection and use of personal information. His arguments were based on a specific understanding of the ways in which the original meaning of personal information was distorted by computer databases, which abstracted this information from its original context, linked together discrete pieces of personal information into an integrated, but extremely problematic "profile" of the individual, and then instantaneously disseminated this information to other persons, who could then use it for purposes that might be entirely different from that for which it had originally been collected. Things had been different in the past, when information had been collected by hand and held in paper form. Information that was collected by government agencies remained to a greater or lesser degree the property of that agency and was only made available to other agencies on the basis of a case-by-case evaluation of the needs of the office requesting the data. In contrast, the proposed creation of an automated, integrated national population information system, which was to become the model for the integrated processing of personal information within the public sector, was based on the principle that personal information should be collected only once and then be made available in up-to-date form on an as-needed basis to all other users. No matter whether in the public or the private sectors, such integrated information systems rendered the individual more transparent to those who controlled this information and thus increased the power of the latter over the former.

Seidel's argument was that such integrated databases removed information from the control of its original owners, who had to some degree ensured that the requesting agency had a legitimate need for the information and that the context and meaning that had inhered in the act of collecting it was not completely lost in the process of its dissemination. The essential point for Seidel was "that the person who originally collected the information ceases to exercise personal control over these secrets, and his protection is superseded by a shimmering spectrum of interests . . . These data collections [then] lead a certain independent existence."[31] The task of privacy protection legislation was, therefore, to compensate for the loss of the "natural" safeguards resulting from this bureaucratic compartmentalization. Such protection was all the more necessary in view of the fact that it was only possible to speak of meaningful consent to the collection of information if this consent took place in a concrete context in which the individual could understand the possible uses to which this information would be put, something that was rendered impossible by the infinite contextual displacement inherent in multifunctional databases.

Existing law did not penalize the collection of protected information, but only its subsequent publication or dissemination, and the law placed no restrictions on the publication of information that did not enjoy special protection. However, their understanding of the impact of computerization led Seidel and others to argue that, since all information bearing on the personal circumstances of an identifiable individual was always potentially harmful to the individual, the traditional logic of privacy would have to be reversed and the exception would have to become the rule. Rather than permitting the collection, storage, combination, and dissemination of all knowledge that did not enjoy special protection, this new conception of informational privacy was based on the principle that all personal information was deserving of protection and that, therefore, the individual should be accorded a much more expansive right to control its collection and subsequent use.

These arguments on behalf of informational privacy did not go unchallenged. The most sophisticated defense of the right to information in the credit sector came from the jurists Klaus Tiedemann and Christoph Sasse.[32] Although the state had developed a number of mechanisms (bankruptcy legislation, mediation procedures, etc.) for remedying the losses caused by credit defaults, Tiedemann and Sasse argued that the state was incapable of taking steps to prevent such defaults without imposing disclosure and regulatory requirements that were inconsistent with the principles of a free-market society. This meant that, in a society in which the individual was in principle free to pursue his or her own well-understood interests and where the state intervened only at the global level to regulate the operation of the market, the only alternative to the forced revelation of relevant personal information was to guarantee the right of individual entrepreneurs to gather the information that they needed to make well-informed credit decisions. Credit reporting agencies represented a mechanism for the collective exercise of this fundamental individual right, a mechanism that enhanced the allocative efficiency of the market by making it possible for merchants and lenders to obtain better information than they could on their own and to do so at less cost.

Tiedemann and Sasse coupled this argument on behalf of the right to information with a critique of the concept of informational privacy, which, they insisted, was no more coherent than the sphere theory that it claimed to replace. If one denied lenders the right to collect and exchange personal information (other than that information culled from publicly accessible sources), then any and all information of potential relevance for credit decisions would be sucked into the black hole of informational privacy, leaving only a residuum of purely factual or statistical data that lacked all predictive power. In such a night in which all cows were black and all personal information private, it would, they claimed, be impossible to distinguish between legitimate and illegitimate privacy interests or to apply such a distinction to real-world problems. As a result, businesses would be prohibited from collecting a substantial amount of information that could be related to a particular individual, but that could not, by any reasonable standards, be considered intimate, secret, or private.

These arguments were based on the belief that it was, in fact, possible to distinguish between that economic information whose unrestricted exchange was essential to the efficient functioning of the market and the purely personal information of the borrower, which could remain private precisely because of its irrelevance to credit decisions. While the proponents of informational privacy tended to regard most financial information as one dimension of personal information, Tiedemann and Sasse inverted this reasoning, arguing instead that "business-related information for commercial needs is, even when it is related to the personal circumstances of the owner or other persons closely connected to the fortunes of the company, different in purpose and extent from information on the private lives of these persons, even though it may partially overlap with this information."[33]

Although Tiedemann and Sasse praised the American Fair Credit Reporting Act for specifically allowing the collection of the kinds of data they deemed necessary, they also argued that Germany did not need the extensive privacy protection guarantees contained in either the Fair Credit Reporting Act or the BDSG, because Germans did not need to be protected from intrusive, American-style credit reporting. For one thing, German consumers relied on credit to a much lesser degree than their American counterparts, who, Tiedemann and Sasse claimed, were more likely to use such credit to support a more spendthrift lifestyle. On top of that, the greater mobility of Americans, together with the absence of both a centralized, nationwide credit surveillance system such as Schufa and a national population registry system, which would have enabled creditors to keep track of the movement of individuals so as to enforce their contractual responsibilities, meant that credit reporting agencies had to dig much more deeply into the private lives of American consumers than was the case in Germany.[34]

Though the arguments of Tiedemann and Sasse represented an incisive critique of the idea of informational privacy, they suffered from their own problems. In addition to overlooking the disciplinary effects of information collection, their arguments were much more plausible with regard to commercial credit reporting, which was the primary focus of their work, than the consumer field, where the fact that credit decisions were based on assessments of how families would husband their income, rather than on audited financial statements, made it more difficult to distinguish between personal and financial information. Moreover, the absence of any objective criteria for distinguishing between financial and personal information meant that the claim that almost any piece of information could, in one context or another, shed light on the creditworthiness of the individual tended to collapse the latter into the former—exactly as privacy advocates feared and just as business argued should be the case. And the belief that credit reporting agencies represented the only means of reducing credit risk in a manner consistent with the principles of the free-market economy led Tiedemann and Sasse to overlook the competing interests of lenders and borrowers in the market itself.

Schufa's commitment to the right to information and the generalized exchange of information within the credit sector was institutionalized in two ways. On the one hand, member firms were obligated to report all credit transactions to a neutral, third-party clearinghouse (Schufa) that had no contractual relationship with the consumer. On the other hand, the Schufa reporting system automatically made the credit information held by one member firm available to every other member organization, while allowing that member, in turn, to benefit from the collective knowledge of the other members. Although such a system may have been well suited for waging a war on economic contingency, the underlying logic of prevention and transparency represented the antithesis of informational self-determination.

Negotiating the Boundaries of Privacy

Giving the individual an unrestricted right to control the use of his or her personal information would have meant that credit reporting agencies would have had to obtain the consent of the individual in order to collect and exchange credit information pertaining to him or her. Such a policy would have rendered credit reporting least effective in precisely those instances where such information would have been most valuable. In response, the representatives of the banking, insurance, and credit reporting industries, which all shared a common desire to prevent fraud, argued that, in a liberal society, individuals enjoyed a right to information and free speech that was no less fundamental than the right to privacy. They also insisted that this right to information trumped the right to privacy not only because the unrestricted exchange of personal information was necessary to secure the collective interest of the community in an efficiently functioning economy, but also because there could be no such thing as a "legitimate" privacy interest in the domain of consumer credit.

In the debates leading to the passage of the BDSG in December 1976, business groups alternated between challenging the federal government's competence to regulate data processing in the private sector and insisting that such regulations would be both costly and unnecessary, because the competitive self-interest of individual firms and the lack of the sovereign power to compel individuals to reveal personal information ensured that information collection in the private sector could never be as intrusive as it was in the public sector.[35] These claims were coupled with the argument that the generalized exchange of personal information in the credit and insurance sectors served the vital interests of both the public and individual lenders by reducing credit risk and cost. To reinforce this point, the federal office charged with regulating the credit sector argued that the information flow among the country's credit institutions had to be as organic and indivisible as the credit sector itself. It even proposed that the Bundestag insert a blanket clause into the BDSG stating that "a legitimate interest in blocking the reporting of personal information does not exist when this information . . . is communicated in order to prevent credit losses or combat white-collar crime," a problem that was also the object of public debate at this time.[36] All of this would, of course, be easy to achieve if the law were not extended to the nebulous domain of "personal information," but rather restricted, as Tiedemann and Sasse had argued, to "details concerning the personal or material (*sachliche*) circumstances of a specific or specifiable natural person insofar as these [did] not pertain to the commercial activity of the person as a businessman."[37] According to the umbrella organization representing Schufa and the installment finance banks, however, the fundamental problem with the draft—one that flowed from its underlying commitment to informational privacy—was that "only the privacy interests of the individual are emphasized, while the draft does not recognize the interests of business in the collection and exchange of information as being of equal importance."[38]

If in the domain of consumer protection legislation Germany opted for what Gunnar Trumbull has called an information model, which was based on the assumption that consumer citizens would make wise decisions concerning quality, safety, and price if provided with adequate information, rather than a protection model, which was based on the belief that citizens had a right to be protected from dangerous or low-quality products, German privacy legislation hewed much closer to the latter.[39] This policy was certainly based, at least in part, on the limited understanding of computers and electronic data processing on the part of the public, though the retention of this principle after the advent of the first natively digital generation points to the role of more deeply rooted cultural ideas about privacy that cannot be addressed here.

The BDSG was based on a blanket prohibition (§3) on the storage and processing of personal information except where specifically permitted by law or where the individual had given informed consent. Though the law included numerous provisions designed to ensure that the individual citizen would be better able to understand the precise uses to which his or her information would be put and thus in a better position to give such consent, the basic assumption underlying the law was that the unrestricted processing of personal information was potentially so harmful and the new technology so opaque that individuals had to be protected from consequences that they could not reasonably be expected to foresee or understand. On the other hand, though, the law did recognize that other individuals and the community as a whole also had a legitimate interest in the collection of personal information, and the text included a number of formulations—"legitimate privacy interests of the individual," "the legitimate interests of those who request or receive information from others," "the preponderant legitimate interests" of the individual or of third parties—through which lawmakers sought to balance the interests of these different parties.[40]

From the very beginning, regulators and state and federal privacy commissioners considered Schufa to be one of the most egregious offenders against the new law. Despite the numerous references to credit reporting during the drafting of the BDSG, Schufa initially claimed that it was exempt from the law because most of its files were held in paper rather than electronic form. The company also insisted that the individual member firms were the storage and processing offices in the sense of the BDSG and that, therefore, they alone were responsible for ensuring the accuracy of the information reported by Schufa. These claims flew in the face of the stated purpose of the law, and state regulators quickly ruled against Schufa on both issues.

Almost everyone involved in the drafting of the BDSG felt that, in its original form, the law did not adequately protect individual rights, and negotiations on revising the law began almost immediately after its passage. One point of particular contention was the fact that, although the BDSG had given individual consumers the right to see the information contained in their credit reports, lenders and merchants were not obligated to explain which individual pieces of information figured into a credit decision or how. To counterbalance this asymmetry, legislators considered modifying the law in one of two ways. Either the law would have to ensure that individuals would suffer no disadvantages for refusing to consent to the reporting of personal information, or it would have to require that lenders reveal the information on which negative decisions were based and then justify those decisions. Businesses, of course, regarded such proposals as completely unacceptable. Not only would such a policy have forced them to reveal both confidential sources of information, which they feared would dry up in the light of such publicity, and proprietary information on business strategy. Giving state regulators the authority to review negative decisions and reverse them if they were deemed unreasonable or discriminatory would, lenders and merchants argued, have deprived them of control over their own property and instituted a "right to credit" that would have amounted to nothing less than a form of informational communism.[41]

But regulatory and judicial efforts to determine the concrete meaning of the law revolved around two issues in particular: the meaning of "legitimate interest" and the role of consent, both of which were crucial to Schufa's heretofore uncontested freedom to determine what personal information was relevant to credit decisions and then to collect this information. Schufa's member firms had long included in their basic customer contracts a provision explaining that, in connection with either a credit application or an application for a bank account with credit privileges,[42] they would report to Schufa the personal information of the credit consumer or account holder. These institutions insisted that this clause was included merely for informational purposes and that they did not have to ask consent to report this data to Schufa. In contrast, regulators argued that, although the member firms were permitted to collect personal information on the buyer or borrower because of their contractual relationship with the person, Schufa had to be treated like a third party. This meant that these institutions could report information to Schufa only if one of two conditions were met: (1) the borrower gave informed consent or (2) if the recipient had a legitimate interest in receiving (or the provider had a legitimate interest in disseminating) such information (which was arguably the case) *and* if the reporting of such interest did not violate the legitimate privacy interests of the borrower (which was much less clear). Regulators and privacy commissioners insisted that, in view of its sensitivity, the reporting of credit information to a third party would almost always entail a violation of the person's privacy rights under the BDSG, and they regarded the existing version of the "Schufa clause" as an obfuscatory attempt to deprive consumers of the rights guaranteed by the law.

In response, Schufa and its member organizations sought to interpret the idea of legitimate interest so as to read an unrestricted right to information into a law ostensibly designed to protect personal information. Although the banks maintained that the informational rights and needs of the credit sector, as represented through Schufa, were intrinsically legitimate, they conceded that, in theory at least, these rights would have to be weighed against the privacy rights of the borrower. In practice, however, things worked quite differently. On the one hand, the banks claimed that it was impossible to balance the concrete interests of the credit sector and the merely theoretical privacy interests of the individual borrower. On the other hand, whenever financial institutions looked at the concrete information available to them and weighed their interest in preventing fraud and default against the borrower's interest in not revealing any derogatory information, these institutions insisted that the potential borrower's privacy interest could not be considered legitimate, because, if asked, borrowers were legally required to disclose whether there were outstanding obligations or other factors that might negatively affect their ability to repay their debts. In other words, from the creditors' perspective, privacy could never be anything other than a cover for fraudulent intent (or, to use the German slogan, *Datenschutz ist Tatenschutz*).[43]

These efforts to negotiate the boundaries of privacy were unsuccessful, and it ultimately fell to the courts to strike a balance between the competing rights to information and privacy in the credit sector. In 1985, the country's highest appellate court for civil and criminal cases ruled that the Schufa system violated the BDSG in numerous respects. The court found that (1) the blanket permission granted by the Schufa clause then in use to report unspecified client information precluded informed consent on the part of the borrower and that, (2) by making the clause an integral part of account agreements in a way that predicated the right to open a bank account on relinquishing privacy rights guaranteed by the BDSG, Schufa's member firms were engaging in an unfair business practice. The court then laid out the conditions that would have to be met for the Schufa system to conform to the requirements of the BDSG: personal information could only be reported to third parties based on a balancing of interests in each individual case; Schufa would have to make sure that the information contained in credit reports provided a complete, accurate, and up-to-date picture of the creditworthiness of the person (even if this required the reporting of more, not less, information); and reports could only be provided to those member firms that had a legitimate interest in such information.[44]

The Changing Face of Informational Power in the Credit Sector

Although the 1985 court ruling forced Schufa to retreat from some of its more expansive claims regarding the right to information and to make corresponding changes in the operation of its credit surveillance system, the decision did not represent an unqualified endorsement of the competing principle of informational privacy. Rather, it coupled an explicit recognition that a broad constitutionally guaranteed right to information was the key to protecting both individual and collective interests in diminishing credit risk and ensuring the smooth functioning of the market economy with a set of procedural safeguards that institutionalized the principle that all personal information could be—depending on context—deserving of protection. In so doing, it ratified the extensively regulated exchange of consumer credit information through the Schufa clearinghouse.[45] The limits of this complex compromise were condensed in one simple fact: merchants and lenders henceforth had to secure informed consent in order to report or collect customer information through Schufa, though they remained free to refuse to open credit accounts or make credit sales to anyone who declined to consent to this exchange of information. Although the court might have imposed more stringent standards on Schufa, it is hard to imagine how it could have ruled otherwise without sharply circumscribing the fundamental liberal rights to information and property. These marginal constraints on the ability of Schufa to follow the logic of its surveillance system to the bitter end may have permitted the survival of some degree of credit risk that might otherwise have been eradicated by a more totalizing apparatus. However, the economic costs resulting from this choice may also be the price that West Germany had to pay to escape from the peculiarly dystopian consequences of an unfettered right to information.

But, as Hegel wrote, the owl of Minerva only takes flight at night, and these issues were being debated at the very moment when social and technological developments were changing the ways in which personal credit information was being collected and used. By the end of the 1960s, the entire financial sector was drowning in paper, and the only hope seemed to lie in office automation.[46] Consumers increasingly relied on electronic funds transfers, and, although debit cards substantially outnumbered credit cards, both kinds of cards generated electronic paper trails. Schufa's manual information system had already become a serious bottleneck for those financial institutions that had the capacity to make electronic inquiries, and in the early 1970s, the organization began a halting move toward automation, which was only completed a decade later.[47] All of this meant that the amount of personal credit information held in digital form was greater than ever before—and growing at an exponential rate. These developments were to have important unintended, yet paradigm-shaping consequences.

For years, merchants and financial institutions had used more or less sophisticated point systems to rate or quantify the creditworthiness of potential customers. Such algorithms gave them a rough handle on ability to pay, willingness to pay, and the likelihood that the person could be sanctioned for failing to live up to contractual obligations. But the combination of affordable computing power and a constantly expanding store of digitized historical transactional data made it possible for financial institutions to approach the question of credit risk in new ways by applying sophisticated statistical methods to determine which factors were the best predictors of credit performance and then, on this basis, adopting those credit scoring or rating techniques that had been pioneered in the United States in the 1960s. This probabilistic turn involved accepting the idea that slow payment, default, and fraud were less sins to be extirpated on an individual basis than an inherent risk of doing business and then shifting focus from the financial morality of the individual to the risk profile of the population. This shift on the part of credit managers—the social therapists of the market domain—from attempting to plumb the depths of the applicant's soul to calculating the probability of repayment (and the profit or loss associated therewith) had its parallel in the decline of clinical decision making elsewhere in the social domain.[48] Although the initial goal was to maximize profit by discovering the most powerful set of discriminant criteria that would enable the institution to extend credit to the maximal number of good risks while at the same time minimizing the number of poor risks, lenders soon moved on to the disaggregation of the population into increasingly more finely grained risk groups, so that they could lend at rates and conditions that were appropriate to their respective risk profiles. This meant that lending or selling to poor credit risks could be profitable if such transactions were priced correctly.[49]

In chapter 10, Silke Meyer argues that creditworthiness should be understood more as a social than an economic phenomenon. She goes on to suggest that the recent explosion in the number of personal bankruptcies in Germany reflects the breakdown of the reciprocal social bonds between borrower and lender. This trend, she argues, is reflected in both the growing number of instant lenders who are no longer concerned about substantiating the financial reputations of prospective borrowers and a more casual, less morally laden attitude toward default on the part of the latter. Accordingly, Meyer interprets recent credit legislation as an attempt to repair the torn social bonds that have allowed the credit industry to spiral out of control in recent years. But how accurate is this reading of recent German credit legislation as a morality tale? In the aftermath of the turn to statistically based credit scoring, lenders have been less concerned with the moral depths of each individual borrower than with his or her actual behavior, the risk profile of the (sub)population to which the person belongs, and the proper calibration of risk and return in their loan portfolios, with individual defaults being viewed as a normal cost of doing business rather than as an original sin eating away at the moral fiber of the community. Without a change in the credit industry's underlying actuarial technologies, it is difficult to see how the reforms described by Meyer will succeed in restoring the sense of reciprocal moral obligations that underlay older notions of trust and creditworthiness.

The same accumulation of electronic transactional information that made possible this paradigm shift in consumer credit reporting and scoring had a similar impact on the related fields of market research and advertising. Here, the ability to more efficiently target ever more finely differentiated segments of the consuming population, and then to mobilize them behind a brand identity, depended on both the collection of vast quantities of personal information through the use of new technologies (point-of-sale tracking [via bar codes], Internet tracking, and electronic processing of credit card purchases, for example) and the development of the statistical techniques and computing power needed to mine this data.[50]

The success of both of these ventures rests on the development of digitized credit surveillance systems. But these developments also intensify the trend noted in the introduction to disaggregate the individual into an infinitude of descriptive characteristics that can be virtually reassembled in constantly changing combinations by those who hold this knowledge. Through this process, the individual becomes, to speak with Deleuze, a "dividual" or, to be more precise, a plurality of "dividuals."[51] Although this predictive analytics may empower us by pointing us toward a new fashion trend or recommending that we buy a book about which we may otherwise not have known, it also gives other people the capacity to single us out for different forms of special treatment as risks to the health, security, or productivity of the community, all depending on how well our virtual credit identity corresponds to the risk profile being employed. In such a world, it is both more important and more difficult for the individual to grasp who knows what about him or her and how this information is being used in what context, and the question remains no less urgent today than it was in the first round of debates over privacy, information, and consumer credit reporting in the 1970s.

Notes

1. The name is an acronym for Schutzgemeinschaft für allgcmeine Kreditsicherung (originally founded in Berlin as the Schutzgemeinschaft für Absatzfinanzierung).
2. Schufa, *Im Dienst des Kreditkunden: 50 Jahre Schufa* (Wiesbaden, 1977), 49, 56.
3. Christine von Hodenberg, *Konsens und Krise: Eine Geschichte der westdeutschen Medienöffentlichkeit, 1945–1973* (Göttingen, 2001) and, more broadly, Ulrich Herbert, "Liberalisierung als Lernprozeß: Die Bundesrepublik in der deutschen Geschichte—eine Skizze," in *Wandlungsprozesse in Westdeutschland: Belastung, Integration, Liberalisierung, 1945–1980*, ed. Herbert (Göttingen, 2002), 7–49.
4. "Massenhaft Material für Erpressungen," *Der Spiegel*, January 1, 1979, 28–33.
5. Alya Guseva and Akos Rona-Tas, "Uncertainty, Risk, and Trust: Russian and American Credit Card Markets Compared," *American Sociological Review* 66, no. 5 (October 2001): 623–46.
6. Ulrich Bröckling, "Vorbeugen ist besser . . . Zur Soziologie der Prävention," *Behemoth: A Journal on Civilisation* 1, no. 1 (2008): 38–48.
7. Timothy Guinnane, "Cooperatives as Information Machines: German Rural Credit Cooperatives, 1883–1914," *The Journal of Economic History* 61, no. 2 (June 2001): 366–89.
8. Kurt Meyer (one of the founders of Schufa), "Neue Wege des Kreditschutzes," *Zeitschrift für Organisation* 1, no. 15 (August 5, 1927): 395–98.
9. Gunnar Trumbull, *Consumer Capitalism: Politics, Product Markets, and Firm Strategy in France and Germany* (Ithaca, NY, 2006), 130.
10. Schelsky, "Gedanken zur Rolle der Publizistik in der modernen Gesellschaft," in *Auf der Suche nach Wirklichkeit* (Munich, 1965), 310–27; and Jürgen Habermas, *The Structural Transformation of the Public Sphere*, trans. Thomas Burger with Frederick Lawrence (Cambridge, MA, 1989).
11. Anthony Giddens, *The Nation-State and Violence* (Berkeley, CA, 1987).
12. Kevin Haggerty and Richard Ericson, "The Surveillant Assemblage," *British Journal of Sociology* 51, no. 4 (December 2000): 605–22.
13. See the excellent discussion of (neo)liberal credit governance in Donncha Marron, *Consumer Credit in the United States: A Sociological Perspective from the 19th Century to the Present* (New York, 2009).
14. Haggerty and Ericson, "The Surveillant Assemblage," 616. For one attempt to marketize this idea, see Steve Lohr, "You Want My Personal Data? Reward Me for It," *New York Times* (July 18, 2010), http://www.nytimes.com/2010/07/18/business/18unboxed.html.
15. The implicit comparison here is with the development of consumer credit reporting in the United States. See Josh Lauer, "The Good Consumer: Credit Reporting and the Invention of Financial Identity in the United States, 1840–1940" (PhD diss., University of Pennsylvania, 2008).
16. On consumer credit in postwar Germany, see Jan Logemann, "Different Paths to Mass Consumption: Consumer Credit in the United States and West Germany during the 1950s and 1960s," *Journal of Social History* 41,

152 • Larry Frohman

no. 3 (Spring 2008): 525–59; and Peter Horvath, "Die Teilzahlungskredite als Begleiterscheinung des westdeutschen 'Wirtschaftswunders' (1948–1960)," *Zeitschrift für Unternehmensgeschichte* 37 (1992): 19–55.

17. The founding members included the various Berlin utility companies, the installment financing institution Kreditanstalt für Verkehrsmittel, the department store Hermann Tietz, Siemens, Singer, and a number of associations representing different branches of commerce (specialty stores, office machines, bicycles); Meyer, "Neue Wege des Kreditschutzes."

18. *Lohnpfändungen: Eine Untersuchung des Deutschen Industrie- und Handelstages anhand von Material aus 88 Betrieben,* Schriftenreihe Deutscher Industrie- und Handelstag 27 (Bonn, 1953). Friedrich Lutz, *Der Konsumentenkredit,* Arbeitskreis für Absatzfragen 1 (Cologne, 1954) provides a critical, but measured account that explores both the individual morality and the macroeconomic effects of consumer credit.

19. "Gelsenkirchener Besprechung über Maßnahmen zur Verhinderung übermäßiger Lohnpfändungen aus Teilzahlungsgeschäften," *Die Teilzahlungswirtschaft* (hereafter TW) 1 (1954): 9–10; "Der Kreditschutz in der Teilzahlungswirtschaft," *TW* 1 (1954): 139.

20. "Der Kreditschutz in der Teilzahlungswirtschaft," *TW* 1 (1954): 10–11.

21. Doris Hallermann, "Der Teilzahlungskredit: Ein Beitrag zur betriebswirtschaftlichen Absatzmarktforschung" (PhD diss., University of Münster, 1966), 154.

22. Uta Kempf, *Konsumentenkredit- und Datenschutzprobleme in Kanada und der Bundesrepublik* (Frankfurt am Main, 1978), 26.

23. On these developments, see Georg von Görtz and Hermut Kormann, "Scheckkarte und Kreditkarte in den USA: Rückblick und Ausblick," *TW* 16 (1969): 9–15 and 88–96; and Josef Henke, "Kreditschutz durch Schufa," *TW* 17 (1970): 8.

24. Gunnar Trumbull, "Between Global and Local: The Invention of Data Privacy in the United States and France," *The Voice of the Citizen Consumer,* ed. Kerstin Bruckweh (Oxford, 2011), 199–224; Abraham Newman, *Protectors of Privacy: Regulating Personal Data in the Global Economy* (Ithaca, NY, 2008), 42ff.

25. Although this reliance on objective data distinguished Schufa from much American credit reporting, the American Credit Data Corporation—later TRW—distinguished itself from its competitors by providing only such information. Alan Westin and Michael Baker, *Databanks in a Free Society: Computers, Record-Keeping and Privacy* (Chicago, IL, 1972), 132–35. Although Credit Data Corporation's practice was praised by Senator William Proxmire in the Congressional hearings leading up to the Fair Credit Reporting Act, its competitors noted that the company could afford to take such a cavalier position, because it did not service those merchants who wanted more detailed information and who often preferred evaluative reporting; ibid., 135.

26. James Rule, *Private Lives and Public Surveillance: Social Control in the Computer Age* (New York, 1974), 38ff, 269ff.

27. Wilhelm Schimmelpfeng, *Die Auskunft und ihre Gegner* (Berlin, 1891).

28. Entscheidungen des Bundesverfassungsgerichts 6, 32, [41].

29. Ulrich Seidel, "Datenbanken und Persönlichkeitsrecht unter besonderer Berücksichtigung der amerikanischen Computer Privacy" (PhD diss., University of Cologne, 1972). For the explicit extension of these arguments to the credit sector, see Otto Mallmann, *Zielfunktionen des Datenschutzes: Schutz der Privatsphäre—Korrekte Information* (Neuwied, 1977), 80ff.

30. Westin defined privacy as "the claim of individuals, groups, or institutions to determine for themselves when, how and to what extent information about them is communicated to others," in *Privacy and Freedom* (New York, 1968), 7.

31. Seidel, "Datenbanken und Persönlichkeitsrecht," 139.

32. Klaus Tiedemann and Christoph Sasse, *Delinquenzprophylaxe, Kreditsicherung und Datenschutz in der Wirtschaft* (Cologne, 1973).

33. Ibid., 135.

34. Christoph Sasse, *Sinn und Unsinn des Datenschutzes* (Karlsruhe, 1976). Gilles Laferté has also made a similar point about the integration of credit information and population registration systems; Laferté, "De l'interconnaissance sociale à *l'identification économique*: vers une histoire et une sociologie comparées de la transaction à credit," *Genèses* 79, no. 2 (2010), 135–49.

35. Such claims did not go unchallenged. Already in 1971, Herbert Auernhammer, Ministerialrat in the Federal Interior Ministry and the architect of the BDSG, had insisted that "all signs indicate that the dangers to the private sphere by the large collections of personal data held by the private sector may be many times as great" as those posed by the public sector. Auernhammer, Vermerk Betr.: Vorbereitung eines Bundesgesetzes zum Schutz der Privatsphäre . . . (January 7, 1971), Bundesarchiv Koblenz (hereafter BAK) B106, Nr. 96305. Similarly, Spiros Simitis, who was appointed Hessian privacy commissioner in 1975, felt that the claim that information was not as centralized in the private sector was a bit disingenuous because the private sector did establish centralized information clearinghouses—such as Schufa and its counterparts in the insurance field—wherever such measures were deemed necessary. Stenographisches Protokoll über die öffentliche Informationssitzung des Innenausschusses (May 6, 1974), 28–30, BAK B 106, Nr. 96319.

36. Bundesaufsichtsamt für das Kreditwesen to BMI (December 18, 1972), BAK B 106, Nr. 96309, Bd. 14.

37. Letter from the Gesamtverband der Versicherungswirtschaft to BMI (February 7, 1973), BAK B 106 Nr. 96308.

38. Zentraler Kreditausschuß, Stellungnahme, BAK B 106, Nr. 96308. This was a written statement of opinion submitted in advance of the August 1972 hearing on the BDSG.

39. Trumbull, *Consumer Capitalism*, 15–17, 170–71.

40. The provisions of the BDSG as they pertained to credit reporting and the various court rulings on the problem through the early 1980s are nicely parsed in Wolfgang Teske, "Die Datenverarbeitung durch die Datenbanken der Wirtschaft am Beispiel der Schufa," in *Datenverarbeitung und Persönlichkeitsschutz: Beiträge*

zu aktuellen Problemen des Datenschutzes in Recht und Praxis, ed. Max Vollkommer (Erlangen, 1986), 131–68.

41. "Demnächst ein Recht auf Zensur und ein Recht auf Kredit," *Die Welt,* August 26, 1982. These same arguments are also advanced in the memoranda submitted by the Bundesverband der Deutschen Industrie (June 11, 1982) and the Gesamtverband der Deutschen Versicherungswirtschaft (June 8, 1982), BAK B 106, Nr. 96340.

42. On the varieties of consumer credit offered by West German banks, including normal personal accounts that one could overdraw, see chapter 2 by Rebecca Belvederesi-Kochs.

43. Bundesverband Deutscher Banken to IM Nordrhein-Westfalen, Betr.: Zulässigkeit der sog. "Schufa-Klausel" (August 28, 1978), Berlin Datenschutzbeauftragter Aktenzeichen 0201/454.

44. *Neue Juristische Wochenschrift,* January 8, 1986, Heft 1/2, 46–48; Ulrich Dammann and Hans-Joachim Stange, "Reform des Datenschutzes im Kreditinformationssystem," *Zeitschrift für Wirtschaftsrecht* 7 (April 25, 1986), 488–93; and Michael Beckhusen, *Der Datenumgang innerhalb des Kreditinformationssystems der SCHUFA: Unter besonderer Berücksichtigung des Scoring-Verfahrens ASS und der Betroffenenrechte* (Baden-Baden, 2004), 148ff.

45. For the most recent round in this continuing debate, see Schufa, ed., *Schutz der finanziellen Privatsphäre: Notwendigkeiten und Risiken in internationalen Kreditmärkten: 2. SCHUFA-Datenschutzkolloquium, 8. März 2007, Berlin* (Wiesbaden, 2007).

46. Axel Boje, "Fortschritte der Datenerfassung im Bankbetrieb," *TW* 15 (1968): 219–22; Karl Heinrich Rüßmann, "Die verborgene Revolution," *TW* 16 (1969): 216–18; and Joachim Milde, "Direkte Datenerfassung—Direkte Datenverarbeitung," *TW* 16 (1969): 232–34.

47. Stefan Kaminsky, "Wie lange noch kann die Schufa ohne Datenverarbeitung bestehen?" *TW* 15 (1968): 222–23; and Josef Henke, "Die Schufa im Jahre 1974," *TW* 22 (1975): 30–31.

48. Pat O'Malley, *Risk, Uncertainty and Government* (London, 2004), 17.

49. Marron, *Consumer Credit in the United States.*

50. Adam Arvidsson, "On the 'Pre-History of the Panoptic Sort': Mobility in Market Research," *Surveillance & Society* 1, no. 4 (2004): 456–74.

51. Gilles Deleuze, "Postscript on the Societies of Control," *October* 59 (Winter 1992), 3–7.

PART III

State Regulation and Credit Policies

CHAPTER 7

Banking on Consumer Credit: Explaining Patterns of Household Borrowing in the United States and France*

Gunnar Trumbull

Americans are famous borrowers. In 2007, household nonmortgage debt averaged 25 percent of disposable income, and 60 percent of households were in debt. If we include equity extracted from housing to make consumer purchases or pay down existing consumer debt, nonmortgage consumer indebtedness rises to 33 percent of disposable income for the same year. Nor was this pattern of indebtedness new. In 1980, at the threshold of financial deregulation, nonmortgage debt averaged 17 percent of disposable income. Why have American households relied so heavily on consumer credit? Two explanations have been proposed. On the one hand, financial liberalization beginning in the late 1970s freed financial markets to supply unmet demand for household credit. On the other hand, innovations in credit rating and risk assessment allowed lenders to overcome the adverse selection problem associated with risky borrowers. While both factors are probably important, they miss a critical feature that distinguished the U.S. credit market from those in most other advanced industrialized countries, namely, the early embrace of consumer lending by commercial banks.

To isolate the sources of American difference, I compare U.S. consumer lending practices with those in France, which has had low levels of household borrowing. From the early 1980s to 2005, French households' nonmortgage debt rose from just 3 percent of disposable income to a peak of 18 percent in 2005. France went through many of the same transformations that

Table 7.1   Household debt as a share of disposable income, 1980–2005

	Nonmortgage debt (%)			Total personal debt (%)		
	1980	1991	2005	1980	1991	2005
United States	17	22	26	70	98	135
France	3	8	18	30	40	64

Source: For the United States, household debt data are from the Federal Reserve Board's Flow of Funds Accounts, and disposable income data are from the Bureau of Economic Analysis; for France, household debt data are from the Observatoire de l'endettement des ménages, Fédération bancaire française.

characterized the U.S. market during this period. Between 1984 and 1987, French financial markets were dramatically deregulated. Quantitative restrictions on credit extension were removed, and French lenders rapidly expanded consumer lending. And, like American lenders, French lenders adopted new technologies that allowed them to evaluate and manage credit risk. By the late 1990s, the French lender Cetelem was the largest consumer lender in Europe. Yet French households never relied on credit to the extent that their American counterparts did. I argue that national differences trace their roots to the structure of the financial sector, and, in particular, the role of commercial banks in U.S. consumer lending. The large number of small unit banks in the United States, together with regulations restricting price competition for deposits, led banks in the 1950s and 1960s to use credit to court new business (table 7.1).

Consumer lending for much of the postwar period was largely unprofitable. Until the mid-1970s, retailers who offered goods on credit typically lost money on the credit component of the sale. Banks that launched credit cards barely broke even. These banks offered credit for a different reason: to attract customers. Given restrictions (Regulation Q) on the interest they could offer on deposits, consumer credit, especially a revolving credit account, was a relatively cheap way to attract new customers. Similarly, the growth and consolidation of local and regional retailers into national chains led them to extend consumer credit on favorable terms to attract new customers. Americans became accustomed to buying on credit at a time when the small size of consumer loans made them largely unprofitable for lenders. In particular, American banks and retailers linked credit card payments to revolving credit facilities that allowed consumers to enjoy a flexible repayment schedule for even small purchases.

In France, where commercial banks were preoccupied with financing industrial development and retailers did not have sufficient scale to offer their own credit, dedicated consumer finance companies emerged to offer personal and sales credit. Unable to subsidize their loans from other lines of business, these lenders emphasized raising revenues and reducing costs. Until the early 1970s, retail clients helped to subsidize credit purchases by accepting delayed payment and shared responsibility in case of nonpayment. Consumer lenders also focused intensively on reducing administrative costs. This sensitivity cost led them to eschew the kinds of revolving credit accounts that became the norm in the United States beginning in the 1950s. The lack of commercial bank lending and revolving credit cards proved consequential. Dedicated consumer lenders continued to be viewed with skepticism; commercial banks had little interest in supporting liberalization; and consumers never came to associate card payments with a revolving credit facility. After a brief experiment with liberalization in the 1980s, French regulators stepped back in to reregulate the market.

The Limits of Market Failure

The most common accounts of national patterns of credit extension focus on the role of institutions in overcoming market failures associated with making consumer loans. The core challenge, identified by Joseph Stiglitz and Andrew Weiss in 1981, was repayment.[1] In the absence of additional information, lenders could not distinguish between borrowers who agreed to higher interest rates because their loans were genuinely more risky and those who accepted higher interest rates because they did not intend to repay. Institutions that helped to overcome this market failure should therefore promote more lending. Economists have emphasized the role of information sharing and legal enforcement in supporting higher lending and lower nonpayment rates, and cross-national studies appear to confirm the relationship.[2] Innovations in microfinance were grounded in the ability of informal social pressure to ensure loan repayment. For lenders in France and the United States, however, repayment was not the primary obstacle to making consumer loans profitably.

Lenders in both countries were already focused on the creditworthiness of their borrowers. In the United States, an informal network of thousands of local commercial and nonprofit credit bureaus existed by the 1950s to address the information needs of lenders. These bureaus tracked the repayment experiences of existing residents, investigated the credit histories of new residents, and collected fees from retailers and banks who sought access to this information. Any new loan was preceded by a call to the local credit bureau. By the late 1960s, these offices were consolidating into large regional networks of credit rating bureaus. In 1970, Retail Credit Company of Atlanta, Georgia (later Equifax), announced plans to computerize the 45 million records in its credit rating database. In the same year, Fair Isaac developed its first formula for standardized, automated credit scoring. These developments made the United States a world leader in consumer credit rating. By the 1990s, credit card companies relied on mailing lists purchased from credit rating agencies to target customers with offers customized to their specific credit profiles.

France never developed this sort of credit rating service for three reasons. First, French consumer lenders relied heavily on retailers to assess the credit quality of potential borrowers. They did offer loans directly, but only after a consumer had successfully repaid a loan provided via a trusted retailer. Successful lenders became good at choosing retail affiliates who made good judgments about customers' likely willingness and ability to repay. Second, France had relatively few lenders. In the late 1950s, when 13,000 consumer lenders had registered in the United States, France had fewer than a hundred registered consumer finance companies. The largest of these, organized in the informal Einstein Club, began in 1974 to share nonpayment records with each other via microfiche. Third, France's banks objected to the creation of a centralized database of positive ("white") credit data on the grounds that it would allow nonbank consumer finance companies to poach their longtime clients. Under the banks' influence, France's powerful data privacy authority (CNIL) decreed that the collection of a positive credit registry constituted an infringement of personal data privacy.

If French lenders enjoyed less access to accurate consumer payments information, the legal environment for enforcing consumer debt contracts in France was more conducive to securing repayment. In the United States, the bankruptcy reform act of 1978 provided consumers access to personal bankruptcy with full discharge of debts. Consumer lenders received a share of any liquidated assets, but no more. In France, debt contracts were strictly enforced, with virtually no means for households to evade them. The first provision for personal bankruptcy, introduced in 1989, emphasized debt renegotiation. Only with reforms in 2003 did French debtors gain access to the sort of automatic discharge that American debtors had long enjoyed. Indeed, it seems likely that the strict enforcement of debt contracts in France might have reduced consumer demand for credit. In any case, the actual repayment experience of French and American lenders was similar: in each case fewer than 1 percent of loans faced nonpayment problems.

The French lag also seems not to reflect any particular technical or innovative deficiency in the financial sector. Historically, the cross-border diffusion of lending innovations has been surprisingly rapid. Indeed, the early American consumer lenders learned how to make small loans mainly from France. Provident loan societies set up in the 1910s to offer charitable pawn loans were modeled on the French *Monts de Piété*.[3] Credit unions introduced in 1909 were based on the French *Crédit Mutuel*. And the first commercially successful consumer lending banks, the so-called Morris Plan industrial banks, were inspired by the small loan success of Crédit Lyonnais. Soon after World War II, lending know-how was flowing in the opposite direction. Bankers from around the world were visiting the United States in the 1950s to track developments in the small loans and credit card sector. French bankers made repeated study trips of this kind in the 1950s and 1960s. These visits meant that most U.S. innovations were quickly emulated in Europe. Credit cards began with an explicitly international focus. The earliest of these, the Universal Air Travel Plan (UATP) launched in 1947 by the International Air Transport Association, was accepted by seventy-two airlines around the world.[4] The first general-purpose travel and leisure cards, Diners' Club and American Express, were also international in their orientation. Diners' Club was launched in 1950 in the United States; its French-owned affiliate opened for business just four years later, in 1954. The American Express card launched in 1958 in the United States and in 1961 in France.

From these early experiments with credit cards, European lenders took their cues on consumer lending technology from developments in the United States. There, J. C. Penney became the first lender to use automated account management when they purchased four IBM 1400 machines in 1962; in France, Cetelem installed two of the same computers the very next year. Computerization began a process that would eventually transform consumer lending in both countries. U.S. lenders were aggressive in embracing technology. From the early 1970s, J. C. Penney's management made substantial investments to improve operations and lower costs. In 1974, they leased 7,000 sales credit communications terminals and eleven System 4000 computers from TRW. In 1975, they completed a nationwide Interconnect System that enabled instant credit authorization from any of the stores, and in 1977, they deployed new statistical risk-evaluation systems at each of their 22 regional credit offices. These systems were expected to increase credit application approval rates by 18 percent.[5] Increasing automation continued when they installed IBM remittance processing equipment in 1978.

Cetelem similarly focused on investments in new technology. Its president, Pierre Boucher, acknowledged, "Computers . . . constitute the hard core of our strategy."[6] The first IBM machines were replaced in 1973 with the IBM 370/145, which was forty times more powerful than the two 1401 machines combined. In 1984, they upgraded to an IBM 3081, again the latest computer technology. Computers allowed the company to take advantage of telecommunications. In 1974, Cetelem installed an internal data network called Transpac that connected all of the roughly 200 Cetelem offices and agencies around France. In 1980, they began making real-time approvals over the network, and by 1981, all approvals were made over Transpac. In 1983, loan approval times were brought below one minute. By 1984, 3,000 affiliated retailers were connected directly to the Cetelem network via France's early public teletex network, Minitel. As one prominent French lender later acknowledged, nearly every credit innovation in France had been directly borrowed from lender innovations in the United States.

Technology and Profitability

The new computer and telecommunications capabilities transformed the economic logic of the sector. By lowering the administrative cost of setting up and maintaining new loan accounts, computerization lowered the threshold for profitable lending. By the 1980s, even small loans could be managed profitably. With automated account tracking and billing, lenders were able to identify late accounts and send automated reminders. For example, this system of prompt and frequent reminders allowed Cetelem to reduce late repayment rates (cases that went to the "contentious" collections department) from 4 to 1 percent. Prior to computerization, consumer loans had been supported by payments from retailers. J. C. Penney's lending business was continuously subsidized from its formation in 1958 until the first year in which it made a profit, 1975.[7] (See figure 7.1.) Likewise, Cetelem's balance sheet showed a net inflow of payments from retailers until 1982, when the payments reversed direction, as Cetelem began offering retailers enticements to provide Cetelem credit to their customers. The new efficiency brought profitability, and that profitability made consumer lending an important business activity in its own right. Within J. C. Penney, the consumer credit division moved in 1975 from a cost center to a profit center, with its own marketing budget.

Financial data from Cetelem's Historical Archive allow us to trace how the costs of lending changed over time. Table 7.2 breaks down the total interest charged on a loan into its cost components. Especially notable was the dominant role of administration and interest payments, as well as the relatively low cost of provisions for nonpayment. The significant increase in the cost of capital from 1960 to 1986 was almost entirely offset by lower administration costs and a reduction in government taxes. The single most important factor in rising profitability was the reduction in administrative costs. From 1973 to 1992, the costs of administering a loan were cut in half. Computerization played a core role in this development.

If technology transformed the economics of consumer lending in the 1970s and 1980s, so too did new insights into consumer preferences. For

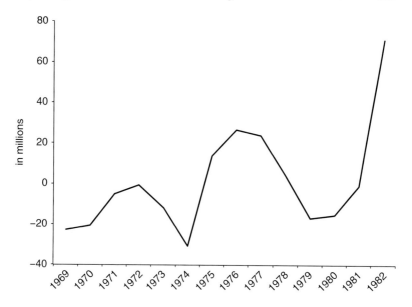

Figure 7.1 J. C. Penney charge card operations, net earnings, 1969–82

Table 7.2 Cost components of Cetelem loans, 1960–92

	1960 (%)	1973 (%)	1986 (%)	1992 (%)
Consumer lending rate	18.7	19.2	18.8	17.6
Breakdown of costs				
Administration	7.0	7.0	5.1	3.8
Interest	6.0	9.4	10.3	8.8
Provision for nonpayment	0.7	0.8	1	1.9
Tax	4.5	1.0	1.2	1.0
Profit	0.8	1.0	1.2	2.1

Source: "Des Tarifs pratiqués dans la vente a crédit des biens de consommation durables," *Revue du Centre d'Information et d'Etude du Crédit*, no. 3 (October 1962); Michel Renault, "La Vente a Crédit s'acclimate en France," *Le Monde*, November 29, 1962; BNPP CHA, "La finance et la trésorerie," *à Découvert*, no. 9, June 1973, 6; CHA, Pascal Bonnet, "Tenir nos taux," *Nous*, no. 2, June–July 1987, 10–11; CHA, *Nous Avons 40 Ans*, April 1993, 25.

France's lenders, the high inflation period from the late 1970s to the early 1980s proved formative. Through the steep fluctuations in interest rates that the inflationary shock demanded, lenders learned that consumer demand for credit was highly insensitive to price. Not only did consumers not seem to care about nominal interest rates, but they also appeared indifferent to real

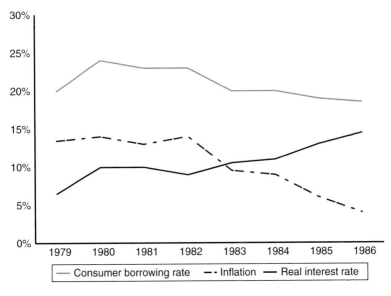

Figure 7.2 Nominal and real consumer lending rates in France, 1979–86

Source: Philipppe Manière, "Les constructeurs auto 'bradent' leurs prêts," *Quotidien de Paris*, April 30, 1986.

interest rates. The first lesson came from the run-up of inflation in the late 1970s. After significant bouts during the 1970s, inflation in France briefly touched 20 percent in mid-1981. In order to maintain reasonable real interest rates, consumer finance companies pushed their consumer loan rates to almost 30 percent. At first they did not know how borrowers would respond. They had long assumed that 25 percent represented a psychological ceiling for borrowers. Yet as this barrier was passed, the head of the Association of French Finance Establishments (APEF) recalled concluding that "30% per year could be adopted without significant consequences . . . "[8] As the crisis deepened, loan applications actually increased (figure 7.2).

The second lesson came with the decline in inflation in the early 1980s. As inflation fell, lenders lowered their interest rates more slowly, because recurring bouts of inflation in the 1970s had taught them to be cautious. The result was higher real interest rates (that is, nominal rates minus inflation). Between 1983 and 1986, average real interest rates for consumer credit in France rose from 10 to 15 percent. Yet demand for credit continued to rise dramatically. By 1986, lenders observing this phenomenon drew the obvious conclusion. The head of one consumer finance company explained: "Consumers pay almost no attention to the absolute level of the rate. They are interested mainly in the monthly payment ... No study has ever shown the least correlation between a rise in the cost of credit and a reduction in consumption."[9] This insight was decisive for Cetelem's strategy. In 1986, CEO Pierre Boucher sent a note to the entire company declaring, "The interest rate is not a decisive element in households' decisions to take a short-term loan."[10] Cetelem would no longer be the lowest cost lender, as it had been in the past. It would instead focus on product features that consumers seemed to value.

The Politics of Deregulation in America

In the United States, reforms relaxed state-level usury restrictions in order to promote national competition in lending. The first blow to usury caps came from the 1978 *Marquette National Bank v. First of Omaha* Supreme Court decision, which applied state-of-origin usury rules to out-of-state credit card lenders. In the case, Marquette National Bank of Minnesota had filed claim against First of Omaha for charging 18 percent, which was permitted under Nebraska state law, to its credit card customers in Minnesota, where usury caps limited interest rates to 12 percent.[11] As large national banks moved their headquarters to South Dakota and Delaware, they were able to charge higher interest rates than local retailers and state banks. Both federal and state regulators responded quickly to eliminate the advantage. A provision added to the 1980 Depository Institutions Deregulation and Monetary Control Act extended the *Marquette* state-of-origin policy to state banks insured by the Federal Deposit Insurance Corporation (FDIC).[12] In order to untie the hands of retail lenders and local finance companies that competed with banks, most states changed their usury policies. By the end of 1981, forty-five states had either raised their usury rate ceilings for consumer loans or eliminated them all together. For states that retained usury laws, smaller local lenders found that they could partner with out-of-state banks to provide loans that exceeded local interest rate caps. A new set of high-interest-rate lenders appeared. Tax preparers began working with banks to make tax refund anticipation loans. These loans had annual interest rates of 150 to 300 percent and were used especially by low-income recipients of the Earned Income Tax Credit. Payday lenders and auto title lenders, whose loans ranged up to 390 percent, also partnered with out-of-state, federally chartered, and FDIC banks to exempt themselves from state usury laws.[13] The Consumer Federation of America lamented, "The result is a set of usury laws that should make a finance company proud."[14]

Marquette left open a range of questions about the scope of state regulatory authority over national banks that would be settled only during the 1990s. In 1996, the Supreme Court heard the appeal of *Smiley v. Citibank,* in which a New Jersey man argued that the late fees charged by Citibank violated state law restricting such fees. Banks, which in the debates leading up to the 1968 truth-in-lending legislation had argued that fees should be treated separately from interest charges, now argued that they were equivalent to interest and thus covered by the *Marquette* precedent. When the Supreme Court found in favor of Citibank, credit card use of late fees expanded from an average late fee of $12 in 1996 to $29 in 2002.[15] Similar cases explored the ability of state regulators to dictate minimum repayment rates. In 2000, the California legislature passed legislation requiring credit card issuers to include a warning on their statement that paying only the minimum balance would increase their principal. In the 2002 case *ABA v. Lockyer,* the American Bankers Association sued the attorney general of the State of California, alleging that the law infringed on a different provision of the National Bank Act that provided for "all such incidental powers as should be necessary to carry out the business of banking."[16] The ABA won, arguing that the cost of printing such a warning made the law "overly burdensome" on banks, and was therefore preempted by the NBA itself. Finally, in 2004, the Office of the Comptroller of the Currency (OCC) issued new rules that preempted states' regulation of a wide range of nationally chartered bank activities, including use of noninterest charges, credit account management, mandatory disclosures, and interest rates and fees.[17] By the time of the 2004 rules, it had become clear that federal preemption of state bank regulations was being treated expansively. Mark Furletti writes, "The agency [OCC] essentially declared that states have little or no authority to impose any consumer-protection-oriented regulation on nationally chartered banks and that any such regulation is the province of federal law."[18]

Deregulation changed the competitive landscape for American consumer lenders. Most credit card lenders increased their lending rates, typically from 16 or 18 percent up to 21 percent. Federal preemption of state fees regulation further increased effective interest rates. The combined impact of a reduced cost of administering small loans and a higher price enabled by liberalized usury caps quickly transformed consumer lending into the most profitable sector in American banking. American banks and consumer finance companies responded with three new innovations. First, banks began in 1986 to securitize credit card receivables. Doing so allowed them to tap into growing financial markets to fund the lending operations. Unbridled by the need to attract deposits in order to make loans, some banks came to specialize in consumer lending. Securitization also allowed banks to remove consumer loans from their balance sheets. Doing so lowered their reserve requirements, further reducing the cost of capital. The result was a dramatic increase in liquidity available for consumer loans.

The second innovation of American lenders was the move to risk-based pricing. Traditionally, consumer lenders pooled the risk of their borrowers, so that the impact of good and bad credit risks would offset each other. The attractiveness of risk pooling was in the power of large numbers: even if a lender did not know the risk of any individual, he knew a lot about the likelihood of repayment in a properly defined population. With automated risk assessment and centralized credit bureaus, lenders could assign a risk to individual consumers. Customers who represented greater repayment risks would still receive loans, but the cost of the loan would be higher than for other borrowers. By weighting price according to risk, lenders could compete on price for reliable lenders and extend credit to risky borrowers that would historically not have been considered creditworthy. Critics of this approach noted that charging higher prices could accentuate risk, making risk scoring a self-fulfilling prophecy for high-risk borrowers. Advocates on the left and right hoped that risk-based pricing would bring credit to marginal groups that had traditionally been the victims of credit rationing.

Finally, as lenders began to compete, the cost of acquiring new customers rose. By the early 2000s, each new credit card customer cost $50 in direct mail costs and retailer incentives to acquire. This led to a change in attitude toward debt administration. With new customers increasingly expensive to acquire, it made little business sense to lose a good customer just because they paid off their loans. By lowering monthly payments, eventually to 2 percent of principle, lenders found they could retain customers longer. These negative-amortization payment plans had two beneficial side effects: with lower monthly payments, nonpayment rates fell and the resulting increase in principle generated greater interest income. The point of the new lending was not to have the loan repaid, but to generate a constant stream of monthly payments without ever reducing the principle.

The new profitability spelled the end for independent retail credit in America. Stores that were too small to have their own brand card began accepting bank credit cards. Retailers that valued their own-brand credit cards but were not large enough to make them profitable contracted out the service to consumer finance companies like HSBC and GE Capital. Retailers with profitable in-house credit programs were made offers they could not refuse. Between 1971 and 1981, retailers' share of the U.S. consumer credit market fell from 12 to 8.9 percent.[19] With financial deregulation in the early 1980s, most major retail credit programs became independent financial operations and were eventually sold. In 1985, J. C. Penney acquired the First National Bank of Harrington, Delaware, and renamed it the JCPenney National Bank.[20] In 1999, GE Capital purchased J. C. Penney's entire credit business. In 1986, Sears launched the general purpose Discover Card with no fees and a 1 percent refund. With the addition of insurance and real estate services, financial services accounted for most of Sears' earnings between 1986 and 1991.[21] The Discover network was ultimately acquired by Morgan Stanley in 1997. The move away from retailer-provided credit changed the logic of consumer credit. For most retailers, the point of credit had been to promote merchandizing. For retailers that ran their own lending operations, the terms of lending and collection were kept amicable in the interest of attracting customers to their stores. These lenders virtually never pursued "hard" collections for fear of scaring away new clients. They also eschewed aggressive credit sales techniques. As profits rose and retailers sold their lending operations, however, lenders embraced a new aggressiveness in sales and collections.

Experimenting with Deregulation in France

Between 1984 and 1987, the French financial sector was dramatically liberalized. This included the elimination of quantitative limits on credit (the so-called credit corset), the privatization of previously nationalized banks, and a shift in authority over banks from the finance ministry to the competition ministry. For France's banks, liberalization initiated a period of rapid expansion into the personal loan business, followed by failure and retrenchment. When France's banks returned to consumer lending in the 1990s, they did so via acquisitions of existing consumer finance companies rather than through in-house lending operations. The experience of French banks in consumer lending shaped the political response to the sector in important ways.

Unlike those in the United States, France's banks had steered clear of consumer credit in the postwar era. The few times when they moved into the area, as in the early 1970s, they failed. Close administrative guidance from the Banque de France also made it difficult for banks to compete in the sector. As recently as 1982, the governor of the Banque de France wrote to all the banks asking that they extend no more personal loans.[22] This sort of stop-go administrative oversight made it difficult to justify the significant investment that large-scale consumer lending would require. More importantly, France's postwar indicative planning had relied on banks to finance its projects, and banks grew dependent on these investments for their profits.

Financial liberalization, however, undermined this line of business, as firms in France began to seek nonbank sources of capital and so turned to the stock market, factoring, and self-financing through retained earnings.[23] Bank corporate lending consequently fell from 159 billion francs in 1982 to 109 billion in 1983. The decline in lending in 1982–83 had coincided with a steep rise in interest rates, but even as rates subsequently fell, corporate borrowing continued to decline. By 1986, outstanding corporate loans were down to 75 billion francs. This trend pushed banks to look for other sources of revenue, and consumer lending became a focus of intensive interest.[24] As one observer noted, "Banks live from lending. Once they realized that companies had less and less need for them, they turned to households with increasing ease as credit was liberalized."[25]

France's large banks allocated large blocks of funds to a new push to extend their consumer lending business. Crédit Agricole alone allocated an additional 20 billion francs to consumer credit in 1986 and 1987.[26] They were thereby able to increase their share of the consumer lending market from 18 percent in 1984 to 25 percent in 1987.[27] They accomplished this feat in three ways. First, they offered lower rates than the consumer finance companies. Whereas the latter were charging in the range from 15 to 18.25 percent at this time, banks began offering rates from 12 to 16 percent.[28] They justified the difference with their lower cost of capital, but also with their detailed knowledge of their clients, many of whom were long-term depositors. They also began aggressively expanding their credit agreements with retailers. For the first time for a French bank, BNP in 1986 allied with a retailer to provide a Carte Bleue credit card co-branded to the retailer, in this case Euromarché.[29] Third, France's big banks started providing their best customers with access to revolving credit accounts. Traditionally, banks lent in the form of personal loans with fixed repayment schedules. In the fall of 1987, however, BNP launched Crédisponible with revolving credit at 15.8 percent. Crédit Lyonnais followed in September 1987 with Crédilion. Societé Génerale offered Crédiconfiance,[30] and Crédit Agricole formed a consumer finance affiliate called Unibanque.

As banks entered the consumer lending market, credit growth boomed. Nonmortgage household debt in France rose from 110 billion francs in 1984 to 370 billion francs in 1989, the peak of the credit boom. Over the same period, the share of indebted households rose from 39 to 53 percent.[31] Average household debt as a share of disposable income increased from 3.5 to 7 percent.[32] By 1990, the credit boom had dramatically slowed, from annual growth of 30 percent in 1987 to 20 percent in 1988, 16 percent in 1989, and 2 percent in 1990.[33] Some attributed the reduced growth to the effect of the first Gulf War; others thought that it was simply an artifact of France having "caught up" after years of credit restraint.[34] The most important cause, however, was the failure of France's large banks in consumer lending.

Their results disappointed for two main reasons. First, banks were not specialists in consumer lending. They had not invested in the skills or equipment that was required for success in it. As Jean-Christophe Goarin, head of the consumer finance company S2P (Société des Paiements Pass), explained,

"The handicap for banks is that they have too many products. We have only a few, but we present them well and they are well adapted to the needs of our clients."[35] Second, although consumer finance companies had embraced the idea of tracking past repayment as a predictor of future repayment, banks were still relying on their relationships with their depositors. They assumed that, because they had known clients for years, they would have low repayment risks, but they found that they faced higher default rates than consumer finance companies. The high rate of defaults was aggravated by the banks' effort to expand their customer base rapidly, which led some to offer loans indiscriminately. Pierre Marleix, head of the trade union–affiliated consumer group AFOC, explained that banks "were increasingly unconcerned about finding reliable borrowers; they simply wanted to increase their loan volume in order to be big."[36]

As banks experimented with consumer loans, consumer finance companies launched a new product: revolving credit. The concept—an open account to which new purchases could be added with a flexible repayment schedule—had its roots in retailing, where the idea that even small purchases could be put on credit was attractive. U.S. banks began adopting the practice in the late 1950s, as they sought to market credit and payment facilities to small retailers that could not afford to offer their own credit plans. By the late 1960s, revolving credit became a requirement for any bank credit card that wished to join one of the new national payments networks, the Bank America Service Corporation (VISA) and Interbank Card Association (Mastercard). In France, by contrast, loans continued to be made on a one-off basis with a fixed repayment schedule until new revolving credit cards were launched beginning in 1985. The reasons for this difference had little to do with innovation or technical capability. Cetelem first experimented with a revolving credit card, called Crédit en poche, in 1965, but it was intended initially only as a reward for especially loyal customers.

The late adoption of revolving credit in France was mainly related to profits, regulation, and the response of the country's banks. First, revolving accounts were more expensive to administer than one-off personal loans. Accounts had to be continuously managed; the smaller size of purchases raised the cost per transaction; and lenders had to constantly monitor the creditworthiness of their customers. For American banks and retailers, this additional cost was not a big deterrent, because they were already losing money on their consumer credit services. For them, credit was a marketing tool. It brought in new customers who would then buy products (retailers) or make deposits and use other financial services (banks). And they quickly found that consumers loved revolving credit. For France's large lenders, who were trying to make profits in a low-margin sector, the additional cost of administering revolving credit accounts made them relatively unattractive.

Second, the Ministry of Finance had, by the early 1960s, begun placing direct administrative restrictions on the quantity of credit that could be extended by different sectors of the economy, and, within those sectors, by individual companies. Each year consumer lenders were informed how much additional lending they could undertake. This posed a problem for managing revolving credit accounts. Because these accounts allowed customers to borrow as they wished up to a fixed ceiling, the lender had relatively little control over the total outstanding volume of credit. With revolving accounts, it was difficult for lenders to take advantage of their full allowance of credit each year. Finally, France's large banks moved to block the rise of payment cards tied to revolving credit facilities. In 1965, as Cetelem was experimenting with its Crédit en poche product, France's large banks collaborated to form their own card-based electronic payments network, Carte Bleue, which specifically separated the payments function from any lending facility. Although some banks did offer overdraft protection on their Carte Bleue accounts, early customers tended to carry large balances and rarely drew on this line of credit. Backed by support from the Banque de France, the Carte Bleue payment network spread rapidly, leaving a whole generation of French consumers to associate card payments with a debit function rather than with credit.

All of this changed with the end of quantitative credit restrictions in 1984. In 1985, Cetelem launched their new Aurore card to counter the aggressive move by banks into personal lending.[37] They offered it as a co-branded card that allowed them to reinforce their ties with retailers. And they already understood the technology, which they had showcased twenty years earlier with their Crédit en poche. By the end of 1987, the Aurore card already had 600,000 users.[38] Other consumer finance companies quickly launched their own revolving products. These included the Accord card by the retailer Auchan, the Plus card by the finance company Cofinoga, and the Pass card by S2P, a finance affiliate of the retailer Carrefour. Another lender, Credit commercial de France (CCF), created an innovative revolving account offering interest rates tied directly to the interbank lending rate.[39] Amid all of the new entrants, the Aurore card came to dominate the field. By 1995, ten years after its launch, Cetelem's Aurore card was used by 5 million French (and 1 million other Europeans).[40] By 2000, there were 13 million Aurore cards in use, with 250,000 points of sale.[41] Interest rates on these loans ranged from 12.4 to 16.1 percent.[42]

Some banks also began launching Carte Bleue payment cards tied to revolving credit accounts, including Alterna by Societé Génerale and Provisio by BNP. Interestingly, bank revolving accounts initially marketed as luxury products did not remain such for long. As France's banks faced a surge in personal loan nonpayments in the late 1990s, they discovered that converting these accounts into revolving credit led to a dramatic reduction in nonpayments. With longer repayment periods and a flexible repayment schedule, write-offs could be avoided. Indeed research at the time found that only 1.1 percent of revolving accounts ended up in legal recovery, compared to 3.2 percent for traditional small personal loans. Driven first by luxury and then by necessity, revolving lending grew from 8.5 percent of consumer borrowing in 1986 to 17 percent in 1990.[43] For consumer finance companies, revolving accounts already accounted for 37 percent of all loans in 1990.[44] By 2000, 26 percent of all nonmortgage household borrowing took the form of revolving credit.

The emergence of revolving credit elicited a new wave of concern from the French public about the likely social and economic impact of the newly liberalized consumer credit markets. Many feared "easy credit" that would drive households excessively into debt. Bankers countered that borrowers with access to revolving credit were able to be more financially responsible because of the greater control that revolving credit gave them. Lenders tended to defend their product by employing developmental and evolutionary metaphors to talk about their revolving credit clients. LaJaques Lenormand, the director of the personal lending department at Crédit Agricole, was typical in claiming, "clients with access to revolving credit are far more adult, more evolved, better informed and, in this sense, better managers."[45] French consumers were evidently more circumspect. A survey in 1992 found that only 30 percent knew what revolving credit was. Among those familiar with it, two-thirds called it "very useful." Yet half—and therefore presumably some significant share of those who called it "very useful"—also called it "a trap from which one never escapes."[46]

A second concern was the potential impact of the new revolving credit arrangements on consumer protection in sales contracts. One of the core pillars of French consumer protection was the 1978 "Scrivener" law, which linked credit and sales contracts. Under the law, installment credit contracts were binding only with the delivery of a product. Conversely, sales contracts were binding only with the approval of a loan. The law also created a seven-day cooling off period for credit sales that required sellers to take back their products if the buyer decided to nullify the credit contract. In practice, sellers commonly waited seven days before making delivery to avoid having to take back used products if a customer opted to reverse a credit purchase.[47] As French consumers moved away from installment borrowing toward revolving credit plans, the benefits of these consumer protections diminished. Yves le Duc, general secretary of the union-affiliated consumer group CSCV, wrote, "The large retailers and banks that offer their own cards no longer need to know if a good is delivered, or if it is in good condition . . . whatever the case, payment is required. This is an important regression with respect to the law of 1978."[48]

Reregulation in France

The growth in the use of credit led to a widespread public debate about the causes and consequences of overindebtedness. Some applauded it for decoupling credit from moral constraints by allowing households to behave more like companies.[49] The dominant interpretation, however, related consumer credit to stagnating purchasing power.[50] From 1980 to 1986, the share of French households with outstanding consumer debt grew from 33 to 40 percent.[51] During the same period, the household savings rate fell from 17.5 to 12 percent.[52] Yves Ullmo, secretary general of the National Council on Credit, described the cause: "Since [1983], disposable income has increased little. To maintain a certain standard of living, use of credit has been a solution."[53] Policy makers on the left and right worried about the sustainability of this strategy. The result was a series of decisions that progressively restricted access to credit for French consumers.

The first target of reregulation was the so-called free credit that had emerged with the relaxation of government restrictions on credit volumes. Free credit referred to loans that were offered without any direct interest charge to increase sales. In the furniture sector, which quickly embraced the practice, 20.5 percent of all credit offered in 1984 was without interest. As a merchandising strategy, free credit seems to have been effective. The two furniture retailers that were most aggressive in offering furniture credit for free—Galeries Lafayette and Castorama—were able to consolidate their position as France's leading furniture retailers. Galeries Lafayette at the time was offering 94 percent of its credit sales at zero interest.[54] For the government of François Mitterrand, who in 1984 was struggling to rein in inflation, free credit raised the old fear that unbridled consumer credit would stoke the flames of inflation and so hurt competitiveness. Laurent Fabius, Prime Minister under Mitterrand, attacked the practice as "pushing customers to purchase using credit they don't really need."[55] In response to these fears, the Banking Law of 1984 restricted free credit sales. Retailers could no longer advertise free credit terms outside the point of sale. More importantly, when free credit terms were offered, retailers were required to display a lower price for goods when they were purchased without free credit. This price was set by a formula—based on the average interest rate plus 50 percent—that for average periods of credit gave prices that were roughly 20 percent below the "free credit" prices.[56] Interestingly, most consumer groups supported the new law, as did small retailers, who did not have the financial means to compete with "free credit."[57]

The second move to restrict credit access focused on the practice of credit rating. In 1988, Jacques de la Rosière, governor of the Banque de France, announced his institution's intention to create and manage a mandatory listing of credit data on all consumer borrowers. This would reestablish a system created in 1946 in which banks reported all of their loans to the central bank. Although this process had been retained for commercial lending, consumer lending had been exempted as part of the credit liberalization campaign of the 1950s. Consumer groups strongly supported the creation of a positive or "white" credit database, in part because they thought it would force France's banks to behave more responsibly. Consumer representative Louis Mesuret warned: "[the banks] do not respect their obligation of prudence and offer credit willy-nilly." The idea was to allow all lenders to know the total debt held by credit applicants so that they could better evaluate the likelihood of repayment. The Association of French Banks came out strongly against the white list idea, which they saw as an attempt by the nonbank finance companies to gain access to their own clients. Banks reasoned that the long-term relationships they had built with depositors would give them an advantage in offering them loans. Consumer finance companies, by contrast, had traditionally offered loans via retailers, and thus had very little direct contact with their customers. By sharing data, banks stood to lose their monopoly on valuable information and gain little in return.[58] Given that banks' own consumer loans were experiencing high rates of nonpayment, they may have overestimated the value of the information they held. Nonetheless, France's large banks are reported to have used their political influence to get France's powerful data privacy body, CNIL, to recommend against the creation of a positive credit listing of the sort proposed by de la Rosière.[59]

With the failure to implement a white list, France's association of finance companies (Association des sociétés financiers, ASF) launched its own debtor black list in October 1988. This list, which was voluntary to its members, included only borrowers who were at least three months late on their payments. Members were encouraged to check applicants against it before making loans. All but the largest lenders participated, accounting for 35 of the 37 member organizations and 70 percent of all finance company lending.[60] The Banque de France responded the following year by creating its own black list. Unlike the ASF list, all consumer lenders were required to check loan applicants against the official government list. And unlike the failed white list proposal, this list included only nonpayment information. The database, called the *Fichier national des incidents de remboursement des crédits aux particuliers* (FICP), was accessible only to credit providers and to individual debtors who wished to view their own record.[61] In practice, the FICP database became a no-credit black list for borrowers. In 1991, it included 800,000 late payers; by 2003, that number had grown to 2.3 million.[62]

After the list's creation, debates periodically surfaced concerning the potential advantages of collecting and distributing more extensive "positive" credit data, including information on outstanding loans, taxes, income, and assets. In one proposal, which came before the National Assembly in 2005, the center-right UDF party argued that a positive registry would give financial institutions a better sense of total borrowing and help them to improve their assessments of a consumer's ability to repay. France's financial institutions were divided on the proposal. Some, including the consumer lending institution Cofinoga, argued that positive data on potential borrowers would help them to minimize an adverse selection of customers and thereby reduce both defaults and credit rationing. But many other financial institutions, supported by the ASF, argued that a positive rating system would only assist foreign financial firms—like UK-based lender Egg—to identify and exploit new clients in France.[63] The country's consumer groups generally agreed, worrying that a positive list would become a tool for the more aggressive commercialization of credit and lead to higher levels of consumer indebtedness.[64] Ultimately, CNIL concluded that the new list would be an illegitimate use of private data and blocked the proposal.

The third major regulatory move was in the area of bankruptcy. With the liberalization of consumer credit in the early 1980s, a rising incidence of overindebtedness led France's consumer and finance associations to negotiate a novel solution. The Neirtz Law of December 31, 1989, named after France's minister of consumption, created a new administrative instrument that worked beside legal structures to help resolve cases of consumer overindebtedness. The core of the new system was a set of Departmental Commissions for Overindebted Individuals managed by France's central bank and to which any consumer could apply for debt restructuring or relief. These commissions had broad authorities. They could suspend payments for up to two years, restructure the payment period for loans, and modify interest rates. New repayment schedules were based on the Commission's assessment of the "minimum vital income" necessary to meet the debtor's most basic needs, and repayment plans could last up to but not longer than ten years. Formally, Commissions could only propose a repayment solution. If both parties to the negotiation did not voluntarily accept it, the case went before a judge, who, from 1995, had the right to enforce the recommendations of the Commission on both parties (or, in rare cases, to design a new repayment scheme).

A series of studies conducted in the 1990s showed that most cases went to the full ten years, that interest rates were reduced on average from 13 to 9 percent, and that average monthly payments were reduced from 6,000 francs to 3,800 francs.[65] Within certain limits—business-related debt was excluded and consumers had to show good faith—nearly all cases were accepted. The number filed with the commissions grew over time—from 90,000 in 1990 to 190,000 by 2004.[66]

Creditors were initially skeptical of the Neiertz procedure and, in 1990, only accepted 45 percent of the solutions proposed by the commissions. Paul Defourny, head of Cetelem, estimated in 1992 that 50,000 of the 160,000 cases heard up until that point represented instances of clear cheating by borrowers who had gone from lender to lender to get as much as they could and who had no intention of repaying. He estimated that the new law had cost the lending industry 1 billion francs in its first two years. As he describes it, "the [Neiertz] law . . . moralized our profession by creating a sort of deontological code."[67] Yet as cases of overindebtedness rose and the commissions showed they could produce workable solutions, industry acceptance of their proposals rose, to 75 percent by the end of the 1990s. The result was a set of responses to consumer overindebtedness that restructured debt but in almost all cases required consumers to make good on their obligations.

By the mid-1990s, concern about the likely social consequences of mounting consumer debt outpaced enthusiasm for credit market access. An incident in 1996 illustrated how different the French approach to credit had become. Since 1967, French law had capped consumer loan interest rates in the range of 20 to 25 percent.[68] In 1996, the UK-based Thorn group launched its first rent-to-sell store, called "Crazy George's," in Bobigny, France, followed with a second site in Le Havre. The store format was based on the company's highly successful Rent-a-Centre chain, launched in 1992 in the United States, and the equally successful Crazy George's rent-to-own chain in the United Kingdom. The idea of the store was to offer goods under a rental contract that would eventually lead to consumer ownership. Their French stores targeted communities with high concentrations of poor and elderly and where credit was not readily available. Although the rentals were not formally credit agreements, the effective interest rate on rent-to-own purchases ranged up to 56 percent. While this implied rate far exceeded the usury cap, it did not formally fall under France's usury restrictions.[69]

Initially, Thorn had envisioned offering the rent-to-own service through its existing French consumer electronics rental company, Visea. To pave the way for this service, Visea began posting billboards in 1994 with slogans that read, "If we lend only to the rich, why did we invent credit?" and "If we deny credit to those who are unemployed, what good is solidarity?"[70] The reference to solidarity was a direct attack on the French idea of equal citizenship without equal access to credit. Concerned about the potential response that the new sales format would elicit, Thorn finally opted to introduce the rent-to-own format as an American import. At the launch of its first Crazy George's store in Bobigny, convertibles festooned with balloons and U.S. flags paraded around town. The French media quickly focused on the new format as an "Anglo-Saxon" import. Public interest heightened when the first store was shut down by France's commercial police (the DGCCRF) on the grounds that it was not accurately reporting the final total price on its goods.

Crazy George's offered many people their only possibility to purchase large household goods. Unlike consumer lenders, Crazy George's accepted social payments as income to qualify for a loan. In fact, a third of all customers reported no household salary income. To manage repayments, the stores sold only to those living within a five-kilometer radius and insisted that customers drop off their payments in person weekly. All applicants were required to give the names and telephone numbers of three friends and two relatives, so that application information could be confirmed.[71] These measures kept default rates below 1 percent.[72] A survey of customers found that 66 percent were first-time buyers of basic household goods like televisions and computers.[73] Critics argued that it was wrong for the poor to pay over twice as much for products. And a public poll found that 70 percent of French opposed the rent-to-sell format.[74] Behind the opposition was a coalition of the Christian right and labor left. France's Catholic newspaper, *La Croix,* took a hard line: "consumer lending . . . is to be condemned, and . . . a total prohibition on the charging of interest, not only abusive interest rates, should be retained."[75] In agreement, if for different reasons, CSCV brought a lawsuit against Thorn for exceeding France's usury cap.[76] In 1998, the company was acquired by Nomura Investment, and its French stores were closed.

Conclusions

The 2008 financial crisis has been traced to excessive U.S. household debt. Although much attention has been directed to mortgage financing, this chapter has instead traced the evolution of nonmortgage consumer debt. In order to understand what was different about U.S. consumer credit, I use the case of French consumer lending as a comparison. Whereas Americans borrowed heavily, their French counterparts took on relatively little debt. Common accounts of such differences in credit extension have emphasized the dual roles of financial deregulation and institutions for managing nonpayment risk. Instead, I trace the origins of heavy credit reliance in the United

States, and relatively limited credit access in France, to the ways in which commercial banks approached consumer credit in the early postwar period.

American banks began extending consumer credit during a period in which this sort of lending was relatively unprofitable. They did so primarily to attract customers rather than to earn income on interest payments. This approach also led them to offer the kind of credit that consumers found most attractive, namely, revolving credit. Because these early credit facilities predated nationwide credit card payments networks, those networks emerged with revolving credit as one of their core functions. For many Americans, secure electronic payments and a revolving credit facility were seen as part of the same service. In France, on the other hand, banks were larger, less numerous, and focused on supporting government-defined goals for economic development. This circumstance left consumer lending in the hands of dedicated consumer loan companies, which in turn meant that France's own secure electronics payments network was not initially associated with a credit facility. Equally important, because banks were not involved in consumer lending, and because small lenders had historically been viewed with considerable suspicion, the consumer loan sector enjoyed little political influence. When politicians called for an economic slowdown, consumer lenders were always the first place the Banque de France looked for credit contraction.

With the invention of profitable, indeed lucrative, consumer lending, these differences in the engagement of banks continued to matter. In the United States, interest rates were deregulated in order to promote competition for consumer loans among national banks. And, because it was felt that banks were responsible actors that were in any case already heavily regulated, politicians and the general public did not worry about the potential lending abuses that had characterized consumer loans in the past. In France, by comparison, the failure of banks to break into consumer lending meant that the sector remained the domain of specialized consumer finance companies. As long as banks were mainly on the outside, any regulation that reined in consumer lending met with little resistance. Indeed, it is a regularity of consumer lending across the advanced industrialized countries that markets with strong bank penetration into the consumer loans market have experienced relatively less regulatory restriction. Consumer lending was invented outside of the banking sector, but it has prospered in countries in which banks were able to win control over the sector.

Notes

*Documents were consulted in the following archives: the archives of the Conseil national de credit at the Banque de France (BdF CNC); the historical archive of the consumer lending company Cetelem (CHA), and the JCPenney Archives at the DeGolyer Library at Southern Methodist University (JCP). Citations to the Conseil national de crédit and the JCPenney Archives are presented as follows: the abbreviation of the archival repository; the box number or name; the folder name; the document title. Because the Cetelem archives had not been classified at the time of consultation, citations include the abbreviation of the archive and nonstandard folder references.

1. Joseph E. Stiglitz and Andrew Weiss, "Credit Rationing in Markets with Imperfect Information," *American Economic Review* 71, no. 3 (1981): 393–410.
2. Tullio Jappelli and Marco Pagano, "Information Sharing in Credit Markets," *Journal of Finance* 48, no. 5 (1993): 1693–718; Simeon Djankov, Caralee McLiesh, and Andrei Schleifer, "Private Credit in 129 Countries," *Journal of Financial Economics* 84, no. 2 (2007): 299–329.
3. These charitable lending societies were not related to Provident Clothing and Supply in Britain and did not engage in doorstep lending.
4. BdF CNC, box 318, Grande Bretagne, Réglementation des ventes à crédit, février 1955-décembre 1968, Correspondence, Sharman Wright, Bank of England, December 31, 1954.
5. JCP, "Report to Credit Management," *JC Penney Management Report* 4/8 (September 1977).
6. CHA, Correspondence from Pierre Boucher, director general, October 4, 1982.
7. JCP, Credit: Credit Growth Campaign, 1975, Steve Kernkraut, "Update: Net Cost of Credit," internal document, Credit Department, September 28, 1975, 1, 8.
8. *Le Matin,* June 29, 1981.
9. Ibid.
10. CHA, Pierre Boucher, internal memo, 1996.
11. U.S. Supreme Court, Marquette Nat. Bank v. First of Omaha Svc. Corp., 439 U.S. 299 (1978), No. 77–1265, 439 U.S. 299.
12. Depository Institutions Deregulation and Monetary Control Act, Public Law 96–221, Sect. 501, 1980.
13. Michael S. Barr, "Banking the Poor," *Yale Journal of Regulation* 21 (2004): 161–73.
14. RLDM, box 212, folder 24, Letter from the Consumer Federation of America to the Senate Banking Committee, June 17, 1982.
15. Mark Furletti, "Credit Card Pricing Developments and Their Disclosure," Fed Discussion Paper, January 2003.
16. National Bank Act, Section 24–7, 1964.
17. Mark Furletti, "The Debate Over the National Bank Act and the Preemption of State Efforts to Regulate Credit Cards," *Temple Law Review* 77 (2004): 425–56.
18. Furletti, "Credit Card Pricing," 16.
19. JCP, JCP Credit—10 Year Strategic Plan, 1983–1993, Part 1, JCPenney Credit Division, Stategic Plan, April 1983, A-1.
20. JCP, JCPenney Credit: 40th Anniversary Booklet, 1998.

21. Ronald D. Michman and Alan J. Greco, *Retailing Triumphs and Blunders: Victims of Competition in the New Age of Marketing Management* (Westport, CT, 1995), 39.

22. François Gomez, "La vente à crédit aux particuliers," *Gestion et Technique Bancaires* 451 (June 1985): 597.

23. Richard Deeg and Mary O'Sullivan, "The Financialization of Europe," paper presented at the Annual Meeting of the American Political Science Association, Philadelphia, 2006.

24. Jean-Pierre Robin, "Credit a la consommation, les français s'americanisent," *La Vie Française,* June 21, 1987.

25. Françoise Fressoz and Philippe Boulet-Gercourt, "Les Français flambent à crédit," *Libération,* August 13, 1987.

26. Florence Paricard, "Consommation: le taux de crédit doit baisser," *La vie française,* March 30, 1986.

27. Fressoz and Boulet-Gercourt, "Les Français flambent a crédit," *Libération,* August 13, 1987.

28. Ibid.; *Journale des Finances,* May 30, 1987.

29. Florance Pricard, "La Carte Bleue fait credit," *La Vie Française,* October 12–18, 1987.

30. Ibid.

31. "Les Français et le crédit," *Figaro-Magazine,* April 8, 1989, 94.

32. Roger Leron, "Rapport surt l'application de la loi No 89–1010 du 31 Décembre 1989 rélative a la prévention et au réglement des difficultés liées au sûrendettement des particuliers et des familles," *Journal Officiel* (1990): 7.

33. *Le Figaro,* May 30, 1991.

34. *La Tribune de l'Expansion,* April 8, 1991.

35. Catherine Rigollet, "Le Bazar des produits financiers," *L'Express,* March 6, 1987.

36. Fressoz and Boulet-Gercourt, "Les Français flambent a crédit," *Libération,* August 13, 1987.

37. The name "aurore" meant dawn, but also sounded like "or-or," or "gold-gold." Rigollet, "Le Bazar des produits financiers."

38. Jean-Philippe Vidal, "L'explosion du crédit à la consommation," *Tribune de l'économie,* October 27, 1987.

39. Paricard, "Consommation: le taux de crédit doit baisser."

40. *Figaro-Economie,* June 19, 1995.

41. Philippe Herail, "Cetelem: une histoire des valeurs, un avenir," Cetelem Historical Archive, August 2002.

42. *Le Figaro,* March 9, 1987.

43. Leron, "Rapport surt l'application de la loi No 89–1010," Annex II.

44. François Henrot, "Les instruments du financement à crédit de la consommation en France," in *La consommation et son financement en France et dans le monde,* ed. André de Lattre (Paris, 1994), 56–57.

45. *Figaro-Economie,* May 14, 1990.

46. Paul Defourny and Josette Bienfait, *Données d'image sur le credit* (Paris, 1992), 7.

47. Law 78–22, January 10, 1978, transcribed as articles 311 and 313 of the French Consumer Code; *La Croix,* May 29, 1976.
48. Philippe Lebellec, "Crédit a la consommation," *La Croix,* November 11–12, 1987.
49. Martine Gilson, "Credit: les français craquent," *Le Nouvel Observateur,* January 26-February 1, 1989.
50. Ibid.
51. *Le Monde,* June 19, 1987.
52. *Le Monde,* January 5, 1989.
53. Leron, "Rapport sur l'application de la loi No 89–1010," 7; Jean-Marc Biais, "Le Piège à mauvais payeurs," *L'Epress,* February 3, 1989, 62.
54. CNC, Direction du Développement, "Credit Gratuit," September 4, 1984.
55. Laurent Chavane, "L'enterrement discret du 'crédit gratuity,' " *Le Figaro,* July 23, 1984.
56. François Renard, "Le credit gratuity va pratiquement disparaître," *Le Monde,* July 25, 1984, 19.
57. Chavane, "L'enterrement discret du 'crédit gratuity,' " *Le Figaro,* July 23, 1984.
58. *Libération,* December 7, 1988.
59. Author interview, confidential, 2007.
60. *Le Monde,* December 8, 1988.
61. Pierre-Laurent Chatain and Frédéric Ferrière, *Surendettement des particuliers* (Paris, 2000), 188.
62. *Libération,* March 20, 1993.
63. Catherine Maussion, "Credit: tout le monde dans le même fichier?," *Libération,* October 5, 2002.
64. Bertrand Bissuel and Anne Michel, "Les établissements de credit accusés de favoriser le surendettement, *Le Monde,* April 28, 2005; Sylvie Ramadier, "La bataille du credit à la consommation," *Les Echos,* January 22–22, 2005, 8.
65. Hubert Balaguy, *Le crédit a la consommation en France* (Paris, 1996), 106–7.
66. The commissions were administrative bodies. Each had four members, representing the Banque de France, the treasury department, a consumer association, and a representative of a lender association. Two nonvoting members were added in 2003: a social worker and a lawyer.
67. Renaud de la Baume, "Surendettement: un banquier dénonce les 'tricheurs,' " *La Tribune a l'Expansion,* March 19, 1992.
68. The exact formula was based initially on the commercial bond rate. From 1989, usury caps were set relative to the average consumer lending rate from the previous period.
69. Crazy George's forty outlets in the United Kingdom operated on far lower effective interest rates, ranging between 20% and 25%.
70. *La Croix,* January 18, 1994.
71. Odette Terrade, "Projet de loi de finances pour 1998—Consommation et concurrence," *Journal Officiel—Sénat* 87/9 (1997).
72. "Crazy George's Déclare forfeit," *LSA* August 27, 1998, 1594.

73. CHA, CSA survey, October 1997.
74. *Le Monde,* November 25, 1996.
75. Hugues Puel, "Crazy George's met l'éthique au défi," *La Croix,* December 11, 1996.
76. *Humanité,* February 20, 1998.

CHAPTER 8

French Consumer Credit Policy in the 1950s and 1960s: From Opposition to Control

Sabine Effosse

France presented almost the opposite pattern of the United States for consumer credit use after World War II, as Gunnar Trumbull emphasizes in the previous chapter. Whereas consumer credit was widely available in the United States, credit access was tightly restricted in France.[1] This article aims to show that this situation was largely the result of French monetary policy. The main problem that dominated French debates over consumer credit from the end of the war to the liberalization of the banking system in 1966 was the question of legitimacy. This issue was illustrated by Pierre Besse, secretary of the National Credit Council, who in 1955 characterized consumer credit as "a necessary disease, which must be restricted as much as possible."[2] This phrase pointed to a paradox in postwar French consumer credit policy: regulatory authorities saw consumer credit as both indispensable and condemnable.

Why were French credit authorities so reluctant to foster consumer credit? Was this policy an exception in an international context? Or was it comparable to policies in other European countries, such as Germany or Great Britain? To answer these questions, this chapter is divided into three parts. In the first, I examine the credit authorities' opposition to consumer credit in the early years after the war, between 1947 and 1952. In the second, I describe the evolution of this attitude in conjunction with the regulatory measures adopted between 1954 and 1957. Finally, by introducing a comparison with other European countries and the United States, I turn to the consequences of these regulatory measures for lenders, for how consumers used credit, and for levels of consumer indebtedness.

Opposition to the Development of Consumer Credit, 1947–52

In the wake of World War II, on December 2, 1945, the French government under Charles de Gaulle decided to nationalize the credit industry and main banks, including the Bank of France. In his announcement, de Gaulle declared, "it is the role of the state to secure credit in order to direct it toward large investments."[3] The credit nationalization law consequently created a National Credit Council to define credit policy and regulate the banking sector.[4] This institution was closely linked to the Bank of France, which was one of its main sources of policy makers, along with the Ministry of Finance, in particular the treasury administration.[5] In October 1947, the minister of finance, expressing concern about the development of illegal lenders and high interest rates, asked the Bank of France to conduct a survey of the consumer credit market.

The Bank of France Survey of the Consumer Credit Market (1948)

In accordance with the banking laws of 1941, all French credit institutions had to be registered.[6] Consequently, even in the absence of a specific regulation on consumer credit, which had been considered in 1942 but had never come to pass, consumer finance companies had to be registered by the National Credit Council before they granted credit.[7] The Bank of France survey, written by one of its auditors, Mr. de Montbrial, only considered banking companies that offered loans—not retail sector lenders.[8] The report confirmed the major role that the consumer finance companies played in postwar French consumer lending, such as those specializing in durable goods discussed by Isabelle Gaillard in chapter 1. Of fifty-nine registered lenders, only two were commercial banks. Moreover, automobile financing initially dominated: 90 percent of consumer loans were granted for cars, in part because car manufacturers had created their own consumer finance companies during the interwar period, including the Diffusion Industrielle Automobile par le Credit (DIAC), founded by Renault in 1924.[9] Most significantly, the survey pointed to a gap between low consumer purchasing power and high demand for consumer durables. Given the limited quantity of legal lenders at the time, this gap fed the growth of an illegal lending market. The report thus suggested the adoption of consumer credit regulations modeled on the so-called Regulation W of 1941 in the United States.[10] Following the American regulation, which was well known by the Bank of France, the survey recommended guidelines for minimum down payments (30 percent for new cars and 40 percent for other goods) and a maximum repayment period (between twelve and eighteen months). Possibly inspired by the British Hire-Purchase Act of 1938, the report additionally emphasized that lenders should publish the cost of credit to consumers. Finally, it suggested setting a limit for the ratio of a bank's outstanding loans to its equity capital.

Transmitted to the National Credit Council at the beginning of 1949, these measures were not followed up on. In spite of the report's conclusions, the council officially refused to regulate consumer credit, defined largely as installment sales during this time. The council rejected this option, because regulating consumer credit would have meant legitimating its development. Thus, all new requests for registration by potential consumer lenders were refused with the exception of sales financing companies for cars.

The National Credit Council's Refusal to Regulate Consumer Credit (July, 1949): Economic, Monetary, and Legal Arguments

The council's rejection of consumer credit in July 1949 was based on three arguments. The first one raised by its members stemmed from their economic priorities. The initial postwar economic plan, the so-called Plan Jean Monnet, had established reconstruction priorities for the period from 1947 to 1952. It aimed first and foremost at rebuilding the industrial and transport sectors. This "fight for production" *(bataille de la production)* called on credit policy to support industrial development. It focused on business investments, especially in state-owned companies such as Electricité de France (EDF) and the national railway company, Société nationale des Chemins de fer français (SNCF).[11] Private consumption needs, even housing, had to take a back seat. Despite an acute housing shortage, little was done to reorganize mortgage loans until 1953.[12] Credit policy had to serve industrial production and not household consumption.

The second argument was monetary. After World War II, inflation was very high in France. Rebuilding and military expenditures (the latter was 28 percent of total government outlays in 1948 due to colonial conflict) generated high budgetary deficits. In this context, the council encouraged the French to save rather than spend. Nevertheless, this inflation risk argument was not extensively developed in council discussions. The Bank of France report had made clear that the volume of installment sales was still too low to seriously influence overall inflation trends (less than 9 billion francs in 1948).

The last argument was legal. The National Credit Council only agreed to register lenders who financed goods that could legally be repossessed and thus serve as security. Since the Malingre law, such goods were limited to new cars or tractors. The council refused to register lenders who granted credit for other goods, which by default were considered "consumption goods." This legal argument brings out a noteworthy point. Contrary to British hire-purchase legislation or the German installment law, both of which gave lenders the possibility to take back goods in case of non-repayment, French legislation did not offer lenders such recourse.[13] According to French Civil Law, as soon as a consumption good was sold, it was the borrower's property, even if it had not yet been paid for in full. This legal characteristic introduced a long-term dichotomy for credit conditions in France between goods that could be repossessed and those that could not; the former carried much lower interest rates.

Against this background, the National Credit Council's rejection of consumer credit seemed logical, especially in the context of the council's overall restrictive credit policy. However, the council's decision also appeared disconnected from social reality. Like their European counterparts during the early postwar years, the French needed new cars less than basic necessities.[14] That is why the main consequence of the council's decision was the development of a black market for consumer credit and the spread of lenders not registered by the National Credit Council.

The Growth of a Black Market for Consumer Credit

Not just the government, but the French people in general had an ambivalent attitude toward consumer credit. However, to many of them, it appeared to be a necessity as well. Wages did not follow the inflationary price development, so that purchasing power initially remained low. In 1950, for example, the price for a washing machine represented seven or eight months of wages for a cleaning woman. The demand for consumer goods after the war concerned mainly motorbikes such as the Vélosolex or scooters like the Vespa, because cars were too expensive for the average household, as well as domestic appliances (radios, refrigerators, washing machines), home furnishings, and also clothes and shoes.[15] Few legal lenders were available to satisfy these needs. The largest consumer finance companies, created by manufacturers of cars and electrical appliances during the interwar period, granted only a small number of loans to households until the early 1950s.[16] Instead, they financed mainly commercial equipment, for example, buses, trucks, and tractors. In 1953, less than 30 percent of the DIAC's outstanding loans involved private automobiles.[17] As discussed in chapter 1 by Isabelle Gaillard, Crédit électrique et gazier (CREG), founded by Philips in 1927, and similar companies started granting loans for households again only in 1953. Meanwhile, illegal lenders emerged.

These lenders were door-to-door salesmen working on their own or for associated retailers, that is, the so-called economic unions, and they were similar in principle to the check credit businesses discussed by Sean O'Connell for Britain (chapter 4) and Andrew Gordon for Japan (chapter 3).[18] The example of economic unions reveals the fluid boundary between the legal and "black market" consumer credit markets particularly well. These economic unions, which were organizations formed by small retailers, had first been created near the beginning of the twentieth century to compete with the big Parisian stores that used credit checks.[19] They were founded mainly in northern France in medium-sized textile cities as well as in the Mediterranean area. Most of them were a type of limited liability company called *société anonyme*. They granted credit by issuing special checks for all consumer goods except food, especially textiles and furniture. They spread during the interwar period, so that there were about one hundred such unions in 1939.

In the wake of World War II, several old economic unions started business again and succeeded; in 1953, they had a turnover of 4 billion francs and a membership of 5,000 retailers. This success caught the attention of shifty entrepreneurs. Attracted by the profits that such operations could yield, some crafty fellows who were not retailers created bogus "economic unions."[20] Using this term, well known and trusted by customers, they founded new companies and granted consumer loans (mainly for motorbikes) at high interest rates. Whereas the interest rates of traditional economic unions were some 25 to 30 percent, "false" economic unions charged rates between 40 and 45 percent, and sometimes even more. By comparison, interest rates for new cars from registered finance companies were about 18 percent, whereas those for textiles from black-market door-to-door lenders were as high as 63 percent (table 8.1).

Newspapers denounced the highest rates as usurious. To protect their reputations, traditional economic unions asked the Bank of France to allow them

Table 8.1 Average consumer credit costs for durable goods, 1953

Product	Annual rate (%)
New cars (subject to repossession)	18.0
Used cars (not subject to repossession)	39.0
Refrigerators	25.0
Furniture	20.5
Textiles	63.0

Source: Bank of France, 1331200301, box 65.

to be registered, but their request failed. Nevertheless, the growth of the illegal consumer credit market caught the government's attention. At the beginning of 1953, Robert Buron, the Christian-Democratic economic minister, prepared a bill that aimed to prevent usury and encourage the development of consumer credit. This plan and an improved overall economic situation moved the credit authorities to change their consumer credit policy.

The Evolution of Credit Authorities: Consumer Credit Regulation, 1953–57

The bill introduced by the economic minister aimed to use consumer credit as a means to boost economic growth. But before any potential expansion of the consumer credit market could be realized, such credit had to be cleaned up or "moralized" in the eyes of authorities. Therefore, regulating it now appeared to be necessary.

The Evolving Economic Situation and the Government Bill

In the immediate wake of World War II, the main problem for the French economy had been to gear up production in the face of widespread destruction, insufficient raw materials, and—especially significant in this context—a shortage of capital. By the beginning of 1953, however, the main problem had become to sell goods.[21] As stated above, wages were not keeping pace with inflation, and French purchasing power remained low. Both the Economic Ministry and the Bank of France observed a phenomenon that they understood as underconsumption. Low levels of consumption threatened budding economic growth, and the government decided to encourage the development of consumer credit as part of a more general program to boost the economy. Other measures entailed support for exports, as well as aid to the mortgage loans market. The latter stressed the close link between an expansive housing policy and related growth in home equipment and consumer durables, which was relevant in the German case, as well.[22] Still, despite the second economic plan's (1953–57) emphasis on home modernization and durable equipment, as well as a finance policy geared more toward housing, government support for consumer credit ran counter to popular expectations.

Indeed, the government performed an interesting semantic shift when talking about consumer credit. As the minister of finance, Mr. Bourgès-Maunoury, declared in Le Monde on February 19, 1953, "what we called consumer credit . . . is really a loan for individual investment."[23] Terminology such as "modernization" and "equipment," which had been used for firms during the first economic plan, was now applied to individual households. Households, like firms, needed to invest in new equipment in order to rationalize their operations. Consumer credit was no longer credit for consumption goods but, instead, financing for domestic equipment. Using the word "equipment" changed everything. This rhetoric comported with developments in the Bank of France and reflected the evolution of consumer credit policy. With the end of the Korean War in July 1953 and a decrease of inflationary risks, thanks to fiscal stabilization under Minister of Finance Antoine Pinay, the central bank became more open-minded about credit expansion.[24] Furthermore, the bank could no longer ignore both the dangers of the illegal lending market and mounting government pressure to regulate consumer credit. After long deliberations, which lasted one and a half years, the Bank of France and the National Credit Council agreed to regulate the consumer credit market and to register new lenders.

The National Credit Council Agreement

In order to clean up the consumer credit market, the National Credit Council first adopted the Economic Ministry's proposal to require lending companies to possess a minimum amount of capital. It also accepted the Montbrial survey's major conclusions to mandate a minimum down payment, a maximum repayment period, the publication of interest rates, and, most importantly, a cap on the ratio of outstanding loans to the equity capital financing them, that is, a cap on the "creditworthiness ratio" or *ratio de solvabilité*. As mentioned above, the Montbrial proposals on minimum down payments and maximum repayment periods were directly inspired by the U.S. Regulation W, which had been briefly reinstated during the Korean War and had been applied in Europe for the first time by Great Britain in 1952, as discussed in chapter 4 by Sean O'Connell. The British Hire-Purchase Credit Control Order set minimum down payments (33 percent of the purchase price, except for motorbikes and bicycles, for which only 25 percent was collected) and a maximum repayment period (eighteen months).[25]

Regarding credit costs and the broader question of defining usury, the council protocols show that regulators were unable to agree on a cap. According to council secretary Pierre Besse, to choose a ceiling cap would have been too difficult: "we must admit that we cannot find a rate above which an offense is committed."[26] Unlike in Great Britain, French regulators preferred simply to require the publication of credit costs in order, occasionally, to refuse to register lenders whose interest rates they deemed too high. Thus, the cap question was postponed until the Money Loans Law, also called the Usury Law, was passed in December 1966.[27] Finally, the creditworthiness ratio—the key measure according to Montbrial's survey—was justified as a measure to curb inflation. Because French consumer finance companies were unable to receive public deposits, they had to maintain a high level of equity capital to limit their own discounting costs. This prevented excessive lending, and the Bank of France considered the measure a guarantee in its fight against inflation.

Finally, the discussion also focused on the types of goods that could be bought on credit. The National Credit Council wanted to encourage the purchase of "useful and durable goods," an effort that would improve "the modernization of family life by saving labor and speeding up the [proliferation of new] home equipment." It aimed especially at introducing domestic appliances such as washing machines, refrigerators, and vacuum cleaners into a greater number of French households. The television, by contrast, was considered a mere leisure product and was thus excluded until 1954.[28] Unlike British regulators, however, the National Credit Council never assembled an official list of goods that were or were not "creditworthy."

Regulation Measures

The earliest National Credit Council measure was adopted on July 28, 1954. First, interest rates had to be published by the lenders, and statistics on consumer credit were to be collected by the Bank of France. Second, the size of the required down payment and the permissible length of the repayment period depended on the types of goods purchased, as well as on economic conditions in the country. A minimum amount for lenders' share capital was also set, and their ability to lend was fixed according to the amount of equity capital they possessed (multiplied by eight or ten).

These measures, however, only concerned the banking sector, which was controlled by the National Credit Council. Retailers remained largely free of limiting regulations. Not surprisingly, consumer credit companies protested against what they considered to be unfair competition. A further decree on May 20, 1955 therefore extended these rules to the retail sector. Still, the application process for retail-based lenders was postponed for political reasons. Small-scale retailers and shopkeepers wielded considerable influence in France during this period. For example, Pierre Poujade (1920–2003), a bookseller turned politician, campaigned to protect shopkeepers from the competition of big stores with considerable electoral success in 1956.[29] Moreover, big firms such as Singer and the French publishing house Larousse lobbied the Economic Ministry for exemptions.[30] On January 11, 1957, the Trade Department decided to make exceptions for some goods, including sewing machines, books and other publications, but also musical instruments.

The Bank of France did not necessarily support this action, but as the credit volume for these goods was relatively insignificant, it did not insist on unified regulation. Thus, by the end of the 1950s, regulation concerned the banking sector and most retailers. Only door-to-door lenders (or *abonneurs*) who traded in credit checks remained unaffected by public regulation until the 1966 Money Loans Law. Still, although between 1947 and 1953 the National Credit Council had generally refused to register new consumer finance companies, the regulatory measures adopted in 1954 opened a new era for consumer lending in France.

Regulating Consumer Credit: Restrictive Credit Policy, 1954–66

These regulations had three major consequences. First, the lending market became more concentrated, and the leading role of consumer finance companies was reinforced. Second, the selective consumer credit policy boosted the development of the French durable goods industries. Third, if we consider access to home equipment, the standard of living did not improve as much as had been expected.

Consumer Finance Companies versus Banks

The National Credit Council encouraged specialized finance companies, rather than banks, to grant consumer credit. According to its general credit policy, banks were to fund the state and firms, but not individuals; consumer credit in the form of housing loans—unless subsidized—was generally granted by finance companies. But, if the French banking sector—commercial banks and saving banks *(Caisses d'Epargne)*—did not directly finance consumer credit, they did so indirectly. In 1961, 89 percent of outstanding consumer loans were financed by the banks and the Bank of France via discounting and rediscounting.[31] This circumstance explained why the Bank of France was so heavily invested in establishing lenders' creditworthiness ratios. Consumer credit companies had to increase their equity capital and find partnership with a banking institution. Therefore, the council preferred to register new large consumer finance companies, not only because they were easier to watch, but also because they had banking partnership, which would limit their rediscounting needs and thus the inflation risk. If nothing else, the Bank of France observed, big companies offered lower interest rates than smaller ones.

The two new largest consumer finance companies had a lot in common. Sofinco and Cetelem (both still exist, and Cetelem is currently the consumer credit leader in continental Europe) were created in 1951 and

1953, respectively, by senior civil servants from the Ministry of Finance, Jack Francès and Jacques de Fouchier, who had quit government service after the war to go into the private banking sector.[32] Both of these finance companies were partnerships between large investment banking groups and industrial manufacturers—of furniture, in Sofinco's case, and electrical appliances, in Cetelem's. These commercial banking groups involved the Banque Générale Industrielle-La Hénin (Sofinco) and the Union Française de Banques (Cetelem).[33] After postwar reconstruction, their activities had changed (one of them had received nationalization indemnities for coal mines) and they sought new activities and capital outlets. The consumer credit market presented a profitable opportunity as demand was high and risks were low.

By the late 1950s and early 1960s, social security, high employment levels, and what might be described as honest financial ethics kept French default rates low. Less than 0.5 percent of consumer loans were not repaid. Because of their connection to banking consortiums, interest rates offered by new specialized lenders such as Cetelem were lower (by as much as 25 percent) than those of competing lenders. This new competition helped to "clean up" the market, insofar as the number of lenders declined and interest rates decreased. The resultant concentration in the consumer credit market was striking. In 1961, 65 percent of all consumer loans for furniture and domestic appliances were granted by only two companies, 73 percent of television loans by four companies, and 64 percent of all car loans by five companies.[34]

As the credit market expanded, banks became increasingly interested in it. In 1959, they bypassed the regulatory framework, which concerned only installment credit, and became directly involved in the consumer loans market. Following the example set by English, Dutch, Swedish, and German banks (on the latter, see chapter 2), they decided to try offering a new credit product, the personal loan, to attract new customers. But this form of direct household financing remained comparatively limited until the liberalization of the banking market in 1966.

Support for the Automobile and Electrical Industries

Next to the lending market, the new regulatory framework also affected the consumer goods industry. Although the National Credit Council did not set a fixed list of consumer durables that could be bought on credit, the selective requirements for down payments and repayment periods, defined differently for different goods, served as tools to encourage key industrial sectors. In decreasing order of significance (table 8.2), durables financed on credit were new cars (half of all new cars were bought on credit in 1965),

Table 8.2 Percentage of consumer durables bought on credit, 1970

Product	Amount (%)
New cars	47
Televisions	47
Washing machines	40
Sewing machines	40
Used cars	32
Refrigerators	29

Source: Bank of France, INSEE survey, 1370198301, box 4.

home appliances (televisions, washing machines, and refrigerators), furniture, and—by the end of the 1960s—leisure goods such as caravans and boats.[35]

Consumer credit policy thus supported industrial interests. With the first steps taken toward European integration and a common market after 1957, French authorities wanted to protect national industries from competition by other European firms.[36] This was especially true for the electrical goods industry, which was not yet as established as the French car industry. Before World War II, most appliances had been imported from abroad, in particular from the United States. In 1958, for example, France produced 410,000 refrigerators, compared to Italy's 425,000 and Germany's 1,350,000.[37] Increases in durable goods production reduced prices and aided national competitiveness. Whereas 8,000 refrigerators had been produced in France in 1947 and sold at 1,000 francs per liter of storage space on average, 1 million were sold at only 700 francs per liter in 1961.[38] The development of consumer credit was thus linked to broader industrial policy. French monetary authorities complied with an expansion of consumer credit markets in part to boost specific national industries.[39] Unlike the United States, however, consumer credit policy in France was less a social policy geared to expanding consumer access to goods; it remained in the first instance an economic policy focused on raising production targets.[40] This partially explains why the growth of consumer credit remained comparatively restricted in France even after the reforms of 1954.

Consumer Credit Development under Control: Low Indebtedness and Backwardness in Home Equipment

Between 1954 and 1967, outstanding consumer credit volume in France grew by a factor of seven in constant currency. The highest increases fell in the

Table 8.3 Average household indebtedness, 1965

Country	Francs
France	154
West Germany	163
Great Britain	212
United States	1, 037

Source: National Credit Council Report, 1965.

Table 8.4 Diffusion of durable goods by household, 1962

Product	Percentage of households that possessed item		
	France (%)	Great Britain (%)	United States (%)
Television	25	78	87
Vacuum cleaner	32	71	75
Washing machine	31	43	95
Refrigerator	37	22	98
Car	33	30	75

Source: Enquête du Centre d'information et d'étude sur le crédit, July 1963.

period between 1959 and 1965, after European economic integration had begun. Still, this increase was relatively small. If we compare the development of consumer credit with that of all loans in France or with the country's GDP, it remained low. Consumer credit in France represented less than 2 percent of all loans during this period, 1 percent in 1954 and 1.7 percent in 1965. It accounted for only 1.6 percent of GDP in 1965—compared to 1.7 percent in West Germany, 2.4 percent in Great Britain, and as much as 6.1 percent in the United States during the same year.[41] Average French household indebtedness remained similarly low compared to these other countries and did not spike as many contemporaries feared (table 8.3).

To be sure, levels of indebtedness varied by area, income, and age. Household indebtedness was highest in industrial cities among workers and salaried employees, as well as newly married couples. Because of their desire to equip their homes, the influence of brides—and women more generally—on household indebtedness was considered to be especially high.[42]

At the same time, France's comparatively low level of average household debt must be seen in the context of its relative "backwardness" in terms of household access to domestic equipment (table 8.4).

In part, this lag in household saturation had technical roots. Electricité de France, the country's main power company, improved household access to electricity only from the mid-1960s, especially with its "blue electricity meter operation," launched in 1963. Before, the lack of a modern electric grid posed a significant restraint on the spread of domestic appliances.[43] But the gap in domestic equipment also had financial roots, as consumer credit long played only a minor role in its spread—with, for example, fewer than one out of three refrigerators bought on credit by 1970. This development was a direct consequence of the monetary authorities' reluctance to fully embrace consumer credit. Even after the turning point of 1953, the Central Bank and the Treasury maintained a comparatively restrictive policy.

Conclusion: A Malthusian Credit Policy

Postwar France's consumer credit policy had an unmistakable "Malthusian" character, insofar as it used quantitative measures to regulate credit. This policy served primarily the interests of the durable goods industry, in particular those of automobile and electrical appliance manufacturers. Even after the recovery, credit authorities continued to think that economic growth rested more on production than consumption. In their view, consumer credit was much more an instrument of industrial policy than a means to raise living standards. Its purpose was mainly to expand the national market in order to facilitate the sale of durable goods. With lower prices, thanks to a broader market and the producers' modernization and standardization, French durable goods manufacturers could also compete elsewhere in Europe after the postwar reconstruction.

This focus on production explains why the social aspect included in initial proposals—the fight against usury—was abandoned.[44] At the same time, the regulation passed in the mid-1950s that mandated "creditworthiness ratios" (unique to France) and minimum capital requirements for lenders indirectly "moralized" the lenders market by eliminating the smallest and most costly of them. But the Bank of France and the treasury agreed not to cap interest rates. For them, high interest rates were also a means to limit the expansion of consumer credit. The restrictiveness of this approach was exceptional in postwar Europe. Even in Germany, where industrial investments and a culture of thrift were similarly encouraged, consumer credit developed more extensively and sooner.

The liberalization of credit ushered in the end of the credit policy shaped in Liberation France and—with the usury law passed in 1966 and the commercial banks' admission to the consumer credit market—ultimately changed this situation. Monetary authorities instead chose to encourage the rise of an effective consumer credit market, that is, a market based on information for consumers about interest rate caps and without any authoritarian restrictions on credit. Still, consumer credit use and its legitimacy remained an important issue of debate in France, as the Lagarde Law on consumer credit reform recently reminded us.[45]

Notes

1. On the history of consumer credit in France, see Rosa-Maria Gelpi and François Julien-Labruyère (both of whom worked for Cetelem, the largest finance consumer company in France), *The History of Consumer Credit: Doctrines and Practices,* trans. Mn Liam Gavin (1994 in French; New York, 2000); Hubert Balaguy (economist), *Le crédit à la consommation en France* (Paris, 1996); Alain Chatriot (historian), "Protéger le consommateur contre lui-même: la régulation du crédit à la consommation," *Vingtième Siècle: Revue d'Histoire* 91 (2006): 95–109; Hélène Ducourant (sociologist), "Du crédit à la consommation à la consommation de crédits: autonomisation d'une activité économique" (PhD diss., Université de Lille 1, 2009); Laure Lacan et al., eds. (sociologists and political scientists), *Vivre et faire vivre à crédit,* special issue of *Sociétés contemporaines* 76 (2009): 5–119; Isabelle Gaillard, "Il credito al consumo in Francia," in *Credito e Nazione in Francia e in Italia (XIX-XX secolo),* ed. Giuseppe Conti et al. (Pisa, 2009), 457–71; Gilles Laferté (sociologist), "De l'interconnaissance sociale à l'identification économique: vers une histoire et une sociologie comparées de la transaction à crédit," *Genèses* 79 (2010): 135–49; Gilles Laferté et al., "Le crédit direct des commerçants aux consommateurs: persistence et dépassement dans le textile à Lens (1920–1970)," *Genèses* 79 (2010): 26–47; Sabine Effosse, "Le développement du crédit à la consommation en France pendant les Trente Glorieuses," in *Los niveles de vida en Espana y Francia en largo plazo,* ed. Gérard Chastagneret et al. (Alicante, 2010), 317–34; Sabine Effosse and Isabelle Gaillard, eds., *Consommer à crédit en Europe au vingtième siècle,* special issue of *Entreprises et histoire* 59 (June 2010): 5–141.

2. Pierre Besse, "Note au sujet du crédit à la consommation," March 24, 1955, Bank of France Archives (hereafter BDF) 1357200901, box 79.

3. Richard F. Kuisel, *Capitalism and the State in Modern France: Renovation and Economic Management in the Twentieth Century* (Cambridge, UK, 1981).

4. Claire Andrieu, "A la recherche de la politique du crédit, 1946–1973," *Revue historique* 271, no. 2 (April-June 1983): 377–417.

5. Laure Quennouëlle-Corre, *La direction du Trésor, 1947–1967: l'etat banquier et la croissance* (Paris, 2000).

6. Claire Andrieu, *La Banque sous l'Occupation: paradoxes de l'histoire d'une profession, 1936–1946* (Paris, 1990).

7. On the 1942 plan, see "Note sur le financement de ventes à crédit d'automobiles," July 7, 1943, BDF 1331200301, box 53.

8. "Rapport sur les entreprises de financement de la vente à crédit," 1948, BDF 1357200901, box 79.

9. Gelpi and Julien-Labruyère, *History of Consumer Credit;* Patrick Fridenson, *Histoire des usines Renault,* 2nd ed. (Paris, 1998), 1:145, 173–74; "French Automobile Marketing, 1890–1979," in *Development of Mass Marketing: The Automobile and Retailing Industries,* ed. Akio Okochi and Koichi S. Shimokawa (Tokyo, 1981), 130, 135, 138. Also, since the so-called Malingre Law of December 29, 1934, new cars and tractors could be repossessed.

10. On Regulation W, see Irving Michelman, *Consumer Finance: A Case History in American Business* (New York, 1966); and chapter 9 by Jan Logemann in this volume.

11. See Richard F. Kuisel and Claire Andrieu, "Le financement des investissements entre 1947 et 1974: trois éclairages sur les relations entre le ministère des Finances, l'Institut d'Emission et le Plan," in *De Monnet à Massé: enjeux politiques et objectifs économiques dans le cadre des quatre premiers plans (1946–1965),* ed. Henry Rousso (Paris, 1986), 41–58.

12. Sabine Effosse, *L'invention du logement aidé en France: l'immobilier au temps des Trente Glorieuses* (Paris, 2003).

13. On this point, see Royston Miles Goode, "A Credit Law for Europe?," *International and Comparative Law Quarterly* 23, no. 2 (1974): 227–91.

14. Jan Logemann, "Different Paths to Mass Consumption: Consumer Credit in the United States and West Germany during the 1950s and 60s," *Journal of Social History* 41, no. 3 (Spring 2008): 525–59; Sean O'Connell, *Credit and Community: Working-Class Debt in the UK since 1880* (Oxford, 2009).

15. Jacques Marseille, "L'ère des industries de consommation," in *Histoire de la France industrielle,* ed. Maurice Lévy-Leboyer (Paris, 1996), 358–73.

16. The modern form of consumer credit in France, with the introduction of a third party between the seller and buyer, spread during the interwar period. The lenders were, on one hand, the check trading companies, which were very close to the department stores. For example, La Semeuse, linked to La Samaritaine (a Parisian department store), was founded in 1913 and was similar to Provident, which Sean O'Connell discusses in chapter 4 of this volume. On the other hand, to respond to these competitors, small local retailers formed economic unions, which also offered sales credit through vouchers. The main difference was that the retailers contributed and pooled their own capital in these unions. Finally, after World War I, the car manufacturers (Citroën, Renault, Peugeot), then the electrical appliances manufacturers (Philips, Thomson), created their own consumer finance companies in order to increase their sales, namely, SOVAC (Société pour la vente à crédit d'automobiles) in 1919, DIAC in 1924, and DIN (Diffusion industrielle nationale) in 1928 for car loans, as well as CREG in 1927 and Radiofiduciaire in 1933 for domestic appliances. In 1938, 15% to 25% of new private cars were bought on credit in France.

17. BDF 1331200301, box 27; BDF 1331200301, box 65; and BDF 1357200901, box 79.

18. On the retailers' black lending market in France, see Laferté et al., "Le credit direct des commerçants aux consommateurs: persistence et dépassement dans le

textile à Lens (1920–1970)." For Great Britain, see Sean O'Connell, "Speculations on Working Class Debt: Credit and Paternalism in France, Germany and the United Kingdom," *Entreprises et histoire* 59 (June 2010): 80–91.

19. Jean Acquier, "Le crédit à la consommation dans les budgets familiaux," *Consommation* 4 (1958): 3–43; Sabine Effosse "Le Unioni economiche: un terzo settore del credito al consume in Francia (1900–1954)," in *Debiti e crediti,* ed. Angiolina Arru, Maria Rosaria De Rosa, and Craig Muldrew, special issue of *Quaderni Storici* 137, no. 2 (August 2011): 577–592.

20. BDF 13312003, box 27; BDF 1331200301, box 83.

21. France shared these overall economic restrictions on credit policy, as well as the shift in emphasis by the mid-1950s, with many of its Western European neighbors, including West Germany, as chapter 2 in this volume by Rebecca Belvederesi-Kochs points out.

22. Logemann "Different Paths."

23. BDF 1331200301, box 61.

24. Hubert Bonin, *Histoire économique de la IVe République* (Paris, 1987).

25. "Note sur le crédit à la consommation en Grande-Bretagne par Philippe Dargenton, inspecteur des Finances, attaché financier de l'ambassade de France à Londres," August 8, 1954, BDF 1427200301, box 318; "Le crédit à la consommation au Royaume-Uni," *Etudes et conjoncture* 4 (April 1954), BDF 1427200301, box 318.

26. "Comité des banques et établissements financiers, séance du 14 janvier 1953," BDF 14272003, box 143.

27. The legislation established a maximum interest rate on loans, which was double the rate of first category bonds.

28. On televisions, see Isabelle Gaillard, "La télévision comme objet de consommation en France des années 1950 aux années 1980" (PhD diss., Université de Paris I, 2006) and chapter 1 by Gaillard in this volume.

29. Herrick Chapman, "Shopkeepers and the State from the Poujadist Revolt to the Early Fifth Republic," in *Les PME dans les societés contemporaines de 1880 à nos jours: pouvoir, representation, action,* ed. Sylvie Guillaume et Michel Lescure (Bruxelles, 2008).

30. Wilfrid Baumgartner (governor of the Bank of France from 1949 to 1959), Wilfrid Baumgartner Archives, 2BA 23, dossier 8.

31. National Credit Council Report, 1961.

32. On Sofinco and Cetelem, see the anniversary books published by these companies: Cetelem, *De la 4 CV à la vidéo: 1953–1983, ces trente années qui ont changé notre vie* (Paris, 1983); Sofinco, *Les 50 ans qui ont changé la France, 1951–2001* (Paris, 2001).

33. Hubert Bonin, *Les groupes financiers français* (Paris, 1995).

34. Rapport du Conseil économique et social, 1961, BDF 13572009, box 78.

35. Kristin Ross, *Fast Cars, Clean Bodies: Decolonization and the Reordering of French Culture* (Cambridge, MA, 1995); Jean-Pierre Rioux, *Au Bonheur la France: Des impressionnistes à De Gaulle, comment nous avons su être heureux* (Paris, 2004).

36. Maurice Lévy-Leboyer, ed. *L'économie française dans la compétition internationale au XXᵉ siècle* (Paris, 2006) and René Leboutte, *Histoire économique et sociale de la construction européenne* (Bruxelles, 2008).

37. "Comment on prépare une crise: l'exemple de l'électroménager," *La Vie française,* August 1, 1958.

38. "La vente à crédit s'acclimate en France," *Le Monde,* November, 28, 1962.

39. The central bank controlled these priorities with rediscounting authorizations.

40. On credit access as a social policy in the United States, see chapter 9 in this volume by Jan Logemann.

41. National Credit Council Report, 1965, 185.

42. Rebecca Pulju, "The Woman's Paradise: The American Fantasy, Home Appliances, and Consumer Demand in Liberation France," in *Material Women, 1750–1950: Consuming Desires and Collecting Practices,* ed. Maureen Daly Goggin and Beth Fowkes Tobin (Farnham, Surrey, 2009), 111–24.

43. Henri Morsel, ed., *Histoire de l'électricité en France* (Paris, 1996), 3:635–73.

44. In 1958, French interest rates were, on average, 15% higher than in Britain for a fifteen-month loan and 18% higher for an eighteen-month loan; see "Le crédit à la consommation en Grande-Bretagne, au Canada et en Australie," *Notes et études documentaires* 2697, September 9, 1960, BDF 1427200301, box 318.

45. This law was passed on July 1, 2010; see Georges Gloukoviezoff et al., "Crédit à la consommation et surendettement des ménages" (debate), *Entreprises et histoire* 59 (June 2010): 112–21.

CHAPTER 9

From Cradle to Bankruptcy?
Credit Access and the American
Welfare State

Jan Logemann

Despite nearly two decades of sustained economic growth both in the United States and across Western Europe, practices of consumer credit still differed notably in the late 1960s. As one contemporary observer pointed out, "About one-half of all Americans both approve of and use installment credit. At the other extreme, only one-fourth of the Germans approve of it, and only one out of ten actually has any installment debt."[1] West Germans, studies found, were much more likely to use their expanding savings to purchase new consumer durables. American households also maintained a considerable savings rate, but for different purposes. Asked in 1966 about the intended purpose of their savings, 45 percent of American family units stated that they were saving for a "rainy day" (such as illness, unemployment, or other emergency), 31 percent for retirement or old age, and 22 percent for education.[2] In the absence of a more elaborate, cradle-to-grave social welfare system, Americans saw a greater need to set aside funds for these life events and risks. In contrast to West Germans, American consumers did not view saving for consumer goods as an attractive alternative to obtaining them through consumer debt.

Fast forward to the late 1990s and early 2000s and research in the field of comparative indebtedness and consumer bankruptcy law. Although both overindebtedness and personal bankruptcies were on the rise on both sides of the Atlantic during the last decades of the twentieth century, Americans significantly outdid Europeans in both categories. The out-of-control consumer debt in the United States was less often the result of excessive spending on consumer goods and more often the result of "passive indebtedness" incurred in changed circumstances such as unemployment and sickness. Particularly significant were medical costs covered through payment plans and consumer credit cards. In other words, American household debt arose more frequently from the very rainy days that Americans once saved for than from lavish lifestyles.[3] These leading causes of consumer bankruptcy in the United States are still much less prevalent in Western Europe. Thus, these snapshots from the 1960s and the present suggest not only a strong interrelationship between consumer credit use and broader social policy, but also a peculiar side to the social practice of credit use in postwar America.

This chapter explores the larger social and political context in which consumer credit in the United States has been embedded. Credit stands, I argue, at the intersection of two powerful narratives in postwar American history. First, credit is instrumental to the story of growing consumer affluence and democratic access to the "American Dream."[4] Second, any research on credit and debt inevitably brings one to the seedy underbelly of America's affluent society and the comparatively circumscribed reach of the American welfare state. Both notions, that of America's affluent "consumer's republic" and that of the United States as the "welfare state laggard," are frequently seen as emblematic of recent American exceptionalism and provide powerful organizing principles for postwar historiography. Credit was central to both narratives, yet a closer look at its role within the fabric of postwar American society can also undermine or complicate the assumptions that inform them.

American policy makers came to conceive of providing credit access as an important social policy tool. This development is significant in two ways. First, considering various subsidies and government provisions for consumer credit, consumption financing has been one way in which recent scholarship has argued for revising the "welfare state laggard" thesis. The American state, the argument goes, simply provided for the welfare of its consumer citizens by different means. At the same time, the development of credit legislation speaks to the very real inequalities that continued to riddle American consumer society and, at times, even helped to create or perpetuate a precarious standard of living for millions of families that calls into question narratives of continuous growth in American affluence.

My goal here is not to relate yet another story of American "exceptionalism." American developments were in many ways neither unique nor outside the context of broader international and transnational developments of the time, as several essays in this volume illustrate. Still, the American story of consumer credit was and remains peculiar and does not lend itself to narratives of postwar homogenization or global convergence toward a uniform American model of consumption. From a comparative perspective, the American case is especially exceptional with regard to the social significance accorded to credit by American policy makers.[5]

Let me briefly outline what I mean when I speak of credit as a social policy. There are several dimensions to be considered regarding access to consumer credit and its role within the context of a welfare regime.

1. Credit access can (at least temporarily) substitute for other forms of income and thus allow access to both necessities of daily life as well as "consumer luxuries." In this form, credit as income can also serve as a "safety net" to bridge periods of unemployment or sickness—areas that also fall within the purview of the traditional social security state.
2. Credit access allows for "consumption smoothing" over the course of a life cycle, for example, by letting young families borrow against future income. Here, credit access can serve as a substitute for welfare state policies such as child or family allowances.
3. Credit can be an important tool in achieving some form of social mobility, for example, by allowing access to homeownership (and with it asset building and social status through emulative consumption) or higher education.

Although the social implications of credit in the first two areas were perhaps mostly incidental, the use of credit to promote social mobility has been a more direct aim of American social policy. It was for this reason, in particular, that credit has been awarded an especially important role in attempts to overcome long-standing structural inequalities in American society based on race, class, and gender.

Finally, consumer credit—here broadly conceived to include revolving retail credit, as well as residential mortgages and student loans—blurs the line between the realm of private consumption in the marketplace and public consumption often relegated to the welfare state. Housing, for example, can be provided through private developers or public entities, and transportation can be provided by a 1957 Chevy or the municipal transit system. To the individual household, rent or mortgage payments and trolley fares or car loan payments are equally consumption expenditures. The postwar American emphasis on fostering various forms of consumer credit has favored market-type consumption over publicly provided consumption and has had a significant impact on the balance between private and public spending in America's affluent society.[6]

Questioning the "Welfare State Laggard" Narrative: Credit Policy and Social Mobility

Studying the development of various forms of consumer credit since the postwar years contributes to recent scholarly efforts that have questioned the long-prevailing paradigm of the United States as a "laggard" in welfare state development. Newer scholarship tends to look beyond direct or redistributive social spending and favors a broader understanding of welfare state regimes, to employ Gøsta Esping-Andersen's term.[7] Political scientist Christopher Howard, for example, has long argued that the American welfare state was effectively bigger than commonly perceived by pointing to a vast array of tax breaks and government subsidies that propped up—among other things—a sizable chunk of private, employment-related welfare spending.[8] Government guarantees for consumer loans and expanded access to credit lines, one can argue, were part of an American welfare state regime that did not develop along traditional "European" lines.

In many ways, the New Deal of the 1930s was a watershed moment for the development of the American welfare state in general as well as for credit-based social policies in particular. There were precursors, to be sure. Making safe, nonpredatory credit available to low-income consumers had been a central issue for many progressive activists since the last decade of the nineteenth century, as societal attitudes toward borrowing became increasingly more accepting.[9] Battling the evils of loan sharks and predatory salary lenders in American cities during the Progressive Era, the Russell Sage Foundation pushed for the abolition of outdated usury laws. Eventually, the adoption of Uniform Small Loans Laws by state legislatures created a safe and legal market for small personal loans. Edward Filene and the Twentieth Century Fund similarly fought for the spread of credit unions to allow low-income households access to safe credit.[10]

In the context of the New Deal, credit access became even more central to progressive politics during the 1930s and 1940s. Lizabeth Cohen has traced the birth of America's postwar consumers' republic to the politically charged decades following the Great Depression, and Kathleen Donohue has shown how American liberalism had come to embrace mass consumption as a central tenet of progressive politics by the Roosevelt era.[11] Credit financing would come to play a special role in New Deal liberalism's approaches to consumer policy. The lessons of the Great Depression, which saw surprisingly low default rates, appeared to suggest that consumer credit was "safe" from a macroeconomic perspective and, therefore, a viable tool for expanding purchasing power and mass demand under an emerging Keynesian policy paradigm.[12]

The increasingly favorable view of consumer debt was partly rooted in a diminishing association of debt with financial distress. Influential economist Rolf Nugent—who had also worked on the credit reform efforts of the Russell Sage Foundation—made a distinction between "deficit financing" and "capital financing" in conceptualizing consumer credit. Deficit financing, he argued, was true debt, because it meant consumers expanded their relative expenditures for consumption and thus their household liabilities without a compensatory increase in their assets. Capital financing, on the other hand, referred to the credit financing of goods such as household durables that tended to offset the additional liabilities incurred over time.[13] Several public social programs instituted with the New Deal had helped to decrease the need for "deficit financing," Nugent contended, and now an expansion of consumer's "capital financing" could be expected.[14] Promoting access to credit thus became a "progressive" means to help a broadening American middle class acquire homes and other capital assets.

The New Deal federal government worked to promote consumer access to credit in several areas. Title I of the 1935 National Housing Act, for example, provided for affordable loans for home modernization. The Electric Home and Farm Administration similarly promoted the purchase of electric household durables on installment credit. Such policies paved the way for a postwar era in which the Federal Housing Administration (FHA) and the Veterans Administration (VA) promoted mass homeownership by guaranteeing millions of inexpensive mortgages and the Federal National Mortgage Association (FNMA) stabilized the secondary mortgage market to ensure mortgage availability. Historian Ronald Tobey has thus called the 1930s a major caesura in the shift from a savings- to a debt-based consumer society.[15]

The early 1940s saw an even more explicit shift to Keynesian purchasing power approaches. Economist Alvin Hansen, at times referred to as the American Keynes, was a key figure in developing the idea of a dynamic economy growing through expanded private consumption (and compensatory government spending). His 1942 *After the War—Full Employment* emphasized the need for a "positive program of postwar economic expansion and full employment."[16] Pent-up demand and increased productive capacities would require a high level of postwar purchasing power. To overcome the postwar "gap" caused by the reconversion from military to civilian consumption, he proposed expanded consumer credit as one key component among several other measures such as increased wages, the liquidation of wartime savings, the reduction of excise taxes, as well as enlarged federal transfer payments. In contrast to France and West Germany, for example, the need for reconstruction capital and consumer savings was relatively low after the war. Indeed, credit policy became an integral part of American "growth liberalism" from the 1940s to the 1960s and part of a set of policies that aimed to promote economic growth and expand mass purchasing power.[17]

The initiatives of the 1930s and early 1940s came to full fruition after World War II. Expanding opportunities for consumer and mortgage credit had aided economic recovery and become a huge factor in expanding private consumption in the postwar decades. Low interest rates were a vital monetary tool in the postwar arsenal of macroeconomic steering, involving several federal agencies. In 1947, Alvin Hansen summarized the social and economic impetus behind such policies as follows: "A low rate of interest tends toward a more equal distribution of income and a higher consumption economy."[18] Particularly under the leadership of Leon Keyserling, the newly created Council of Economic Advisers (CEA) similarly advanced an ideology of "purchasing power" as a framework for social and economic policy. By 1949, the CEA felt that the U.S. economy had shown its potential for growth and that "efforts to promote expansion of the total production and income are more significant than measures to 'redistribute' the current product."[19] Easy credit was a central element of this growth strategy under the purchasing power paradigm, and expanded access to credit rather than direct redistribution became a preferred social policy tool in the postwar era.

By the 1950s, consumer credit had not only attained a sense of respectability in public perception, but it was contrasted with the poverty and backwardness associated with the Depression era. Consumer credit promised a new suburban lifestyle with ranch houses and automobiles for (nearly) everybody. The power of this image of credit as the great "democratizer" and its employment by pro-business interests became clear in the vehement opposition to Regulation W credit restrictions on loan lengths and minimum down payments during the late 1940s and early 1950s.[20] Although Regulation W merely aimed at smoothing temporary cyclical swings, it came under heavy criticism from various sides. Commerce organizations, such as the National Retail Dry Goods Association and the National Retail Credit Institute, as well as banks, attacked the regulatory efforts as an affront to the notion of consumer credit as democratic access to the American Dream. Alfred Dietz, President of the CIT Financial Corporation explained that— if unregulated—"consumer credit will enable millions of families in lower income brackets to satisfy their needs for new products as these become available."[21] Other critics called Regulation W a "gross discrimination among the American people, dividing them according to the size of their pocket books and excluding millions from access to the American products which they need and to which they have a right . . . ."[22]

Especially the credit industry increasingly framed consumer credit as central to an "American standard of living." As economist Clyde Phelps summarized, installment buying is "one of the significant factors which influence the American standard of living, level of living, and plane of consumption, which are, in material terms, quantitatively the highest in the world."[23] The charge that credit regulation was discriminatory because it effectively raised the price of credit reverberated with unions as well. In 1952, during the reinstatement of credit restrictions due to the Korean War, CIO Secretary-Treasurer James Carey told the House Banking and Currency Committee that curbs on installment buying "discriminate against small wage-earners."[24] Some observers at the time likened proponents of expanded consumer credit (ironically often banks and financial institutions) to the populists and Greenbacks of the late nineteenth century in their fight for a looser money supply.[25]

It is no surprise, then, that provisions propping up consumer credit featured prominently among those postwar policies that Chris Howard has termed "America's hidden welfare state." Tax deductions—although less visible than direct governmental social spending—represented a substantial area of government spending in the United States. Until 1986, the U.S. tax code allowed for the deduction of interest payments on consumer credit (including credit cards).[26] Interest on mortgage debt was similarly deductible in many instances, making household debt significantly more affordable and providing a tremendous subsidy for attaining homeownership. The most important and well-known aspect of indirect public funding during the postwar years, of course, were those federal subsidies for purchasing a home. Millions of mortgages were made affordable by mortgage guarantee programs through the FHA and the VA, as well as through the operation of the FNMA in the secondary mortgage market as standard repayment periods were extended from twenty-five to thirty years.[27]

In further areas, too, credit access served as an alternative to other forms of social spending to provide opportunities for mobility. The Higher Education Act of 1965 remains a watershed for higher education in the United States and provided federal financial aid directly to students through Educational Opportunity Grants to poor students and subsidized loans to lower-middle-class students. The number of students eligible for subsidized student loans grew significantly during the 1970s, and the 1978 Middle Income Student Assistance Act (MISAA) eliminated means-testing and vastly expanded access to the Stafford loans program. Loans thus became a central aspect of higher education in the United States in ways that remain uncommon in Western nations to this day.[28]

Such policies should be included in any consideration of postwar American social spending, which was more extensive than frequently recognized. This social policy regime, however, was ultimately skewed toward middle-class consumers and their consumption patterns.[29] Furthermore, in its emphasis on providing loans for homeownership or easy credit terms for car loans rather than the provision of public housing or public transportation, it contributed to postwar America's overall preference for private over public consumption. A few critical voices such as John Kenneth Galbraith did ask if "the bill collector [should be] the central figure in the good society."[30] For the most part, however, Americans of all stripes tended to see credit as the great democratizer during the postwar decades, provided it was considered safe. Paternalistic concerns voiced by government officials and social elites about the use of credit—as was still common, for example, in Germany or France at the time—were largely absent in the American case.[31] Instead, progressive advocates by the 1960s and 1970s increasingly worried about overcoming obstacles to credit access faced by women and minority groups as part of a larger agenda of social inclusion. Yet, the inherent precariousness of credit-based elements in the American welfare regime would become increasingly obvious by the last quarter of the twentieth century as the postwar economic boom faded.

Questioning the "Affluent Society" Narrative: Access Inequalities and the Return of "Deficit Financing"

An examination of postwar credit policies in America's "affluent society" complicates narratives of democratic access to the American Dream and throws continuing inequalities of postwar America's consumer society into sharp relief, as Lizabeth Cohen has so emphatically pointed out. The last quarter of the past century saw various legislative efforts to combat such social discrimination and, indeed, access to credit soared to ever new heights. At the same time, however, a dramatic rise in personal bankruptcies and the resurgence of "deficit credit" underscored the precariousness and unevenness of this path to affluence.[32]

As Lawrence Bowdish discusses in chapter 5 of this volume, one significant area of credit discrimination was demarcated by gender. Women—especially if they were married, widowed, or divorced—faced numerous obstacles to obtaining credit. The 1974 Equal Credit Opportunity Act (ECOA) aimed to prevent discrimination in the credit market and was originally intended to battle discrimination solely on the basis of gender. Later amendments, however, came to include race, age, and income from public programs. The legislation recognized that access to credit during the postwar decades had been far from equal for many groups in spite of the democratic rhetoric of credit proponents.[33] By the 1970s, credit had come to be regarded as a democratic right for all American consumers and, tamed by state and federal legislation, a key to achieving the middle-class consumer lifestyle of the postwar decades.

Racial discrimination especially limited credit access in the area of mortgage lending in the postwar era. For some time, FHA policies even supported so-called redlining practices, which effectively excluded many minority neighborhoods from access to loans. With other forms of consumer credit as well, place of residence—for example, the zip code of a predominantly African American neighborhood—could impact loan approval or conditions.[34] The 1977 Community Reinvestment Act (CRA) was one effort to remedy discriminatory lending practices. The act required deposit-taking banks to extend loans in all the neighborhoods of the communities in which they maintained branches. While many of the act's provisions have become outdated in today's world of specialized interstate mortgage lending, the CRA achieved some success in providing minority neighborhoods with access to loans.[35]

Although discrimination on the basis of race and gender frequently barred well-qualified consumers from access to credit, efforts to extend credit to low-income consumers proved even more difficult and problematic. During the late 1960s, the disadvantages faced by poor consumers in accessing credit had been the subject of Federal Trade Commission studies. With regard to credit, "the poor paid more," as sociologist David Caplovitz found, and social activists fought for credit as a basic right.[36] In Washington, D.C., for example, Kann's Department Store teamed up with the United Planning Association in 1969 to provide $50 in credit to 500 poor consumers, half of whom were welfare recipients. Nationwide, the National Welfare Rights Organization started a campaign to compel Sears department stores to extend $150 credit lines to welfare families.[37] Such efforts to open up credit access to underprivileged consumers culminated in a 1982 ECOA amendment that prohibited discrimination based on income from a public assistance program. Credit providers began to issue "secured credit cards" to help consumers with "damaged" credit improve their credit record. By the 1980s, however, a changed calculus on the banks' part also helped the expansion of credit to low-income consumers who had previously not enjoyed full access to lines of consumer credit.

Finally, a 1978 bankruptcy reform act made the accumulation of consumer debt considerably less risky for consumer households. Not only did the act remove many sanctions (making it more difficult, for example, to garnish wages), but it also rejected the "moralization of failure for the consumer debtor."[38] Although bankruptcy remains a definite burden on consumer households and jeopardizes future access to credit (especially after changes in the law in 2005[39]), the law provided for the possibility of a "fresh start" by establishing either a "clean slate" (Chapter 7 bankruptcy) or a schedule of monthly payments (Chapter 13 bankruptcy) under less stringent conditions (for example, allowing for the retention of some home equity or an auto-mobile). In combination with the subsequent deregulation of credit markets, the stage was set for a further expansion of consumer credit since the 1980s. Some, like Federal Reserve Board member Mark Olson, hailed this expansion in access as the ultimate "democratization" of credit, whereas to others it represented the precariousness and increasing inequality of America's affluent society.[40]

To be sure, the post-1980s credit expansion was not simply a result of legislative efforts, but coincided with a "supply-side revolution" in consumer lending that drew on a number of factors. The deregulation of financial services began with the 1978 Marquette ruling, by which the Supreme Court effectively eliminated state usury levels on unsecured loans. Mortgage rates were affected by the Depository Institutions Deregulations Act of 1980.[41] At the same time, advances in credit scoring models enabled automated approval processes.[42] The same innovations that would ultimately allow for the emergence of a subprime sector in mortgage lending also made risk-based pricing of other forms of consumer credit possible.[43] Whereas credit applicants deemed "unqualified" had once been screened out, new models now allowed for "razor sharp segmentation games... [and] *credit control-by-risk* characterized by a segmented accommodation of varying credit qualities," as financial sociologist Martha Poon puts it.[44] At the same time, the availability of general-purpose credit cards grew during the 1980s, reaching ever new segments of society: first lower-middle-class and working-class consumers, then college students and the elderly, and finally the working poor and the recently bankrupt. The underlying rate differentials inherent in risked-based pricing ironically often meant that less well-off "revolving debtors" now subsidized the credit card use of wealthy "convenience users."[45]

The economic growth of the 1990s was uneven. Although credit-financed consumption soared, an increasing number of households found themselves at the brink of financial collapse. By the middle of the decade, expanded debt and a declining savings rate had deprived many American consumer households of the savings that had once protected them on rainy days.[46] In 1996, the national savings rate was negative for the first time during the postwar era. At the same time, changes in the labor market left more and more Americans unprotected by the traditional safety net of America's welfare regime. A "fringe banking" sector emerged that catered to the credit needs of a growing segment of American society that once again borrowed out of destitution and that had exhausted more traditional sources of credit. Pawnbroking experienced a renaissance from the 1980s, particularly in inner-city, minority neighborhoods that commercial banks had successively abandoned. Pawn chains such as EZ Pawn, Pawn Mart, and Cash America once again operated as the "poor man's banks"; the number of outlets grew from 6,900 in 1988 to about 13,000 in 1998, proliferating especially in Hispanic and African American neighborhoods.[47] Auto-title lenders and payday lending chains reemerged and have seen even more astounding increases in their business, particularly among low-income consumers. Although they were virtually nonexistent in 1990, 12,000 to 14,000 outlets gave cash advances on paychecks by 2001, often at exorbitant interest rates.[48] Most of these loans constituted "deficit" and not "capital financing," to recall Rolf Nugent's 1930s distinction. This observation is underscored by the rise in personal bankruptcy filings from 350,000 in 1985 to 1,400,000 in 1998.[49]

As inequalities in America's affluent society have grown in recent decades, credit has served as a means to compensate for limited social security.[50] Credit cards are routinely used to temporarily make up for lost income in times of unemployment. Skyrocketing medical bills are a significant contributing factor to bankruptcy filings. In 2007, 41 percent of the adult American population (ages nineteen to sixty-four) reported they had accrued debt because of medical expenses, and 28 percent were currently paying off medical bills. These problems were especially prevalent among the un- and underinsured, and as many as 33 percent of those with bill problems were using general-purpose credit cards to cover at least some of the expenses.[51] Credit card use has similarly expanded to cover the growing expenses attached to college education. In 2006, one study found 71 percent of college students using credit cards to cover parts of the average $6,000 gap between financial aid and actual college expenses. Although much of this usage concerned textbooks and living expenses, according to the National Association of Student Financial Aid Administrators (NASFAA), nearly a quarter (24 percent) of students charged part of their tuition on credit cards.[52]

In light of such numbers, some legal scholars have argued for the need to reassess credit contracts in a society in which "consumer credit contracts are not risk-taking gambles in the commodity market but often a method of attaining the 'standard package' of consumer goods and services." This circumstance, they argue, raises the question of whether household and consumer goods should be protected from seizure and sale. Such arguments further call for "consumer welfarism" as an organizing framework for credit contract law. Future bankruptcy reform, comparative legal scholar Iain Ramsay has suggested, should include the principle of "social force majeure." Cases of unemployment, illness, and so on should fall under the general pillars of the welfare state by "providing a legal entitlement to reschedule payment of debts."[53] Instead, however, U.S. bankruptcy law has long since barred the discharge of student loans and has recently seen efforts come to naught that would have excluded medical debt from tightened bankruptcy provisions.[54]

Conclusion: The American Credit Model in Transatlantic Perspective

In many ways, the expansion of consumer credit in the United States in the postwar era and especially in recent decades is emblematic for an American consumer society that economist Avner Offer has described as characterized by high levels of inequality and risk that are offset in some ways by equally high levels of consumption.[55] Credit access as a social policy has served to expand the possibilities of material consumption for many Americans. Public policies subsidizing credit and battling credit discrimination have contributed to some degree to this expansion, which became a hallmark of the American welfare regime, broadly conceived. At the same time, credit expansion has kept millions of consumer households in a precarious situation that belies the promise of steadily increasing affluence long made by optimistic credit advocates. With the end of the boom era, the absence of a well-developed traditional social security state has forced many Americans once again to fall back on various forms of consumer credit as a safety net to cover their rainy-day deficits.[56]

Transatlantic comparisons serve to highlight the peculiarity of the American approach. Europeans have added to their consumer debt burdens, too, but Americans still take on considerably more liabilities. In 2007, consumer debt accounted for 25 percent of disposable income in the United States, as opposed to only 16.2 percent in Germany.[57] In many ways, this is less a consequence of differences in cultural attitudes toward consumer debt and consumption and more one of incentives given to households. The U.S. credit industry has certainly been particularly aggressive in tempting consumers to take on ever more debt, and financial deregulation has spurred on their efforts.

Still, it would be one-sided to overlook the progressive intentions that overlapped with free-market policies to make the American case unique. From the FNMA to the ECOA and the CRA, U.S. policies toward consumer credit were driven in part by progressive hopes for social democratization. Expanding access to credit proved politically less controversial than some of its alternatives. Rather than redistributive spending, public services, or extensive social safety nets, consumer credit provided opportunities for social mobility and a safety net in case of a rainy day. The underlying premise, of course, was that the rainy day would be the exception and continuous growth the norm. Herein lies the dilemma of the American social model of postwar "growth liberalism." Debt-financed consumption has become central to its continued viability; however, at the same time, it poses a fundamental threat to the system, as the recent mortgage crisis so painfully underscored.[58]

To many European observers, the American credit model has lost some of its luster in recent decades.[59] Whereas American credit institutions symbolized modern consumer prosperity to many if not all Europeans in the 1950s and 1960s, the explosion of consumer debt and the fringe banking institutions that came with it exposed aspects that certainly ran counter to European social models. On issues such as bankruptcy law reform, the American model may yet have a few lessons to teach Europeans. Overall, however, consumer credit is one area in which the limits of postwar convergence or "Americanization" appear especially palpable.

Notes

1. George Katona, Burkhart Strumpel, and Ernest Zahn, *Aspirations and Affluence: Comparative Studies in the United States and Western Europe* (New York, 1971), 3.
2. University of Michigan Survey Research Center, "Surveys of Consumer Finances," cited in ibid., 97–98.
3. On "passive indebtedness" as a leading cause for bankruptcy in the United States, see, for example, Elizabeth Warren and Amelia Warren Tyagi, *The Two-Income Trap: Why Middle-Class Mothers and Fathers Are Going Broke* (New York, 2003), which criticizes the overconsumption thesis.
4. For a critique of the triumphalist narrative of credit as the great "democratizer," see Lendol Calder, "The Evolution of Credit in the United States," in *The Impact of Public Policy on Consumer Credit,* ed. Thomas Durkin and Michael Staten (Boston, MA, 2002), 23–34. Calder similarly rejects cultural jeremiads that decry the expansion of consumer credit as a decline in thrift; instead he emphasizes the social disciplining nature of increased credit obligations.
5. On the shifting policy coalitions supporting expanded consumer credit, see chapter 7 in this volume by Gunnar Trumbull.
6. On transatlantic differences in the significance of private and public consumption, see Jan Logemann, "Is It in the Interest of the Consumer to Pay Taxes? Transatlantic Differences in Postwar Approaches to Public Consumption," *Journal of Consumer Culture* 11 (2011): 339–65. For historical context on the broader transatlantic contrast in social models, see, for example, Avner Offer, *The Challenge of Affluence: Self-Control and Well-Being in the United States and Britain since 1950* (Oxford, UK, 2006); and Tony Judt, *Postwar: A History of Europe since 1945* (New York, 2005). A recent comparative study on the development of the welfare state in Germany and the United States: Marcus Gräser, *Wohlfahrtsgesellschaft und Wohlfahrtsstaat: Bürgerliche Gesellschaft und Welfare State Building in den USA und in Deutschland 1880–1940* (Göttingen, 2009).

7. On the notion of welfare regimes, see Gøsta Esping-Andersen, *The Three Worlds of Welfare Capitalism* (Princeton, NJ, 1990).

8. See, for example, Christopher Howard, "Is the American Welfare State Unusually Small?," *Political Science and Politics* 36 (2003): 411–16.

9. On changing attitudes toward credit buying, see esp. Daniel Horowitz, *The Morality of Spending: Attitudes towards the Consumer Society in America, 1875–1940* (Baltimore, MD, 1985); and Lendol Calder, *Financing the American Dream: A Cultural History of Consumer Credit* (Princeton, NJ, 1999). For the spread of consumer credit during the interwar years, see also Martha Olney, *Buy Now, Pay Later: Advertising, Credit, and Consumer Durables in the 1920s* (Chapel Hill, NC, 1991).

10. On the campaigns against loan sharks and for the introduction of small loans banks, see Michael Easterly, "Your Job Is Your Credit: Creating a Market for Loans to Salaried Employees in New York City, 1985–1920," *Enterprise & Society* 10 (2009): 651–60; and Bruce Carruthers, Timothy Guinnane, and Yoonseok Lee, "Bringing 'Honest Capital' to Poor Borrowers: The Passage of the Uniform Small Loan Law, 1907–1930," Yale Economics Department Working Paper 63 and Yale University Economic Growth Center Discussion Paper 971, June 3, 2009.

11. Lizabeth Cohen, *A Consumer's Republic: The Politics of Mass Consumption in Postwar America* (New York, 2003); Kathleen Donohue, *Freedom from Want: American Liberalism and the Idea of the Consumer* (Baltimore, MD, 2003).

12. See, for example, "Business and Finance: Mass Credit," *Time*, August 31, 1931: "no inhalation has come about; installment selling has withstood Depression well." On the limited number of defaults (and the problematic economic consequences that this entailed), see also Martha Olney, "Avoiding Default: The Role of Credit in the Consumption Collapse of 1930," *Quarterly Journal of Economics* 114 (1999): 319–35.

13. Rolf Nugent, *Consumer Credit and Economic Stability* (New York, 1939), 122.

14. Ibid., 138 and 238.

15. See Ronald Tobey, *Technology as Freedom: The New Deal and the Electrical Modernization of the American Home* (Berkeley, CA, 1996). On credit expansion during the New Deal, see also Jordan Schwarz, *The New Dealers: Power Politics in the Age of Roosevelt* (New York, 1993), esp. 235.

16. Alvin Hansen, *After the War—Full Employment* (Washington, D.C., 1942), 1.

17. On the notion of "growth liberalism," see Robert Collins, *More: The Politics of Economic Growth in Postwar America* (Oxford, UK, 2000).

18. Alvin Hansen, *Economic Policy and Full Employment* (New York, 1947), 131.

19. Council of Economic Advisers, *Business and Government: Fourth Annual Report to the President* (Washington, D.C., 1949), 6.

20. This Federal Reserve policy, born in response to wartime circumstances, was employed into the early 1950s as a Keynesian tool to achieve economic stability by temporarily restricting access to consumer credit by means of controlling minimum down payments, interest rates, and maturity rates. Regulation W, it

should be noted, was by and large not an attack on the institution of consumer credit itself. The ability of consumer credit to increase mass purchasing power and spur aggregate domestic demand was always acknowledged, as was its ability to boost domestic durable goods consumption during peacetime conversion. On Regulation W, see Irving Michelman, *Consumer Finance: A Case History in American Business* (New York, 1966), 256–77.

21. "Consumer Credit Expected to Rise," *New York Times,* January 2, 1947, 46.

22. "Credit Curb Eased for Home Repairs," *New York Times,* September 26, 1945, 29. Even though little empirical evidence could be mustered to prove that regulation of credit terms actually crowded out potential low-income buyers, critics such as Milton Friedman largely succeeded in likening Regulation W to an arbitrary and discriminatory tax conceived by elitist administrators. See Milton Friedmann, "Speech Published in Symposium on Consumer Credit and Consumer Spending," *University of Pennsylvania Bulletin* 57 (1957): 67.

23. Clyde Phelps, *Financing the Installment Purchases of the American Family* (Baltimore, MD, 1954): 29–31. The same argument was made by CIT Financial Corporation president Arthur Dietz, "Die 36-Milliarden Dollar-Frage: Die Bedeutung des Teilzahlungskredites in amerikanischer Sicht," in *Schriftenreihe des Wirtschaftsverbandes Teilzahlungsbanken e.V.* 7 (Dortmund, 1956), translation of speech in English given by Dietz on April 6, 1956.

24. "CIO for Ending Time Buying Curbs," *New York Times,* May 7, 1952, 14.

25. "The Great Credit Debate," *Time,* January 30, 1956.

26. Richard Brown and Susan Burhouse, "Implications of the Supply-Side Revolution in Consumer Lending," *Saint Louis University Public Law Review* 363 (2005): 363–99. As these deductions were phased out after 1986, home equity loans (which were exempt from the reform) became the financial product of choice for tax-subsidized debt. See "Playing the New Tax Game," *Time,* October 13, 1986.

27. See Charles Haar, *Federal Credit and Private Housing: The Mass Financing Dilemma* (New York, 1960) for a more detailed discussion. Taking the *Survey of Consumer Finances* as his basis, economist Paul Merz estimated that personal deductions for housing expenses amounted to well over 1 billion dollars in 1954 alone and closer to 3 billion annually by the late 1950s—a substantial number if one considers that total income tax revenue in 1954 amounted to $29.5 billion and federal outlays to individuals (mostly Social Security) $12.6 billion. See U.S. Office of Management and Budget, Budget of the United States Government, Historical Tables, http://www.whitehouse.gov/omb/budget/Historicals, tables 2.1 (Receipts by Source) and 11.3 (Outlays for Payments for Individuals).

28. On the development of student lending, see Patricia Somers, James Hollis, and Tim Stokes, "The Federal Government as First Creditor in Student Loans: Politics and Policy," *Educational Evaluation and Policy Analysis* 22 (2000): 331–39.

29. Preferential treatment to home owners amounted to discrimination against those who were compelled to rent, as economist Paul Merz pointed out. It also skewed the equity of the personal income tax as middle- and upper-income groups were the main beneficiaries of these tax subsidies. See Paul Merz, "The Income Tax Treatment of Owner-Occupied Housing," *Land Economics* 41 (1965): 247–55.

30. John Galbraith, *The Affluent Society* (Boston, MA, 1958).

31. This is not to say that paternalist rhetoric was completely absent from the American discourse. One example was a 1968 *New York Times* essay that addressed the problems of an overspent American middle class in medicalized terms and linked buying on credit to addictive behavior: "For those with severe compulsion to buy unneeded items, an investment in medical advice has often been worthwhile . . . Many [companies] find that their credit drunks have wives who drink and gamble or are unstable." The cure for such "credit drunks": "the magic words . . . 'we can't afford it' . . . Not only has this been known to convert debts into healthy bank balances, but it has also helped breadwinners cure other problems, including neurotic wives and children." H. J. Maidenberg, "Personal Finance: Credit Drunk," *New York Times,* July 18, 1968, 47 and 52. Although the author's prescription may have been somewhat tongue-in-cheek (one hopes), it certainly reflected the predominant gender biases during the postwar decades.

32. For a recent survey of postwar credit developments in the United States that emphasizes the growing risks for consumers, see Andrea Ryan, Gunnar Trumbull, and Peter Tufano, "A Brief History of U.S. Consumer Finance," *Business History Review* 85 (2011): 461–98.

33. On the debate surrounding the ECOA, see, for example, "Credit Where Credit Is Due—Without Sex Bias," *Los Angeles Times,* May 15, 1974, and Eileen Shanahan, "U.S. Issues Tighter Rules to Outlaw Bias in Credit," *New York Times,* October 17, 1975, 1. See also Cohen, *Consumer's Republic,* 369–70.

34. See, for example, "Feds Ban on Racial data on Credit Application Hits," *Washington Post,* August 13, 1976, and Nancy Ross, "Minority Applicants, Single Men Facing Discrimination by Lender," *Washington Post,* June 14, 1980, E1. Racial biases remained pronounced in automobile financing, as lawsuits reveal: Diana Henriques, "New Front Opens in Effort to Fight Race Bias in Loans," *New York Times,* October 22, 2000, 1. On credit discrimination in an urban context and legislatives efforts to remedy these problems, see Dan Immergluck, *Credit to the Community: Community Reinvestment and Fair Lending Policy in the United States* (New York, 2004).

35. On increases in lending to minorities (despite continuing inequalities) and the difficulty of ascertaining the role of the CRA and similar legislation (such as the Home Mortgage Disclosure Act of 1975) in these changes, see Rapahel Bostic, "Trends in Equal Access to Credit Products," in *The Impact of Public Policy on Consumer Credit,* ed. Thomas Durkin and Michael Staten (Boston, MA, 2002), 171–203. On the CRA, see also William Apgar and Mark Duda, "The Twenty-Fifth Anniversary of the Community Reinvestment Act: Past Accomplishments and Future Regulatory Challenges," *FRBNY Economic Policy Review*

9 (June 2003): 169–91; and Therese Wilson, "Responsible Lending or Restrictive Lending Practices? Balancing Concerns Regarding Over-Indebtedness with Addressing Financial Exclusion," in *The Future of Consumer Credit Regulation: Creative Approaches to Emerging Problems,* ed. Michelle Kelly-Louw, James P. Nehf, and Peter Rott (Aldershot, 2008), 91–106.

36. David Caplovitz, "Consumer Credit in the Affluent Society," *Law and Contemporary Problems* 33 (1968): 641–55.

37. Robert Samuelson, "Common Purpose: Extending Retail Credit to the Poor," *Washington Post,* July 6, 1969, 85. On the Sears campaign, see also Cohen, *Consumers Republic,* 382–83, and esp. Felicia Ann Kornbluh, *The Battle for Welfare Rights: Politics and Poverty in Modern America* (Philadelphia, PA, 2007), chap. 5.

38. See Iain Ramsay, "Comparative Consumer Bankruptcy," *Illinois Law Review,* no. 1 (2007): 241–74. At the same time, separate legislation such as the Fair Debt Collection Practices Act of 1978 limited some of the more abusive practices of collection agencies.

39. Matt Olson, "Medical Debtors to the Poorhouse," *The Progressive* 65, no. 7 (July 2001): 30.

40. Federal Reserve Board member Mark Olson noted in a 2003 speech that "one result of the ongoing financial-market changes [including deregulation, low interest rates and increased competition] has been the democratization of credit.... Notably, the strongest growth in the proportion of families having any debt occurred in the lowest two quintiles of income distribution." To Olson, this was not a sign for concern but encouragement: "the benefits that the democratization of credit have conveyed can...be seen by looking at the growth of consumers' holding of non-monetary assets, including homes, automobiles and business." Mark Olson, "Increased Availability of Financial Products and the Need for Improved Financial Literacy," Speech at the America's Community Bankers 2003 National Compliance and Attorney's Conference and Marketplace, San Antonio, TX, September 22, 2003, http://www.federalreserve.gov/boarddocs/speeches/2003/20030922/default.htm.

41. See Brown and Burhouse, "Implications," 381.

42. The FICO score used for many automatic underwriting processes is based on the Fair Isaac & Co. model for generating scores via a combination of repayment history (25%), usage of available credit lines (30%), length of credit history (15%), types of credit used (10%), and usage pattern (10%). See ibid.

43. On this shift, particularly in the mortgage market, see Martha Poon, "From New Deal Institutions to Capital Markets: Commercial Consumer Risk Scores and the Making of Sub-Prime Mortgage Finance," *Accounting, Organizations and Society* 34 (2009): 654–74.

44. Ibid., 659.

45. Robert Manning, *Credit Card Nation: The Consequences of America's Addiction to Credit* (New York, 2000), esp., 11, 21–22 and 161–63. On the generation and recruitment of debt "revolvers," see also Brett Williams, *Debt for Sale: A Social*

History of the Credit Trap (Philadelphia, PA, 2004), chap. 3, an academic exposé of the social consequences of the "supply-side revolution."

46. Notably, the traditionally rather optimistic coverage about credit developments developed an increasingly concerned tone during the 1980s, as credit problems more and more affected not "just" the poor but ever more "middle-class" households as well. Although there was a persistent tendency to blame increasing debt problems on relaxed bankruptcy regulations or the supposedly looser financial morals of a new, hedonistic generation that had never learned to save or defer gratification, attention was paid to underlying structural problems in the consumer finance market as well. See, for example, "The American Way of Debt," *Time,* May 31, 1982.

47. See Robert Johnson and Dixie Johnson, *Pawn-Broking in the U.S.: A Profile of Customers,* Credit Research Center, Georgetown University, 1998, http://faculty. msb.edu/prog/CRC/pdf/mono34.pdf. On the development of "fringe banking," see also Williams, *Debt for Sale,* chap. 5; and Manning, *Credit Card Nation,* chap. 7.

48. On the emergence of the industry and the prevalence of repeat borrowing, see Michael Stegman and Robert Faris, "Payday Lending: A Business Model that Encourages Chronic Borrowing," *Economic Development Quarterly* 17 (2003): 8–32.

49. Brown and Burhouse, "Implications," 363. By 1999, 50% of filers claimed health problems, childbirth, a death in the family, or medical bills as primary reasons for their bankruptcy, as opposed to only 11% three decades earlier. See Melissa Jacoby, Teresa Sullivan, and Elisabeth Warren, "Rethinking the Debates over Health Care Financing: Evidence from the Bankruptcy Courts," *New York University Law Review* 76 (2001): 375–418. On consumer bankruptcy in the United states generally, see also Teresa Sullivan, Elizabeth Warren, and Jay Westbrook, *As We Forgive Our Debtors: Bankruptcy and Consumer Credit in America* (Washington, D.C., 1999) and Teresa Sullivan, Elizabeth Warren, and Jay Lawrence Westbrook, *The Fragile Middle Class: Americans in Debt* (New Haven, CT, 2000). Charles Luckett, "Personal Bankruptcies," in *The Impact of Public Policy on Consumer Credit,* ed. Thomas Durkin and Michael Staten (Boston, MA, 2002), 69–102, summarizes the results of numerous studies conducted during the 1990s.

50. Although the notion of a "retrenchment" in American welfare state policies in recent decades is contentious in the scholarship, Jacob Hacker has suggested the term "policy drift" to capture the reality of an increasingly outdated welfare regime that relies on employment-based benefits in a fundamentally changing job market; see his "Privatizing Risk without Privatizing the Welfare State: The Hidden Politics of Social Policy Retrenchment in the United States," *American Political Science Review* 98 (2004): 243–60.

51. Michelle Doty et al., "Seeing Red: The Growing Burden of Medical Bills and Debt Faced by U.S. Families," *The Commonwealth Fund Issue Brief* 42, pub. 1164 (August 2008). The practice is not entirely a recent phenomenon, however;

many medical facilities began accepting charge cards as early as the 1960s. See "Credit: The Importance of Being in Debt," *Time,* October 30, 1964.

52. Angela McGlynn, "College on Credit Has Kids Dropping Out" *Hispanic Outlook in Higher Education* 16 (January 30, 2006): 26–27; Manning, *Credit Card Nation,* chap. 6.

53. Iain Ramsay, "Consumer Credit Law, Distributive Justice and the Welfare State," in *Oxford Journal of Legal Studies* 15 (1995): 177–97.

54. Olson, "Medical Debtors," 30.

55. Offer, *Challenge of Affluence.*

56. The recent economic crisis serves to highlight the financial inability of many households to avoid losing ground during tough times, instead frequently accruing high debt burdens and filing for bankruptcy. Bankruptcies were expected to reach a record 1.4 million in 2009. See, for example, Hibah Yousuf, "Personal Bankruptcies Surge 9%," CNN Money, November 4, 2009, http://money.cnn. com/2009/11/04/news/economy/October_consumer_bankruptcy/index.htm.

57. European Credit Research Institute data cited in Ramsay, "Comparative Consumer Bankruptcy." On transatlantic differences in household lending patterns, income-to-debt ratios, reasons for default, etc., see Nicola Jentzsch and Amparo San Jose Riestra, "Consumer Credit Markets in the United States and Europe," in *The Economics of Consumer Debt,* ed. Giuseppe Bertola, Richard Disney, and Charles Grant (Cambridge, MA, 2006), 27–62.

58. It has become commonplace in recent debates over consumption and credit to cite President George W. Bush's exhortation of Americans to keep spending and consuming after the terror attacks of September 11, 2001. The structural problem of an economy increasingly dependent on consumption-driven growth (even if that entailed growing deficits), however, dates back at least to the postwar decades and had been widely recognized as a fundamental problem during the "stagflation" period of the 1970s. See, for example, "Merchants of Debt," *Time,* February 28, 1977.

59. This, to be sure, is not universally true. The European Union has seen efforts over the past decade to cut regulations on consumer credit with proponents arguing for the economic growth potential of increased household debt. See, for example, Giuseppe Bertola, Richard Disney, and Charles Grant, "The Economics of Consumer Credit Demand and Supply, in *Economics of Consumer Debt,* ed. Bertola, Disney, and Grant, 1–26.

PART IV

Cultures of Credit

CHAPTER 10

Economic Agents and the Culture of Debt

Silke Meyer

It is during times of crisis that the economic system shows its other, incalculable, constructivist face. Terms such as "credit crunch," "credit binges," and "toxic loans" offer graphic descriptions of an ailing regime we no longer trust. Indeed, when banks and states go bankrupt, when anxious customers storm the branches to withdraw their money, and when millions of people face unemployment and homelessness, the notion of trust—or rather its loss—dominates newspaper discussions of the otherwise soberly presented ups and downs of the stock market, national debt levels, and currency exchange rates. Without trust, the global market and our daily banking routines cannot work, for money and the credit business are less matters of fact, less material and palpable, than we commonly assume. Economic markets are cultural and social constructions, and consumers act not only as economic agents, but also as cultural and social entities.

If credit relationships can thus be interpreted as constructions of "trust," the recent credit crisis can benefit from the perspective of an anthropologist as much as from that of an economist or policy analyst. The key contribution from an anthropological credit study is the focus on the market tool of consumer credit from the point of view of the economic agents involved. I begin this chapter by placing relationships of credit and debt within the framework of economic anthropology and economic history. Subsequently, I illustrate the topicality of the recent consumer credit crisis in Germany and elsewhere by utilizing statistical data from Schufa, the German credit reporting agency. I then explore the cultural logic of credit motivation and credit decisions in a case study. The collision of current developments in the market with this logic, that is, the high percentage of overindebted consumers, is briefly contextualized within the longer history of the culture of borrowing in Germany. Even if German consumers have been comparatively less prone to credit use and overindebtedness than their counterparts in some other areas of the world—as several contributions to this volume suggest—significant recent changes can be observed in the German case as well. My hypothesis is that credit follows not only an economic, but also a cultural logic, which plays an important role in the individual's decision making and credit behavior. Methodologically, my research is based on qualitative interviews with forty-five debtors and debt counsellors.[1] Proceeding from an agent-oriented perspective, I aim to arrive at an understanding of credit transactions as social and cultural practices.

In the context of an interdisciplinary volume, culture could be defined as the historical and discursive framework that channels collective and individual systems of perception and constructions of meaning. While the analytical category of "culture" encompasses collective patterns of orientation and interpretation, it also describes individual performances and practices. Culture contains frameworks for the construction of meanings through those practices, but individual practices shape cultural patterns at the same time by updating, innovating, and transforming them. Thus, culture is never a secluded and self-contained system but is characterised by variety, openness, and contingency.[2]

Economic Transactions and the Analysis of Culture

From an economic point of view, both partners in a credit transaction benefit from it: the debtor has money available at short notice, and the creditor receives monetary gain from the added interest. Prerequisite to the latter's gain, however, is trust in the debtor. For the creditor, trusting pays off in interest, and interest and the modalities of credit are subject to a contract that regulates the interaction and cooperation of the two partners. This concept of trust has been institutionalised by credit rating systems, so that the creditor has multiple ways of making sure of the partner's trustworthiness.[3] From the creditors' point of view, the agency determines the degree of trust in the debtor. From the debtors' point of view, however, the agency's role is merely a statistical mirror of consumer behavior, void of the motifs of need, intention, good will, cooperation, and individual circumstances.

Thus, economic agents act in two worlds simultaneously.[4] While they negotiate their choices and decisions within the principle of maximising their economic benefit, they also act within or against collective ideas of cooperation, sociality, and common welfare. Pierre Bourdieu captures this idea of simultaneity in his concept of a *general economy of practice*. The economic habitus as "conditioned and limited spontaneity" is the product of collective and individual history with a subjective system of preferences and tastes; as such, it in no way represents purely economic behavior but rather cultural behavior. The agent can be described as "a collective individual"[5] whose actions are guided by discourses and patterns of orientation, but who nevertheless finds room for—what might sometimes seem irrational—emotions, spontaneity, contingency, resistance, and wilfulness.[6]

Today, this perspective is common currency across many academic disciplines. The gap between the model of an ahistorical and universal *homo oeconomicus* and the idea of an individual whose decisions are shaped by the cultural specifics of its social environment has long been overcome. For the last ten years, approaches like the New Economic Criticism have provided a framework for interdisciplinary studies that successfully bridge the divide between culture and the economy.[7]

But how can cultural analysis help us understand the credit business? Maximizing strategies through cooperation can only be successful if the behavior of my partner or partners is predictable. This is where culture provides a crucial link: an anthropological concept of rational choice does not universally proclaim individual benefit as the best outcome, but instead focuses on individual decisions under specific conditions. A cultural theory of credit does not ask whether people maximize their benefit but, rather, how different forms of benefit are ranked and converted into each other individually and group-specifically. Maximizing is not a universal human strategy but becomes a cultural construction shaped by individual and collective histories. In other words, the *homo oeconomicus* is a *homo sociologicus* and a *homo culturalis* at the same time.[8]

Credit as Exchange Relation

Economic behavior as a social act is the seminal interpretation of economic transactions in anthropology. Following Marcel Mauss's key study, *The Gift* (1923–24), giving, taking, and reciprocating are elementary representations of a social order created by exchange. According to Mauss, if we want to understand a society, then we have to learn how to interpret its patterns of exchange, the key to which can be located in its understanding of the gift. Mauss describes the character of each gift, even if it appears selfless, voluntary, and spontaneous, as "constrained and self-interested."[9] The constraint lies in each received gift having to be reciprocated within a certain time limit. The more time that lies between giving and reciprocating, the higher the giver ranks the creditworthiness of the receiver.[10] If reciprocity is impossible for economic or social reasons and the exchange created debts, the process results in a social bond between the two relevant parties. These obligations turn the gift into a structural element that allows social ties to form over distance and outside a community of relatives and neighbors. Credit can be regarded economically as a gift with a countergift of repayment plus interest. Socially, credit is a gift of trust with the countergift of obligation, sometimes accompanied by gratitude and loyalty. The logic of credit as a gift highlights the character of loaned and borrowed money as social glue. Debts build relationships, and they help to determine one's position in society. Therefore, credit possesses cohesive power and creates networks of obligations.

Economic Markets and Social Networks: Historical Credit Culture

Credit as a network of obligation has long been the focus of economic history. Recent studies underline that both the economic benefit and the network character are leading principles for premodern and modern economies alike. This research reveals the coexistence of personal and institutional credit systems from the seventeenth to the twentieth centuries. Credit and debts retained their informal character parallel to the development of cooperatives and banks.[11] Historical research thus demonstrates a plurality of institutionalized and private credit sources, which means that the credit machinery was based on personal, as well as institutionalized, notions of trust (Niklas Luhmann), as Georg Fertig can show for the Westphalian country market. Although lawyers and contracts increased in importance throughout the nineteenth-century credit market, they did not eliminate private credit or loans with informal conditions based on the personal reputations of the debtors within their communities.[12]

Reputation was social and economic capital in historical credit cultures. With regard to prestige, standing, and symbolic capital, Craig Muldrew refutes Max Weber in his interpretation of the individual's market behavior as an expression of the spirit of capitalism. In the case of the early modern credit market at King's Lynn, Muldrew shows that all the guidebook advice given to tradesmen about diligence and frugality—for example, in Daniel Defoe's *The Complete English Tradesmen* (1727)—was not directed inward to the individual's beliefs but outward into the community with the aim of establishing a reputation. "What mattered was not an internalised or autonomous self, but the public perception of the self in relation to a communicated set of both personal and household virtues."[13]

Credit was nothing new in sixteenth-century society, as Muldrew freely admits. What was new, however, was the volume of transactions and the number of private consumers who used credit. The reason was the limited amount of paper money and coins in the face of a quickly growing desire to consume and thus an increasing number of transactions. When there was literally not enough money to buy commodities, one could always possess them on credit. And debts brought together all walks of life: the poor, as well as the rich, were drawn into credit relationships, city people and country people alike. Credit was a necessity, experienced throughout society, and thus it transformed society as a whole. Communities might have been divided by religion and politics, but they were united through a tight web of obligations by loaning and borrowing money. Because one could not survive without credit, people lived with an eye toward reputation, monitoring their own conduct and keeping up their social standing.

Other studies underscore this socially disciplining role of credit. Laurence Fontaine shows that, in the High Dauphiné region, credit relations extended for extremely long periods and in complex structures.[14] Many people were debtors and creditors at the same time, as can be seen in a Nuremberg broadsheet that shows "the death of credit." Credit is laid out in the middle of the marketplace and surrounded by distressed tradespeople, wringing their hands over what they will do without her. The same trades can be found in the booths and stores around the marketplace in the background of this illustration, this time in the role of creditors. "The death of credit" motif was widespread in Europe. Folklorist Adolf Spamer has collected Polish, English, French, and German examples that date back to the sixteenth century. His most recent examples, from the 1920s, are banners and pictures in the style of obituaries that announce the death of credit in taverns and bars (figures 10.1 and 10.2).[15]

Rather than paying back the money they borrowed, people maintained their debts in order to make sure of loyalties. On the one hand, creditors did not always demand payment in order to maintain their network of credit and reputation. On the other hand, even debtors did not always strive to become free of their obligations, as Margot Finn shows with the example of the painter Benjamin Haydon. Haydon, chronically in debt, was disappointed with his baker, who had deferred his bills but was now demanding his money: "This debt was for my baker's bill whom I had always promised to pay in my troubles out of the first sum of any amount I received. Does he thank me? Not he. He is just as likely, now that he is safe, to behave ill as a stranger."[16]

Owing money meant participating in a network of obligations, and repaying those debts amounted to canceling this membership. Reinhard Johler investigates the local community of St. Leonhard in Austria where, until the beginning of the twentieth century, all monetary transactions were undertaken on a specific day. On the first Monday of Lent, debtors and creditors

Figure 10.1   The death of credit, ca. 1925
Source: Estate Adolf Spamer, Institut für Sächsische Geschichte und Volkskunde, e.V., Dresden

Figure 10.2   Death announcement
"I hereby announce to all my customers, guests, and friends that my best friend credit just passed away. Therefore, I ask you all to kindly pay straightaway."
Source: Estate Adolf Spamer, Institut für Sächsische Geschichte und Volkskunde, e.V., Dresden.

came together on a bridge to settle their affairs. If a debtor was unable to pay, he still had to pay his dues by showing up. In many cases, the meeting was not about repaying the money and liquidating the debts. New deals were negotiated, and debts were passed on and exchanged. If a debtor failed to make an appearance, however, he lost his honor within the community and could no longer rely on obtaining credit in this region. The local newspaper *Burggräfler* described conditions in 1890: "A debtor who does not come to St. Leonhard on this day loses his creditworthiness not only with his creditors but in the entire valley. . . . If he cannot pay, the creditors are willing, in neighborly fashion, to make new arrangements, but everyone with an obligation must come."[17] Historical studies agree on one aspect: while the credit system witnessed a process of professionalization with the establishment of banks, the spread of cooperatives, and the increasing importance of lawyers in the process of lending and borrowing money, it maintained its personal character well into the twentieth century. Informal arrangements accompanied the emergence of a formal credit market. To place historical and contemporary credit practices into merely an economic sphere would thus overlook the variety of their social and cultural implications.

Credit in Contemporary Society

Most anthropologists and historians accept the argument of credit as a social obligation in regard to peasant societies and face-to-face communities past and present. Contemporary credit culture, however, is often viewed in a different and somehow colder light. But the evolutionary and slightly romanticizing narrative of a "Great Transformation" (Karl Polanyi) from intact societies with socially embedded forms of monetary relationships to modern societies with disembedded and abstract economic transactions does not suffice for the complexity of either historical or modern societies.[18] In both cases, credit must be analyzed as an economic and a social transaction, for the two transactional orders might create contrasts within a society or group, but not between societies. There is no good or bad, no personal or impersonal, embedded or disembedded way of dealing with credit that might reflect on better or worse social structures.[19] As will be shown below in interviews with contemporary consumers in Germany, the notion of credit as a social obligation with cohesive power also prevails in our contemporary society. It is worth giving modern societies some "credit" and examining their debt relations as social relations, too.

The German Consumer Credit Crisis in Numbers

Sociocultural analysis becomes all the more relevant when everyday practices and needs collide with the economic system. In other words, sociocultural factors become particularly important in times of crisis, when debts become excessive, which the data below shows is increasingly the case for consumers in Germany.

For the German credit market, Schufa has collected the credit histories of consumers since the 1920s, as Larry Frohman discusses in chapter 6.[20] The total number of people with excessive levels of debt in Germany is difficult to determine; however, estimates for 2009 range around 6.2 million, which would amount to more than 9 percent of the population.[21] Almost 40 percent of all households finance their consumption partially on credit, which includes installment plans, credit cards, overdrawn bank accounts, and other forms of consumer loans.[22] About 8.5 percent of all people aged eighteen and older have negative entries on their Schufa records; that is, they have displayed conspicuous credit behavior in the form of delays in repayments, defaults, or even personal bankruptcy filings.[23] In absolute numbers, 5.5 million people find themselves on the often slippery slope from indebtedness to overindebtedness.

Overindebtedness occurs when a debtor's spending—including loan payments and added interest—exceeds his or her income on a regular basis.[24] However, this condition does not automatically equal personal bankruptcy. Credit counsellors use the term "relative indebtedness" to describe people whose income does not cover all their financial obligations, but whose living expenses have been reduced to a limit that exempts their property from seizure. In Germany, this limit is fixed at €989.99 for a single person (€1,359.99 with one child, €1,569.99 with two children). Child allowances and other social benefits are not seizable. "Absolute indebtedness," by contrast, refers to a debtor's inability, by and large, ever to fulfil his or her obligations. Taken into account in such cases are only consumer debts stemming from rent and alimony payments; gas, water, and telephone bills; obligations to telecommunication, mail order, and insurance companies; and money borrowed from friends and family. Mortgages, however, are not included.

In contrast to the United States and other countries in which this option has long been available, filing for personal bankruptcy only became legally possible in Germany in 1999.[25] Between 1999 and 2007, nearly 800,000 consumers have made use of this new way out of debt. Whereas in 1999 average debt levels before bankruptcy amounted to around €180,000, that sum decreased to €59,000 in 2007.[26] This reduction can be explained in part by the option, since 2002, to defer legal fees, which opened the solution of personal bankruptcy to destitute debtors, too.[27] The lower sum could also suggest, however, that debtors find their way to court earlier and more easily and that bankruptcy has become less socially stigmatized.

Living with Debts: Credit Practices between Inclusion and Exclusion

From the hypothesis that debts operate as networks, we can deduce the anthropological function of credit. As the objectification of a social relation, credit plays an integrative role for the individual. In contrast to a simplistic reading of debts as exclusively tainted with embarrassment and feelings of social exclusion, credit on a praxeological level includes individuals in two ways.[28]

First, credit enables affiliation with a consumer society by allowing the individual access to a symbolic language of membership. People borrow money to purchase status symbols and means of distinction that promise social acceptance and integration. Expressions in interviews like "to be part of something," "to participate," or "to join in" show how important the role of membership in consumer society is for individual credit motivation. For their part, banks advertise aggressively with images of status symbols and luxury goods.[29] Obtaining a loan means gaining access to a world of dreams and unlimited possibilities beyond the boundaries of class or income. Credit allows immediate fulfilment of desires without years of tedious waiting or the crushing difficulties of work. The discourse of inclusion through consumption is a powerful tool of the credit industry.

Second, consumption on credit enables more than participation in a consumer society by owning prestigious goods. Credit approval and freshly borrowed money from the bank are symbols of creditworthiness and therefore markers of social acceptance and trust. In this cultural logic of debts, credit itself becomes an indication of creditworthiness and thus a symbol of social status and respectability. Georg Simmel recounted the story of an English tradesman who once explained, "a common man is he who buys goods by cash payment, a gentleman one to whom I give credit."[30] In this way, Simmel designated receiving credit as a more reputable transaction than paying in cash.

Creditworthiness means passing the credit assessment, experiencing competence, and enjoying trust. Credit approval turns into a positive experience of inclusion, as can be seen in the interview with a thirty-nine-year-old architect from Dortmund, whom I shall call Milena Basiç. Her debts entailed bank overdrafts, three maxed-out credit cards, a loan with her bank, and debts to family members. At the time of the interview, the single mother was €18,000 in debt and had no job to provide regular income. In 2004, she filed for personal bankruptcy, and she was out of debt by 2010.

Milena Basiç's responses are exemplary for an economic agent acting in two worlds. She speaks about the first debts she incurred as a student as if they had been investments at the stock exchange. In fact, she bought some shares during that time, too. "Well, it was not really taking a risk, the stocks were high and I did some real research. . . . I checked all the options and the fine print, compared the different offers, talked to people. It was a sound investment, also in my own future, my degree. . . . Well, and then, yeah, the market went bust and I had to write it off." Although she lost most of the money she had borrowed from the bank on the stock market, she felt self-supporting during her student years: "I made it alright through my studies and for myself. I always had a job when I was a student and thus enough money. And, after my studies, it was normal for me that things would look up and I would be able to afford more."[31]

In a sense, by relying on her education and qualifications, Milena Basiç took out a loan on her biography. She assumed that her profession as an architect would provide for a better lifestyle than she could afford as a student and kept spending on travel, changing apartments, and leisure. "Everybody did this. We had finished our studies and had free time, and I so longed to finally afford something for myself after all those years as a student." Her habitus as a professional—not her actual income, for she was not working as an architect at the time—directed her toward anticipatory consumption.

The interview reveals different layers of her understanding of credit. She regarded her first loan as an investment in the future and speaks about the credit deal with business terms: "stocks," "fine print," and "writing off." She reframes this loan to make clear that she was not under pressure and valued the money as a capital asset.

Subsequent debts guaranteed her standard of living and her participation in consumer society. For her, this mostly entailed traveling. She is not embarrassed to be in debt, because "many people have debts, especially these days. That's quite common." At the same time, she distances herself from an image that in her view describes the usual situation: "In my case, it is not your typical debtor who orders on the internet and cannot stop consuming." It is interesting to note how she addresses her debts openly and confidently, but conjures up an image of indebted consumers from which she fervently distinguishes herself.

When she needed more money and again turned to the bank, she recounts the situation as a positive experience. The fact that the bank was willing to refinance her debts and give her a bigger sum than she needed gave her confidence in herself: "I felt all grown-up that they would give me that much money. As long as they give me money, I thought, it can't be that bad. And you can decide for yourself. You are an active part in this. . . . And as long as they talked to me and made me new offers, I was not all that upset. Only when they stopped talking to me at the bank, then I felt like an outcast."

Milena Basiç's response is exemplary for an understanding of credit as recognition. She interprets the symbolic function of credit as inclusion in a social structure. The economic logic of credit is thus turned around. Whereas creditworthiness comes first and is logically followed by credit approval, the cultural logic of credit works the other way around. Milena regards the fact that she received money as a sign of her creditworthiness. Credit is allocated an almost indexical character of creditworthiness. Especially in those situations when she cannot offer any security to the creditor and yet still receives money on her bank account, this debtor looks upon credit approval as an act of integration.[32]

Further motivators are the experiences of competence and choice; she calls this "[feeling] all grown-up." Many interviews show that credit conveys and—in some cases—restores the freedom of choice and decision making in consumption as a means of defining identity. Milena Basiç says that—apart from the first loan—she borrowed money for no special purpose: "Well, that's the thing. Nothing much really. It is not that I had something in mind which I had always wanted and now I could go and get it. And it certainly was not the luxury holiday or the pretty designer dress. It was more the having of the money, being able to spend it on this and that. Of course, I needed those things too. But perhaps not in that price range and not at that time." Her answer shows an individual credit practice at odds with the advertising discourse. She derides the common credit motivation of luxury and status symbols. To her, the freedom that money conveys was motivation enough to obtain credit. The freedom of making one's own decisions accompanied the economic benefit of having money available on short notice. Milena Basiç could do the math. She knew about the unfavourable interest rates of 12 to 18 percent. But crucial for her decision was the social benefit of inclusion and self-determination.

The effectiveness of the social character of debts can be seen in Milena Basiç's attitude toward personal bankruptcy. This procedure plays an important role in the interview. "I was really afraid of it. Not to pay back my debts, how is that going to work?" When she filed for bankruptcy, she no longer had any debts with her friends or family. Thus, although the only outstanding debts were with banks, mail-order, and telephone companies, she suffered from a bad conscience—and not because she could not repay her debts, but because she had ended the credit relation. The social character of credit still works between an individual and an institution: "Of course, I would have wanted to pay my debts. Like this, I feel bad every time I walk past the bank. I know that this is wrong, just leaving. If everybody did it, it would not work. And if I need money now, who should I turn to?" With the declaration of bankruptcy, she shed her obligations to the banks. At the same time, however, she also disposed of the social relationship that might have helped her out of a potential predicament in the future. Her refusal to reciprocate by filing for bankruptcy severed all social ties.

Precarious Relations: From Saving to Borrowing

With the caesurae of two world wars and their drastic effects on the economy, postwar credit culture in Germany witnessed a number of consumerist developments. The first high demand for loans took place from the mid-1950s to the mid-1960s, when the scars left by World War II had begun to heal. In the immediate aftermath of the war, lending and borrowing in order to cope with daily needs had still been stigmatized as a last resort in times of crisis. In the mid-1950s, however, when the economic situation started to consolidate with increasing incomes and a secure job market, people began to consume more than the bare necessities, and they increasingly did so on credit. Sought-after products included radios, furniture, and white goods such as washing machines, as well as scooters and cars.[33]

With plenty of money in their safes, banks began to find the credit business attractive, too. As discussed by Rebecca Belvederesi-Kochs in chapter 2, German savings banks were the first to introduce consumer credit in 1952. Still, those credit offers were initially purpose-bound, which meant that potential borrowers had to explain to the bank's loan officer what they intended to do with the money, where, and when. Such purpose-specific access to credit declined during the 1960s, as the customer experienced revaluation as a responsible consumer and credit underwent a process of democratization.[34] To borrow money for any purpose became a possibility for almost everybody, and credit turned into an integral part of consumer life, an everyday helper.[35] Pierre Bourdieu has called this process—slightly ambivalently—the "personalization of credit." With this personalized credit plan, the guarantee was established in the notion of every client having a permanent income. What used to be conveyed only to clients with calculable and predictable careers was now open to the new clientele of middle-class wage earners. Their creditworthiness was defined bureaucratically with a set of data based on expected earnings, family size, life expectancy, and so on. In this way, credit became available to a larger group of consumers and was turned into a support of their purchasing power.[36]

Whereas in 1954 the conservative voice of national economist Wilhelm Röpke still proclaimed the superiority of saving over spending, warning against taking out consumer loans, which he characterized as "disruptive, irresponsible, gypsy-like," and freeloading,[37] by the 1960s consumer credit had become a driving force of the new economic prosperity in Germany. The stigma of "squandering money one did not have" slowly yielded to a pattern of consumption and distinction.

The credit market peaked again in the 1990s, following German reunification and another period of higher incomes, as well as a sound job market. Whereas the first peak was partially mirrored in the boom experience of many other Western nations, it was also rooted in the more nationally peculiar experiences of war and heavy inflation. This second peak seemed even more in tune with broader global developments.[38] Why, however, did this credit behavior now lead to a credit crisis? Are we witnessing a new "pathology of affluence"?[39]

Conversations with debtors about their dealings with banks and finance companies frequently point to how things appeared "really quick," that they received money "immediately" and that the whole affair was "easy" and "not complicated" at all. It is noticeable that the interviewees' responses repeat bank advertisements for products like instant credit or online credit. One twenty-three-year-old nurse—let us call her Denise Stamm—exemplifies this trend: "I received a flier in the mail and they said it was really easy, apply online and all that, and that I could do with the money whatever I wanted. And it was like that, at first." When asked if she had ever spoken to a clerk, she replied, "No, I was not so keen on getting another refusal in person. They did not want to know much in the form, just wanted a copy of my paycheck and a picture ID and that was it . . . . It was so quick, I did not take it all that seriously myself."[40]

Denise Stamm's answer not only shows her hesitation to contact the bank personally for fear that she would feel rejected and excluded, but it also highlights how the online credit offer seemed less binding, less effectual, so that she "did not take it all that seriously." Debt counsellors also note that the highest failure of credit repayment occurs with exactly these new consumer options. These loans are advertised and sold by focusing on the immediacy of the moment. And when credit itself is a means of interfering with the order of time,[41] because it allows instant indulgence of desired goods without saving or waiting, instant credit exponentiates this notion even further. Time, however, is needed in order to establish an exchange relation: with quick credit offers online or over the phone, the exchange is one-sided and without the duty to reciprocate.[42]

Bank advertisements verbally and visually express the anonymity and the lack of personal counselling. Many images seem like personal holiday photos, or they are cropped like snapshots. The advertising language is deliberately simple, like spoken language: "know what's up right away" (*sofort wissen, was geht*); "just off to get some money" (*nur mal eben Geld holen*). Promises of fairness, convenience, and security carry the signature of the chair of the board.[43]

All in all, one can interpret this advertising strategy as compensation for the lack of face-to-face contact between borrower and lender. The individual circumstances of the client—his or her real income and obligations—play no role in the transaction. The credit agreement is virtual rather than personal.

Conclusion

Credit is an incorporating transaction that establishes and maintains social relations. From the point of view of the private debtor, the sociocultural mechanism of gift and countergift holds true in our contemporary society, too. This understanding of debts has not undergone a transformation; credit relations are still based on the reciprocity of a culture of trust and creditworthiness. But with the lack of personal contact and individual counselling, the cultural logic of credit as a means of distinction and long-term social obligation no longer prevails. The results are overindebtedness, defaults, and even bankruptcy. Debts have become mere consumer options; social relations have turned into precarious relations.[44]

Now is it rational to take on more debt than one can afford? Do borrowers not see the false promises of advertising and the tricky conditions of their credit policy? Why do they choose to overlook certain details and focus on others? An initial answer must link their choices to the dominant discourse on consumption. Symbols of freedom, luxury, and prestige are sold easily in modern credit economies, in which credit industries play upon the utopian notion of total social mobility. But there is more to the matter than the temptation of affluence.

Debtors' choices are rational with regard to their economic habitus: the need to keep up appearances pays off emotionally and socially; habitus as orientation saves on time, calculations, and information costs; the interpretation of credit as creditworthiness corrects biographical narratives and shifts perceptions of identity. All in all, the economic habitus does not distinguish between financial, emotional, or social decisions.[45] As Thorstein Veblen put it, the economic agent is not merely a "bundle of desires . . . but a coherent structure of propensities and habits."[46] Consumer habits do not rely solely on rational planning in the narrow economic sense but rather also on experience and cultural patterns, and the level of consumer spending is affected not only by present income, but also by past or future income. Therefore, borrowing beyond one's economic means can make sense, simply because the social, emotional, and cultural gains by far outweigh even the high interest rates.

Anthropologists cannot solve the debt crisis, but we can contribute to understanding this development in our societies by examining agents' reasons for running up debt. Credit relations are embedded in a system of social integration and cultural values. If one separates economic acts from their cultural context, like the new business models of instant credit or online credit have done, individuals act contrary to the structural patterns of their previous practices, society collides with its own cultural premises, and the consequences reverberate throughout the socioeconomic system.

Luckily, interdisciplinary research is no mere hypothetical intellectual game. One of the reactions to the debt crisis is a renewed legal directive of the European Parliament and Council that corrects shortcomings in banks' credit offers, effective as of October 31, 2009.[47] It prescribes that credit advertising has to become more tangible inasmuch as the contract must be documented on paper or a permanent data carrier, not online, and it must provide the address and other contact details for the creditor or credit intermediary (art. 10), thus conveying a bricks-and-mortar character to the credit business. There must be a cooling-off period of fourteen days, during which the consumer may retreat from the contract (art. 14), thus removing speed from credit deals and reintroducing the element of time lacking with instant credit. Most importantly, the lending institution is obliged to confirm the creditworthiness of the consumer (art. 8) and grant credit only where credit is economically warranted. Together, these rules restore the cultural logic of debts and reestablish the prerequisite of credit transactions as exchange relations. In short, credit transactions are reembedded in culture.

Notes

1. The names given in this article have been changed in order to preserve the anonymity of the interviewees.
2. Therefore, culture indeed makes a difference for individual economic transactions, but definitely not "all the difference" in terms of economic behavior as part of an assumed national culture, as David S. Landes concludes in *The Wealth and Poverty of Nations: Why Some Are So Rich and Some So Poor* (London, 1998), 516.
3. On the history and development of the German credit rating agency Schufa, see chapter 6 of this volume by Larry Frohmann.
4. In 2002, Vernon L. Smith and Daniel Kahnemann were awarded the Nobel Prize in Economic Sciences for their theories of social preferences and reciprocity in economic behavior.
5. Pierre Bourdieu, *The Social Structures of the Economy,* trans. Chris Turner (Cambridge, UK, 2005), 211.
6. For an overview of the intersectionality of rational economy and individual behavior, see Frank Adloff and Steffen Mau, "Zur Theorie der Gabe und Reziprozität," in *Vom Geben und Nehmen: Zur Soziologie der Reziprozität,* ed. Frank Adloff and Steffen Mau (Frankfurt am Main, 2005), 9–57. See also

Hartmut Berghoff and Jakob Vogel, "Wirtschaftsgeschichte als Kulturgeschichte: Ansätze zur Bergung transdisziplinärer Synergiepotentiale"; Christoph Conrad, " 'How much, Schatzi?' Vom Ort des Wirtschaftens in der New Cultural History"; and Jakob Tanner, "Die ökonomische Handlungstheorie vor der 'kulturalistischen' Wende: Perspektiven und Probleme einer interdisziplinären Diskussion"; all three in *Wirtschaftsgeschichte als Kulturgeschichte: Dimensionen eines Perspektivwechsels,* ed. Hartmut Berghoff and Jakob Vogel (Frankfurt am Main and New York, 2004), 9–41, 43–68, 69–98. For an economist's point of view, see Armin Falk, "Homo Oeconomicus versus Homo Reciprocans: Ansätze für ein neues wirtschaftspolitisches Leitbild?," Working Papers of the Institute for Empirical Research in Economics 79 (Zurich, 2001), http://e-collection. library.ethz.ch/eserv/eth:25582/eth-25582–01.pdf; and Robert M. Axelrod, *The Evolution of Cooperation,* rev. ed. (New York, 2006).

7. Mark Osteen and Martha Woodmansee, eds., *The New Economic Criticism: Studies at the Intersection of Literature and Economics* (London, 1999); Mark Osteen, ed., *The Question of the Gift: Essays across Disciplines* (London, 2002); Elizabeth Hewitt, "The Vexed Story of Economic Criticism," *American Literary History* 21, no. 3 (1990): 618–32. Exemplary studies from philological disciplines: Richard Gray, *Money Matters: Economics and the German Cultural Imagination, 1770–1850* (Seattle, WA, 2008); Fritz Breithaupt, *Der Ich-Effekt des Geldes: Zur Geschichte einer Legitimationsfigur* (Frankfurt am Main, 2008); Catherine Ingrassia, *Authorship, Commerce, and Gender in Early Eighteenth-Century England* (Cambridge, UK, 1998); Margot Finn, *The Character of Credit: Personal Debt in English Culture, 1740–1914* (Cambridge, UK, 2003).

8. Margrit Grabas et al., "Kultur in der Wirtschaftsgeschichte: Panel des Wirtschaftshistorischen Ausschusses des Vereins für Socialpolitik," *Vierteljahrschrift für Sozial- und Wirtschaftsgeschichte* 94, no. 2 (2007): 173–88.

9. Marcel Mauss, *The Gift: Form and Reason of Exchange in Archaic Society,* trans. W. D. Halls (London, 1990), 4.

10. Ibid., 84.

11. An excellent overview is offered in Carola Lipp, "Aspekte der mikrohistorischen und kulturanthropologischen Kreditforschung," in *Die soziale Praxis des Kredits: 16.–20. Jahrhundert,* ed. Jürgen Schlumbohm (Hannover, 2007), 15–36. See also Mark Häberlein, "Kreditbeziehungen und Kapitalmärkte vom 16. bis zum 19. Jahrhundert," in *Die soziale Praxis des Kredits,* ed. Schlumbohm, 46.

12. Georg Fertig, "Zwischen Xenophobie und Freundschaftspreis: Landmarkt und familiäre Beziehungen in Westfalen, 1830–1866," *Jahrbuch für Wirtschaftsgeschichte,* no. 1 (2005): 53–76.

13. Craig Muldrew, *The Economy of Obligation: The Culture of Credit and Social Relations in Early Modern England,* 2nd ed. (Basingstoke, 2001) 156.

14. Laurence Fontaine, *L' économie morale: Pauvreté, crédit et confiance dans l'Europe préindustrielle* (Paris, 2008); Laurence Fontaine, "Die Bauern und Mechanismen der Kreditvergabe," in *Schuldenlast und Schuldenwert: Kreditnetzwerke in der europäischen Geschichte 1300–1900,* ed. Gabriele Clemens (Trier, 2009), 109–30.

15. The Nuremberg broadsheet: Herzog August Bibliothek Wolfenbüttel, Flugblatt IE 191. It also appears on the title page of Jürgen Schlumbohm, ed., *Soziale Praxis des Kredits: 16.–20. Jahrhundert* (Hannover, 2007). For more on this common motif, see Adolf Spamer, "Kredit ist tot: Zur Geschichte eines volkstümlichen Scherzbildes," in *Volkskundliche Gaben: John Meier zum siebzigsten Geburtstag dargebracht,* ed. Harry Schewe (Berlin and Leipzig, 1934), 223–43.

16. Tom Taylor, ed., *Life of Benjamin Robert Haydon, Historical Painter: From His Autobiography and Journals* (London, 1853), 2: 351, entry for September 23, 1832.

17. Quoted in Reinhard Johler, "Bäuerliches Kreditwesen im Alpenraum: Vorbemerkungen zu einer *Economic Anthropology,*" *Historische Anthropologie* 7 (1999): 146.

18. Karl Polanyi, *The Great Transformation: The Political and Economic Origins of Our Time* (Boston, MA, 2001).

19. Jonathan Parry and Maurice Bloch, "Introduction," in *Money and the Morality of Exchange,* ed. Jonathan Parry and Maurice Bloch (Cambridge, UK, 1989), 29. For a similar point of view on the social aspect of money and economic transactions, see, for example, Bill Maurer, "An Anthropology of Money," *Annual Review of Anthropology* 35 (2006): 15–36; Viviana A. Zelizer, *The Social Meaning of Money: Pin Money, Paychecks, Poor Relief and Other Currencies* (New York, 1994); Arjun Appadurai, "Introduction: Commodities and the Politics of Value," in *The Social Life of Things: Commodities in Cultural Perspective,* ed. Arjun Appadurai (Cambridge, UK, 1986), 3–63. I pursue this hypothesis from a broader perspective in Silke Meyer, "Prekäre Beziehungen: Zur kulturellen Logik des Kredits," in *Österreichische Zeitschrift für Volkskunde* 114 (2011): 3–25.

20. Schufa has annually published a "Debts Compass" since 2003; see http://www.schulden-kompass.de.

21. This number is given in a consumer marketing agency census; see Microm Creditreform, "Schuldner-Atlas Deutschland, 2009" at http://www.creditreform.de/Deutsch/Creditreform/Presse/Archiv/SchuldnerAtlas_Deutschland/2009/Analyse_SchuldnerAtlas_Deutschland_2009.pdf. In 2004, 8% of German households were overindebted; see Statistisches Bundesamt, *Datenreport 2004* (Bonn, 2004), 600.

22. Bankenfachverband, ed., "Grundlagenstudie zur Konsum- und Kfz-Finanzierung," GfK Finanzmarktforschung (Oktober 2009), 8, http://www.bfach.de/media/file/4343.GfK_Studie_Konsum-Kfz-Finanzierung_2009_bfach.pdf.

23. Schufa Holding, ed., *Schufa Kredit-Kompass 2010: Empirische Indikatoren der privaten Kreditaufnahme in Deutschland: Auswirkungen der Wirtschaftskrise auf den Konsumentenkredit* (Wiesbaden, 2011), 46, chart 1.15.

24. For an in-depth discussion, see Gunther E. Zimmermann, "Private Ver- und Überschuldung im Analysekontext: Ansätze und Verfahren der Definition sowie der empirischen Erfassung von Überschuldung," in *Schuldenkompass 2007,* ed. Schufa Holding (Wiesbaden, 2007), 133–42. Zimmermann also lists subjective

overindebtedness, which is when debtors feel overly strained by their financial situation regardless of—and in many cases without looking at—the numbers.

25. For a comparative view of consumer bankruptcy and overindebtedness in the context of national debt adjustment and regulation laws, see Ian Ramsay, "Comparative Consumer Bankruptcy," *Illinois Law Review,* no. 1 (2007): 241–74.

26. Jürgen Angele, Brigit Frank-Bosch, and Jenny Neuhäuser, "Überschuldung privater Personen und Verbraucherinsolvenzen," *Wirtschaft und Statistik* (Statistisches Bundesamt), no. 11 (November 2008): 963–64. For a more detailed description of the procedures for private bankruptcy in Germany, see Wolfram Backert et al., "Bankruptcy in Germany: Filing Rates and the People behind the Numbers," in *Consumer Credit, Debt and Bankruptcy: Comparative and International Perspectives,* ed. Johanna Niemi, Iain Ramsay, and William C. Whitford (Oxford, UK, 2009), 273–88.

27. Schufa Holding, ed., *Schuldenkompass 2008: Analyse B: Auswertung Schuldnerberaterdaten* (Wiesbaden, 2009), 106–108.

28. For a comparative view of credit as a means of social inclusion in the United States, see chapter 9 in this volume by Jan Logemann.

29. For an overview of the historical development of credit advertisements, see Peter Borscheid, "Sparsamkeit und Sicherheit: Werbung für Banken, Sparkassen und Versicherungen," in *Bilderwelt des Alltags: Werbung in der Konsumgesellschaft des 19. und 20. Jahrhunderts,* ed. Peter Borscheid and Clemens Wischermann (Stuttgart, 1995), 294–349.

30. Georg Simmel, *Philosophy of Money* [1900], ed. David Frisby, 3rd ed. (New York, 2004), 479.

31. All quotes taken from my interview with Milena Basiç on May 4, 2008, my translations.

32. See also Meyer, "Prekäre Beziehungen," 17–20.

33. Britta Stücker, "Konsum auf Kredit in der Bundesrepublik," in *Die bundesdeutsche Massenkonsumgesellschaft,* ed. Alfred Reckendrees, special issue of *Jahrbuch für Wirtschaftsgeschichte,* no. 2 (2007): 82–86. For the development of the mass consumer society in West Germany, see the entire aforementioned special issue of the *Jahrbuch für Wirtschaftsgeschichte,* as well as Arne Andersen, *Der Traum vom guten Leben: Alltags- und Konsumgeschichte vom Wirtschaftswunder bis heute* (Frankfurt am Main, 1997), 196–205.

34. Stücker, "Konsum auf Kredit," 64–68.

35. See chapter 7 in this volume by Gunnar Trumbull for the democratization of credit in the United States, where access to credit has been associated with economic opportunity, social solidarity, and even national identity.

36. Bourdieu, *Social Structures of the Economy,* 153–55.

37. Wilhelm Röpke, *Borgkauf im Lichte sozialethischer Kritik* (Cologne, 1954), 112.

38. See Johanna Niemi, Iain Ramsay, and William C. Whitford, eds., *Consumer Credit, Debt and Bankruptcy: Comparative and International Perspectives* (Oxford, UK, 2009).

39. See Iain Ramsay, " 'Wannabe WAGS' and 'Credit Binges': The Construction of Overindebtedness in the UK," in *Consumer Credit, Debt and Bankruptcy,* ed. Niemi, Ramsay, and Whitford, 75–90.
40. Interview with Denise Stamm on February 2, 2008. See also Silke Meyer: "Sofortkredit: Zur kulturellen Praktik der Verschuldung," *Jahrbuch für Europäische Ethnologie,* 3rd ser., no. 2 (2007): 105–20.
41. Pierre Bourdieu, *Die feinen Unterschiede: Kritik der gesellschaftlichen Urteilskraft* (Frankfurt am Main, 1987), 271.
42. A counterexample would be the credit procedures at Crazy George's stores, at which personal contact, vicinity, and references by friends and family members prevent repayment failures; see chapter 7 in this volume by Gunnar Trumbull.
43. Flyer by easyCredit, eC 8S.80.01/07 (2007), in possession of the author.
44. See also Meyer, "Prekäre Beziehungen," 23.
45. Gary Becker, *The Economic Approach to Human Behavior* (Chicago, IL, 1976).
46. Thorstein Veblen, "Why Is Economics Not an Evolutionary Science?," *Quarterly Journal of Economics* 12, no. 4 (July 1898): 390.
47. A pdf-version can be downloaded from http://eur-lex.europa.eu/LexUriServ/ LexUriServ.do?uri=OJ:L:2008:133:0066:0092:EN:PDF. I am grateful to Dr. hab. Fryderyk Zoll, Krakow University, for pointing out these new regulations to me.

CHAPTER 11

Japan and the Western Model: An Economist's View of Cultures of Household Finance*

Charles Yuji Horioka

It is commonly believed that the Japanese and other Asians are penny-pinchers and savers and that Americans and other Westerners are spendthrifts and borrowers, but do the data bear out this conventional wisdom? The purpose of this chapter is to shed light on this question using data on household wealth (assets) and indebtedness (liabilities) from the Organisation for Economic Co-operation and Development (OECD) on the Group of Seven (G7) countries, the world's seven major industrialized countries. I then explore why the conventional wisdom is—or is not—correct.

Looking at previous analyses of this topic,[1] Andrew Gordon also explores the prevalence of consumer credit in Japan but takes a more historical approach, confines his comparisons to the United States, and focuses primarily on installment plans used to finance the purchase of consumer durable goods. Charles Horioka also considers whether the Japanese are unique, looking not only at their assets and liabilities, but also at their saving rates, consumption levels, and consumption patterns. The present investigation differs from these earlier studies in that it takes an economic approach, compares Japan to all of the other G7 countries, considers the total liabilities of households, focuses on liabilities and assets, and analyzes data for a longer period of time, that is, 1955–2008 for Japan and 1980–2008 for the other countries.

In the first section, I present data on household wealth and indebtedness for the G7 countries; in the second section, I discuss trends over time in

Japan; and in the third section, I speculate about the causes of household borrowing behavior in Japan.

Data on Household Wealth and Indebtedness for the Group of Seven Countries

In this section, I present data on the household wealth and indebtedness of the G7 countries taken from the *OECD Economic Outlook,* a semiannual publication of the OECD.[2]

Before turning to the results, I provide definitions of the various categories of wealth and indebtedness. Household wealth or assets can be broken down into two broad groups: financial assets (consisting of bank and postal deposits, negotiable securities such as bonds and equities, life insurance, etc.) and nonfinancial assets (consisting mostly of land and housing).

Similarly, household indebtedness or liabilities can be broken down into two broad categories: mortgages (housing loans) and all other liabilities. However, this breakdown is not available in some countries (France and Italy), and in these countries, loans are broken down by the period of maturity (short- and medium-term loans versus long-term loans in France and short-term loans versus medium- and long-term loans in Italy). However, for ease of exposition in these cases, I will use the term "mortgages (housing loans)" even when the data pertain to long-term or medium- and long-term loans and the term "nonhousing loans" for all other liabilities.

Finally, I use two measures of household wealth that take account of both wealth (assets) and indebtedness (liabilities), because indebtedness (liabilities) should be regarded as a negative asset or as an offset to assets. Net financial wealth is calculated as financial assets minus total liabilities, and net wealth (the broadest measure of household wealth) is calculated as total assets minus total liabilities.

Table 11.1 shows data on the ratios of these various categories of household wealth and household indebtedness to household disposable income for the G7 countries between 1980 and 2008 (for the end of each respective calendar year at five-year intervals between 1980 and 2005, as well as for 2008), except that 2007 data are shown in cases for which 2008 data were not yet available. For ease of exposition, I will write 2008 even when the data pertain to 2007.

Data on Household Indebtedness

Because the focus of this chapter is consumer credit, I look first at data on household indebtedness (liabilities). As can be seen from table 11.1, Japan

Table 11.1 Household wealth and indebtedness in the OECD countries, 1980–2008

	1980		1985		1990		1995		2000		2005		2008	
Canada														
Net wealth	405.0	5.5	400.7	4	416.5	7	476.5	6	502.2	7	534.5	7	544.5	6
Net financial wealth	151.0	2	167.2	4	177.5	5	219.0	4	240.1	5	216.5	5	210.5	5
Nonfinancial assets	254.0	5	233.5	4	239.0	6	257.6	6	262.0	6	318.0	6	333.9	6
Financial assets	238.0	2	243.1	4	270.4	4	322.4	4	352.7	5	345.9	5	352.1	5
of which: equities	58.0	2	56.3	1	49.6	5	60.5	3	84.3	3	79.4	3	94.3	1
Total assets	492.0	4	476.6	4	509.4	7	580.0	6	614.8	6	663.8	7	686.0	6
Share of nonfinancial assets	51.6	5	49.0	5	46.9	6	44.4	5	42.6	5	47.9	5	48.7	5
Liabilities	87.0	1	75.9	4	92.9	3	103.4	3	112.6	4	129.4	4	141.6	2
of which: mortgages	53.0	2	47.4	3	59.2	3	68.8	2	69.6	3	79.1	3	88.2	3
of which: all other loans	34.0	5	28.5	4	33.7	3	34.6	3	43.0	2	50.2	2	53.3	2
Share of mortgages	60.9	5	62.5	4	63.7	5	66.5	4	61.8	5	61.2	5	62.3	5
France														
Net wealth	405.0	5.5	388.3	5	541.8	4	462.7	7	552.5	5	748.2	3	750.1	3
Net financial wealth	85.0	7	98.4	7	169.6	6	154.2	6	205.7	6	200.5	6	185.1	7
Nonfinancial assets	319.0	3	289.8	3	372.2	5	308.5	4	346.8	5	547.7	1	565.0	2
Financial assets	147.0	6	161.7	6	248.3	6	219.8	7	282.5	6	291.5	6	285.3	7
of which: equities	21.0	5	43.4	3	114.1	1	53.3	4	83.5	5	77.5	4	64.5	5
Total assets	466.0	6	451.5	5	620.5	5	528.3	7	629.3	6	839.2	6	850.3	4
Share of nonfinancial assets	68.5	2	64.2	1	60.0	4	58.4	3	55.1	2	65.3	2	66.5	1
Total liabilities	62.0	4	63.3	5	78.7	5	65.6	6	76.8	6	91.0	6	100.2	6
of which: long-term loans	40.0	3	42.9	4	53.4	5	49.6	5.5	53.4	6	65.3	5	76.4	4
of which: all other loans	22.0	5	20.4	5	25.3	5	16.0	6	23.4	7	25.7	7	23.8	7
Share of long-term loans	64.5	4	67.8	2	67.9	4	75.6	1	69.6	1	71.8	3	76.3	1

Table 11.1 (Continued)

	1980	1985	1990	1995	2000	2005	2008
Germany							
Net wealth	n/a	n/a	535.6 [5]	497.6 [5]	536.6 [5]	581.2 [6]	628.0 [5]
Net financial wealth	139.0 [3]	172.8 [3]	130.8 [7]	126.6 [7]	151.4 [7]	180.0 [7]	198.0 [6]
Nonfinancial assets	n/a	n/a	404.8 [3]	371.0 [3]	385.2 [3]	401.2 [4]	430.0 [4]
Financial assets	154.0 [5]	189.3 [5]	200.7 [7]	223.8 [6]	265.9 [6]	287.1 [7]	300.0 [6]
of which: equities	7.0 [7]	13.3 [7]	11.6 [7]	41.2 [7]	75.2 [6]	71.3 [7]	72.0 [4]
Total assets	n/a	n/a	605.5 [5]	594.8 [5]	651.1 [5]	688.4 [6]	730.0 [5]
Share of nonfinancial assets	n/a	n/a	66.9 [1]	62.4 [1]	59.2 [2]	58.3 [2]	58.9 [3]
Total liabilities	15.0 [6]	16.5 [6]	70.0 [6]	97.2 [4]	114.5 [4]	107.2 [5]	102.0 [5]
of which: mortgages	10.0 [6]	10.4 [6]	53.6 [4]	58.7 [4]	71.7 [4]	71.0 [4]	69.2 [5]
of which: all other loans	5.0 [6]	6.1 [6]	16.4 [6]	38.5 [2]	42.8 [3]	36.2 [4]	32.8 [5]
Share of mortgages	66.7 [2]	63.0 [3]	76.6 [1]	60.4 [5]	62.6 [4]	66.2 [4]	67.8 [4]
Italy							
Net wealth	498.0 [3]	324.7 [3]	636.9 [2]	703.2 [2]	762.7 [2]	833.6 [1]	863.9 [1]
Net financial wealth	109.0 [6]	138.5 [6]	196.3 [4]	213.9 [5]	329.9 [4]	311.2 [3]	298.6 [2]
Nonfinancial assets	388.0 [1]	186.2 [1]	440.5 [2]	488.5 [1]	432.8 [1]	522.4 [3]	565.4 [1]
Financial assets	118.0 [7]	147.8 [7]	225.4 [6]	245.5 [5]	382.7 [5]	376.4 [4]	370.7 [4]
of which: equities	8.0 [6]	14.9 [6]	46.0 [6]	37.6 [7]	98.0 [7]	84.2 [2]	76.8 [3]
Total assets	506.0 [3]	334.0 [3]	665.9 [3]	734.0 [2]	815.5 [7]	898.7 [2]	936.0 [2]
Share of nonfinancial assets	76.7 [1]	55.7 [1]	66.2 [2]	66.6 [1]	53.1 [3]	58.1 [3]	60.4 [2]
Total liabilities	8.0 [7]	9.2 [7]	29.1 [7]	31.6 [7]	52.8 [7]	647.6 [7]	72.1 [7]
of which: medium- and long-term loans	6.0 [7]	6.5 [7]	13.7 [7]	18.7 [7]	28.5 [7]	36.9 [7]	41.2 [7]
of which: all other loans	2.0 [7]	2.7 [7]	15.4 [7]	12.9 [7]	24.3 [6]	610.7 [6]	35.2 [4]
Share of medium- and long-term loans	75.0 [1]	70.7 [1]	47.1 [6]	59.2 [6]	53.9 [6]	5.7 [6]	57.2 [6]

Japan														
Net wealth	2	504.0	2	561.9	1	943.2	1	735.8	1	747.7	3	740.4	4	727.8
Net financial wealth	5	124.0	5	164.7	5	261.9	1	281.2	3	335.7	3	397.2	1	383.3
Nonfinancial assets	2	380.0	2	397.3	1	681.3	1	454.6	2	411.9	2	343.2	5	344.5
Financial assets	3	201.0	3	253.4	3	393.3	1	411.4	1	470.3	2	529.1	1	511.0
of which: equities	3.5	24.0	3.5	29.9	4	51.7	4	45.9	5	41.5	7	75.6	6	46.5
Total assets	2	581.0	2	650.7	1	1074.6	3	866.0	1	882.2	2	872.2	3	855.5
Share of nonfinancial assets	3	65.4	3	61.1	2	63.4	6	52.5	4	46.7	4	39.3	6	40.3
Total liabilities	2.5	77.0	2.5	88.8	1	131.5	1	130.2	1	134.6	1	131.9	2	127.7
of which: mortgages	5	31.0	5	35.6	5	50.7	6	49.6	5.5	61.1	5	64.1	6	64.7
of which: all other loans	1	46.0	1	53.2	1	80.8	1	80.6	1	73.5	1	67.7	1	63.0
Share of mortgages	7	40.3	7	40.1	7	38.6	7	38.1	7	45.4	7	48.6	7	50.7
United Kingdom														
Net wealth	4	431.0	4	491.2	2	611.0	3	568.7	3	768.1	1	827.0	2	759.6
Net financial wealth	4	133.0	4	179.2	2	214.1	3	288.5	2	380.3	1	304.3	4	242.8
Nonfinancial assets	4	297.0	4	312.0	2	396.9	4	280.1	5	387.8	3	522.7	3	516.8
Financial assets	4	190.0	3.5	265.0	2	329.9	3	394.8	3	497.4	1	466.6	2	424.3
of which: equities	3.5	24.0	5	26.7	5	61.2	2	78.3	2	113.6	2	76.0	5	50.1
Total assets	5	487.0	5	577.0	2	726.8	2	674.9	2	885.2	1	989.3	1	941.0
Share of nonfinancial assets	4	61.0	4	54.1	4	54.6	5	41.5	6	43.8	5	52.8	4	54.9
Total liabilities	5	57.0	5	85.8	2	115.8	5	106.3	2	117.1	2	162.3	1	181.4
of which: mortgages	4	33.0	4	52.3	1	81.3	1	78.3	1	85.4	1	121.2	1	137.3
of which: all other loans	4	24.0	4	33.5	2	34.5	2	28.0	5	31.7	5	41.1	3	44.1
Share of mortgages	6	57.9	6	61.0	6	70.2	2	73.7	2	72.9	1	74.7	2	75.7

Table 11.1 (Continued)

	1980		1985		1990		1995		2000		2005		2008	
United States														
Net wealth	507.0	1	478.7	3	474.5	6	509.3	4	579.4	4	634.1	5	489.7	7
Net financial wealth	259.0	1	251.9	1	259.0	2	302.0	1	355.5	1	335.3	2	256.7	3
Nonfinancial assets	248.0	6	226.8	5	215.6	7	207.6	7	223.9	7	298.8	7	233.0	7
Financial assets	336.0	1	332.0	1	345.6	2	395.4	2	456.2	3	466.4	3	388.3	3
of which: equities	61.0	1	48.2	2	52.1	3	105.1	1	148.9	1	127.6	1	86.3	2
Total assets	584.0	1	558.8	3	561.2	6	603.0	4	680.1	4	765.2	5	621.2	7
Share of nonfinancial assets	42.5	6	40.6	6	38.4	7	34.4	7	32.9	7	39.0	7	37.5	7
Total liabilities	77.0	2.5	80.1	3	86.6	4	93.4	5	100.7	5	131.1	3	131.6	3
of which: mortgages	50.0	2	49.5	2	60.3	2	63.2	3	67.2	4	97.5	2	98.9	2
of which: all other loans	27.0	3	30.6	3	26.3	4	30.2	4	33.4	4	33.6	5	32.7	6
Share of mortgages	64.9	3	61.8	5	69.6	3	67.7	3	66.8	3	74.3	2	75.1	3

Note: The left-hand figures show the ratio of each category of assets or liabilities (at the end of the year) to net household disposable income (in percent). The figures pertain to the household sector inclusive of nonprofit institutions serving households except in the case of Italy. The right-hand figures show the rank of each country among the G7 countries.
Source: OECD *Economic Outlook*, no. 54 (December 1993), table A-64, for 1980 data; no. 65 (June 1999), annex table 58 of the same for 1985 data; vol. 2002/2, no. 72 (December 2002), annex table 56 of the same for 1990 data; vol. 2007/2, no. 82 (December 2007), annex table 58 of same for 1995 data; and vol. 2009/2, no. 86 (November 2009), annex table 58 of the same for 2000, 2005, and 2008 data.

(the only Asian country in the sample) ranks first with respect to the ratio of total liabilities to household disposable income in four of the seven years (1985, 1990, 1995, and 2000) and relatively high in the other years, too (second in 1980 and 2005 and fourth in 2008). This ratio ranged between 77 and 135 percent in Japan between 1980 and 2008, meaning that total liabilities exceeded household disposable income in most years!

Americans are believed to be far more prolific borrowers than the Japanese, partly for cultural reasons and partly because housing loans and other forms of consumer credit developed far sooner and to a far greater extent in the United States than they did in Japan; however, according to table 11.1, Americans are only about average with respect to the ratio of total liabilities to household disposable income, ranking between second and fifth in all seven years for which data are shown, below Japan in six of the seven years, and tied with Japan in the remaining year (1980). Thus, the conventional wisdom concerning Japan and the United States seems to be totally mistaken; the behavior of households in the two countries is the opposite of what it is purported to be.

Looking at the other G7 countries, the ratio of total liabilities to household disposable income is relatively high in Canada and the United Kingdom, relatively low in France and Germany, and lowest by far in Italy, where this ratio ranges from only 8 to 72 percent. Thus, there is considerable variation even among the Western countries, but virtually all of them rank below Japan with respect to the ratio of total liabilities to household disposable income.

I look next at the two major components of household indebtedness (liabilities)—namely, mortgages (housing loans) and nonhousing loans to see which is responsible for Japan's surprisingly high liability-to-income ratio. It is widely believed that the availability of mortgages (housing loans) was expanded in Japan before the availability of other types of consumer credit. For example, the former Housing Loan Corporation (Juutaku Kin'yuu Kouko), whose purpose was to make low-interest housing loans to low- and middle-income households, was established by the Japanese Government in 1950, whereas the expansion of consumer credit came much later, hindered in large part by government regulations, as discussed by Gordon in chapter 3. Moreover, the ratio of housing prices to household disposable income is much higher in Japan than it is in most other countries. For both reasons, one would expect the ratio of mortgages (housing loans) to household disposable income to be relatively high in Japan. However, this expectation is contradicted by the data in table 11.1, which show that the ratio of mortgages (housing loans) to household disposable income in Japan is near the bottom of the G7 countries (fifth or sixth in all seven years), ranging from 31 to 65 percent.

By contrast, the ratio of mortgages (housing loans) to household disposable income in the United States is near the top of the G7 countries (second in most years, third in one year, and fourth in one year), reaching between 50 and 99 percent. (Note parenthetically that this ratio increased sharply—by 30 percent—during the 2000–05 period, presumably as a result of U.S. government policies to increase the availability of housing loans to the low-income population, an action that precipitated the subprime-related financial crisis that spread from the United States to the world economy as a whole.)

Thus, the relative rankings of Japan and the United States are reversed, depending on whether one looks at total liabilities or mortgages (housing loans), which suggests that the relatively high ratio of total liabilities to household disposable income in Japan is the result of the relatively high ratio of nonhousing loans to household disposable income.

The other G7 countries have similar ranks, whether one looks at total liabilities or mortgages (housing loans), with Canada and the United Kingdom ranking relatively high for both, France and Germany relatively low, and Italy seventh (last) in all years.

Looking next at direct evidence on the importance of nonhousing loans, the data in table 11.1 show that Japan ranked first with respect to the ratio of nonhousing loans to household disposable income in all seven of the years for which data are shown, with this ratio ranging from 46 to 81 percent.

By contrast, the United States ranks between third and sixth—lower than with respect to the ratio of housing loans to household disposable income in all but one year, and below Japan in every year with respect to the ratio of nonhousing loans to household disposable income, this latter ratio ranging from 26 to 34 percent. As for the remaining countries, the ranks of Canada, Germany, and Italy are roughly the same in the case of both housing and nonhousing loans, whereas France and the United Kingdom ranked lower with respect to nonhousing loans than they did for housing loans.

In sum, Japan devotes a relatively high proportion of total consumer credit to nonhousing loans (more than 50 percent except in 2008); France, Germany, the United Kingdom, and the United States devote a relatively high proportion of total consumer credit to housing loans; and Canada and Italy are somewhere in-between. Thus, contrary to the conventional wisdom, the Japanese have been the most prolific borrowers among the G7 countries, at least until 2000, and they have been especially prolific borrowers of nonhousing loans. However, it should be noted that nonhousing loans include not only noncollateralized loans used to finance consumption, but also other items such the interfirm credit and trade credit of private unincorporated enterprises, which are part of the household sector. It could well be that nonhousing loans are relatively more important in Japan because interfirm and trade credit are comparatively more important, which in turn could be because private unincorporated enterprises are relatively more prevalent in Japan.

Data on Household Wealth

The present discussion has focused on the ratio of indebtedness (liabilities) to household disposable income, but this can be a misleading indicator of the magnitude of indebtedness because it does not take account of the opposite side of the household balance sheet—namely, household wealth (assets). A high liability-to-income ratio is not necessarily a problem if the household has a considerable amount of wealth (assets), that is, a high wealth-to-income ratio. Conversely, even a low liability-to-income ratio may be problematic if the household has little or no wealth (assets), that is, a low wealth-to-income ratio. Thus, I now turn to data on household wealth (assets).

Looking at the ratio of total assets (the broadest measure of household assets) to household disposable income in table 11.1, Japan ranked first with respect to this ratio in three out of the seven years for which data are shown, second in two out of the seven years, and third in the remaining two years, with this ratio ranging from 581 to 1,075 percent. Thus, Japan has a relatively high liability-to-income ratio, as well as a relatively high asset-to-income ratio, so that its relatively high liability-to-income ratio is not necessarily cause for concern.

By contrast, the ratio of total assets to household disposable income is relatively low in the United States, ranking between third and seventh (except in 1980, when it ranked first) and ranging from 561 to 765 percent, but the United States is about average with respect to the ratio of total liabilities to household disposable income. Thus, the situation in the United States is of more concern than the one in Japan, but it is not necessarily cause for grave concern.

Turning to the other G7 countries, Italy and the United Kingdom rank relatively high with respect to the ratio of total assets to household disposable income, whereas Canada, France, and Germany rank relatively low for this ratio. Thus, the correlation between total liabilities and total assets is high but imperfect, with the United Kingdom ranking high for both, France and Germany low for both, and Canada high for liabilities but low for assets. It therefore appears that Canadians are the least financially healthy.

Turning next to data on net wealth, which take account of assets as well as liabilities, the ratio of net wealth to household disposable income has been relatively high in Japan, ranking between first and fourth and ranging from 504 to 943 percent. This is because, although the liabilities of Japanese households are relatively high, their assets are high by an even larger margin.

By contrast, the ratio of net wealth to household disposable income is below average in the United States, ranking between third and seventh (except in 1980, when it ranked first) and ranging from 475 to 634 percent. This is because its asset-to-income ratio is below average and its liability-to-income ratio is about average. These results show that the financial position of the Japanese is much healthier than that of Americans and are consistent with our earlier findings concerning total assets. Thus, our results suggest that the Japanese are more frugal than Americans and that the conventional wisdom is correct, after all. However, the difference between the United States and Japan can be explained both by differences in culture and by differences in policies and institutions (for example, the timing and extent of financial sector development), and it is not clear from just looking at the data which is the real culprit.

Among the other G7 countries, Italy and the United Kingdom rank relatively high with respect to the ratio of net wealth to household disposable income, whereas Canada, France, and Germany rank comparatively low. These results mirror those for the asset-to-income ratio, which is not surprising, because variations in the magnitude of assets exceed variations in the magnitude of liabilities. Canada's relatively low rank is consistent with our earlier finding that Canada ranks high with respect to liabilities but low with respect to assets, thus providing further evidence that the financial health of Canadians is not very good.

Turning finally to the share of nonfinancial (housing) assets in total assets, this share is relatively high in France, Germany, and Italy, and relatively low in Canada, Japan, the United Kingdom, and the United States. There does not seem to be much correlation between the net-wealth-to-income ratio and the share of nonfinancial (housing) assets: some countries with relatively low housing shares (such as Japan and the United Kingdom) have relatively high net-wealth-to-income ratios, whereas other countries with relatively low housing shares (such as Canada and the United States) have relatively low net-worth-to-income ratios. This suggests that portfolio choice does not have a significant impact on one's financial health.

Trends over Time in Japan

In this section, I look at trends over time in Japan using the OECD data for the 1980–2008 period shown in table 11.1 as well as the data for the 1955–75 period shown in table 11.2 and taken from the National Accounts

Table 11.2   Household wealth and indebtedness in Japan, 1955–75

	1955	1960	1965	1970	1975
Net wealth	330.9	363.6	332.6	398.8	415.4
Net financial wealth	56.9	75.4	77.8	97.1	98.9
Nonfinancial assets	274.0	288.2	254.8	301.6	316.5
Financial assets	79.6	114.8	131.5	157.2	161.2
of which: equities	9.5	13.0	14.8	24.0	20.1
Total assets	353.6	403.0	386.3	458.8	477.7
Total liabilities	22.7	39.4	53.7	60.0	62.3

Note: These figures show the ratio of each category of assets and liabilities (at the end of the year) to net household disposable income (in percent). The figures for 1955–65 pertain to the household sector inclusive of private nonprofit institutions serving households, whereas the figures for 1970 and 1975 pertain to the household sector exclusive of private nonprofit institutions serving households.
Source: Keizai Kikaku-chou, Keizai Kenkyuu-sho, ed., *Kokumin Keizai Keisan Houkoku: Chouki Sokyuu Suikei: Shouwa 30-nen—Shouwa 44-nen* (Tokyo, 1988); Keizai Kikaku-chou, Keizai Kenkyuu-sho, ed., *Kokumin Keizai Keisan Nenpou* (Tokyo, 2000).

of the Japanese Government.[3] (Unfortunately, pre-1980 data are not readily available for the other G7 countries.)

As can be seen from tables 11.1 and 11.2, the ratio of total liabilities to household disposable income in Japan was only 23 percent in 1955 but increased rapidly until 1990, before leveling off at the 128-to-135 percent level. Thus, the Japanese were not always prolific borrowers, but rather their propensity to borrow increased sharply over time, at least until 1990. Thus, the conventional wisdom that the Japanese have an aversion to borrowing used to be correct, although the data alone do not reveal whether this is the result of differences in culture or differences in policies and institutions.

On the asset side, the ratio of total assets to household disposable income was only 354 percent in 1955. It increased steadily until 1990, when it peaked at 1,075 percent, and it has been fluctuating in the 856-to-882 percent range since then.

Turning finally to net wealth, which takes account of both assets and liabilities, the ratio of net wealth to household disposable income was only 331 percent in 1955. It increased steadily until 1990, when it peaked at 943 percent, and it has been fluctuating in the 728-to-748 percent range since then.

In sum, all three aggregates (the ratios of total liabilities, total assets, and net worth to household disposable income) have shown similar trends over time, increasing until 1990 before leveling off. The increase in liabilities was more than offset by the increase in assets during the 1955–90 period, so that net wealth (the difference between the two) increased. Thus, the sharp increase in liabilities during this thirty-five-year period was not a worrisome or unhealthy trend.

Speculation about Causes

What about the determinants of trends over time in Japanese household borrowing behavior? If culture were the dominant explanation of household behavior and if culture were slow to change over time, the Japanese might be expected to have always been prolific borrowers or to have always shunned borrowing. From this perspective, the dramatic increase in household borrowing over time, at least until 1990, suggests that culture cannot offer the dominant explanation for Japanese household borrowing behavior. However, culture can and does change over time, and thus we cannot conclude that culture is not important just because Japanese behavior changed over nearly four decades. In fact, it could well be that the Japanese had previously shunned borrowing for cultural reasons and that they subsequently showed a sharp increase in household borrowing because traditional values eroded over time.[4]

That the sharp increase in household borrowing was largely the result of a strong increase in mortgages (housing loans) suggests that factors relating to housing—for example, sharply rising land and housing prices, as well as an increased demand for housing induced by higher income levels and the rapid urbanization of the population—also contributed to this trend.

Moreover, changes in government policies and regulations can also help explain trends over time in household borrowing. During the high-growth era of the 1950s, 1960s, and early 1970s, the Japanese government made a conscious decision to allocate virtually all available credit to the business sector to enable it to invest in plant and equipment and thus to expand its productive capacity as rapidly as possible. However, the former Housing Loan Corporation (Juutaku Kin'yuu Kouko), whose purpose was to make low-interest housing loans to low-to-middle-income households, was established by the Japanese Government in 1950 and gradually increased the supply of housing loans over time, with private financial institutions also getting a piece of the action as time passed.

Conclusion

To sum up, I have analyzed data on household wealth and indebtedness for the G7 countries, and the conventional wisdom that the Japanese and other Asians are penny-pinchers and savers and the Americans and other Westerners are spendthrifts and borrowers appears, at first glance, to be mistaken.

The Japanese were the most prolific borrowers among the G7 countries, at least until 2000, whereas Americans were not unusually prolific borrowers. However, what matters more than the level of liabilities is the level of liabilities relative to the level of assets, and the Japanese rank relatively high with respect to both total assets and net wealth (the most comprehensive measure of household wealth that takes account of both assets and liabilities), whereas Americans rank relatively low with respect to both. Thus, the Japanese are more frugal than Americans and most other Westerners, and the conventional wisdom is correct, after all. However, the difference between the United States and Japan can be explained by differences both in culture and in policies and institutions (for example, the timing and extent of financial sector development), so that it is not clear just from looking at the data which the real culprit is. Turning to trends over time, Japan has shown a sharp increase in household borrowing, at least until 2000. One possibility is that the erosion of traditional values over time caused this trend. However, the fact that the sharp increase in household borrowing was due largely to the sharp increase in mortgages (housing loans) suggests that factors relating to housing may also have contributed to this trend.

Looking, finally, at the broader implications of my findings, what do they imply about the applicability of the "Anglo-American credit model"? My analysis found that liabilities are only about average in the United States but among the highest in the United Kingdom, which constitutes only weak evidence in favor of the conventional wisdom that Americans and the British are unusually prolific borrowers. The fact that both total assets and net wealth are relatively low (even though liabilities are relatively low) in the United States suggests that the financial position of Americans is indeed relatively weak, but the fact that both total assets and net wealth are relatively high in the United Kingdom (even though liabilities are relatively high) suggests that the financial position of the British is relatively strong. Moreover, both countries have shown dramatic but diametrically opposed changes, with the United States falling from first to last with respect to both total assets and net wealth during the 1980–2008 period but the United Kingdom rising in the ranks with respect to both during the same period. In other words, the financial health of Americans has deteriorated badly whereas the financial health of the British has improved markedly. Thus, the financial positions and trends over time of the Americans and British are dissimilar from one another but not necessarily from the other G7 countries, suggesting that there is no "Anglo-American credit model."

If I had to divide the G7 countries into two groups, I would do so using household net wealth (the broadest measure of financial health) as the criteria, and, if I did so, Italy, Japan, and the United Kingdom would end up in the relatively healthy group and Canada, France, Germany, and the United States in the relatively unhealthy group. However, it should be noted that neither of the two groups is homogenous. For example, Japan and the United Kingdom have relatively high liabilities, whereas Italy has comparatively low liabilities, even though they are all in the same (relatively healthy) group. Similarly, Canada and the United States have relatively high or average liabilities, whereas France and Germany have comparatively low liabilities, even though they are all in the same (relatively unhealthy) group. Thus, it can be seen that it is not easy to categorize the G7 countries and that each has its own peculiarities. This circumstance is not surprising, because economic behavior is determined by culture, policies, institutions, and a host of other factors.

Notes

*I presented an earlier version of this chapter at the workshop "Cultures of Credit: Consumer Lending and Borrowing in Modern Economies," which was held at the German Historical Institute (GHI), Washington, D.C., on February 5–6, 2010. I am very grateful to Lawrence Bowdish, Sheldon Garon, Andrew Gordon, Jan Logemann, and the other workshop participants, as well to Shizuka Sekita and the other participants of my graduate seminar at Osaka University for their helpful discussions. I would also like to thank Andrew Gordon for his valuable information about data issues.

1. Andrew Gordon, "From Singer to Shinpan: The Growth of Consumer Credit in Japan," in *The Ambivalent Consumer: Questioning Consumption in East Asia and the West,* ed. Sheldon Garon and Patricia L. Maclachlan (Ithaca, NY, 2006), 137–62; Andrew Gordon, "Credit in a Nation of Savers: The Growth of Consumer Borrowing in Japan" (unpublished manuscript, Department of History, Harvard University, 2010); Charles Yuji Horioka, "Are the Japanese Unique? An Analysis of Consumption and Saving Behavior in Japan," in *Ambivalent Consumer,* ed. Garon and Maclachlan, 113–36.

2. Organisation for Economic Co-operation and Development (OECD), ed., *OECD Economic Outlook,* nos. 54–86 (December 1993-November 2009).

3. Keizai Kikaku-chou, Keizai Kenkyuu-sho, ed., *Kokumin Keizai Keisan Houkoku: Chouki Sokyuu Suikei: Shouwa 30-nen—Shouwa 44-nen* (Tokyo, 1988); Keizai Kikaku-chou, Keizai Kenkyuu-sho, ed., *Kokumin Keizai Keisan Nenpou* (Tokyo, 2000).

4. Chapter 10 of this volume by Silke Meyer argues—from an anthropological perspective—that household borrowing behavior is embedded in culture.

CHAPTER 12

"Ahead a Good Deal": Taking the Long View of Household Debt and Credit in American Life

Lendol Calder

To a lot of people, it must seem like Americans have a suicidal debt wish. Travel writer James Salter remembers a conversation with a Frenchman who sat next to him on a plane:

> To throw him off I took the position that life in Europe, in his own country in particular, was in many ways better than life in the United States, a perhaps exuberant point of view but I was just seeing how things would go. "The bread is better," I said. "The bread? Yes, perhaps." "The food is better," I continued. He shrugged and almost at the same time nodded a little. Between us there was the enthusiasm of men comparing wives. "The attention to the details of life," I went on. "Yes, yes," he said, "but the United States has given something more important to the world. The modern world could not exist without it." "What's that?" "They invented credit."[1]

The Frenchman exaggerated, of course. Americans did not invent credit. But it is not wrong to regard the United States as the oldest and most developed consumer credit market in the world, and arguably the most innovative. Americans invented the credit reporting firm, the installment plan, revolving credit, and the credit card. Americans may no longer be the world's biggest borrowers, as Charles Horioka points out in the previous chapter. Still, American consumers use and abuse credit with an exuberance that astonishes the world's savers. In 2009, the average American household owed $121,953 in mortgage loans and consumer debts. A figure as large as this leads one to wonder, what's the deal with Americans and indebtedness? Why do Americans go into debt so much?[2]

There is little agreement on an answer to this question. Broadly speaking, some say that structural factors are responsible for the zip and cornucopia of American credit markets, while others look to culture to explain the American way of debt. These broad categories of explanation can be seen in the essays in this volume, even when the focus is not on the United States. For example, Charles Horioka, an economist, claims that rising Japanese indebtedness is a consequence of changing government regulations. He is unconvinced that culture has had much to do with it. On the other hand, Silke Meyer examines the German debt crisis with an anthropologist's eye and insists that we pay attention to how tectonic shifts in credit morality are reshaping German consumer culture. Traditionally, Meyer observes, Germans viewed credit as a form of personal obligation. But recent advertisements portray credit as a consumer's right, thus reframing time-honored social understandings of debt. In the case of Japan, Horioka believes that mounting debt is the result of changing structural features in the country's credit markets. In the case of Germany, Meyer claims that rising indebtedness has everything to do with changing moral authorities and the messages that they convey about how people should make sense of the world. What are we to make of these very different explanations for mounting indebtedness? Can the economist and the anthropologist still be friends?

Gunnar Trumbull thinks so. Searching for the roots of the American debt crisis of 2008, he recognizes value in both approaches. Trumbull's main argument is that high levels of household debt in the United States are the result of a deliberate public policy—a structural explanation, in other words. Comparing the United States to France, Trumbull claims that the American state encouraged private sector lending because political leaders viewed easy credit as an alternative to public provision of social welfare. On this view, laws and regulations that empowered consumers with a right to consumer credit were intended to forestall the creation of a progressive, social democratic welfare system. The argument makes a lot of sense. But Trumbull's explanation also highlights ideological intentions that influenced the structure of American credit markets—culture, in other words. Trumbull recognizes that his structural argument is incomplete until we ask why Americans would prefer private sector credit to public sector welfare. This is exactly the kind of question Silke Meyer urges us to ask when she writes that "Economic markets are cultural and social constructions, and consumers act not only as economic agents, but also as cultural and social entities."[3] Structures matter, yes. But culture matters, too. If we want to understand rising levels of indebtedness,

American or otherwise, all hands are going to be needed on deck: economists, anthropologists, and other scholars, too.

In this essay, my intention is not to take sides between economic and anthropological explanations. Like Trumbull, I presume that robust accounts of the American knack for getting into and out of debt must combine insights from both perspectives. As a historian, however, I maintain that, if we want to know why Americans take on so much debt with such little fear and trembling, then the explanations we come up with ought to consider accounts of the subject that are properly *historical.* That is to say, we need to go back to the beginning of what we are trying to explain, and maybe just a little before. My point is that discussions of American indebtedness too often ignore the long view. For example, many who have tried to make sense of the Great Recession of 2008 look no further back than the housing bubble and low interest rates of the previous decade. To his credit, Gunnar Trumbull thinks it is necessary to look back to the late 1970s, but this is not far enough. Long before the American banking sector reorganized itself in the 1980s to provide convenient revolving credit to consumers, Americans were securing prosperity and luxury with the magical phrase "Charge it!" The phrase first appears in Mark Twain's *The Gilded Age,* a satire saluting "Beautiful credit! The foundation of modern society." Twain wrote these words in 1873.[4]

When the *longue durée* of historical continuities is not kept in mind, present-minded explanations of the American debt wish multiply, encouraging latent misunderstandings, false hopes, half-truths, and wishful thinking. The most common error is supposing that massive indebtedness is something new in American life, that thriftlessness was invented by the present generation. To suggest why I believe this view is mistaken, I offer the credit history of a nineteenth-century American Everyman named Walter Post. This man's story is worth thinking about because it is a thread that, once pulled, begins to unravel pervasive myths about household borrowing in the United States. Replacing folklore with evidence, we can fashion new and better explanations for the contemporary American debt wish.

The Debts of Walter Post

In the archives of the Minnesota Historical Society, several file folders contain the yellowing letters of Walter T. Post, a late nineteenth-century railroad clerk who lived in obscurity all his life.[5]

Born on a farm in Michigan in 1867, Post felt the lure of town life, so he set off for Detroit to attend business college. In 1889, he landed a job as an accountant with the Northern Pacific Railroad in St. Paul, Minnesota. For the next seven years, Walter wrote weekly letters to his parents back home on the farm. The letters provide details of his thoughts, activities, and finances. Many offer monthly budget figures with outlays recorded down to the penny. This correspondence between Post and his parents offers an unusually transparent window into the money management of a lower-middle-class, white-collar worker who aspired to bourgeois respectability.

The young man revealed in the letters was certainly no spendthrift. Walter Post was a man who aimed to do right, whose great passion in life was evangelical Protestantism. But on a clerk's salary of $55 a month, Walter had a hard time making ends meet. While still single, he did all right. Though he regularly bought goods on credit from local retailers and traveling salesmen, and though he occasionally obtained loans from friends, some months saw him in the black and lending money to coworkers or sending a surplus home to his folks.

But once Walter got married in 1894, balanced budgets were a thing of the past. The remaining two years of letters in his file show him and his wife Lilly going deeply into debt. It began the month after the wedding. After renting a house, the Posts felt it necessary to furnish the bare rooms, floors, and walls in a manner befitting a middle-class couple. After comparison shopping and some whittling down of their wish list, the couple purchased furniture and carpets from the Schuneman and Evans department store on terms of two-thirds down and the balance in sixty days. For the kitchen, Walter bought a used stove from a friend for six dollars down and fifteen dollars later. As the debts mounted higher, it turned out to be much later. By the spring of 1895, as the Posts looked forward to the birth of their first child, the couple owed money to the dentist, the doctor, the grocer, the butcher, a tailor, the hardware store, and a sewing machine agent. They also still owed money on the furniture and stove, extending these loans several times over. As the creditors became insistent, Walter tapped his brother Charlie for a loan. After rent, groceries, ice, fuel, and other fixed expenditures, Walter's disposable income that spring was about ten dollars a month; the Posts' debts totaled $78.50. It was this kind of economic behavior that led labor leader Ira Steward twenty years earlier to ask, "Has not the middle class its poverty? Very few among them are saving money. Many of them are in debt, and all they can earn for years, is, in many cases, mortgaged to pay such debt."[6]

Some might think the Posts were reckless overspenders, but that is not the image that comes through in the letters. To his brother Charlie, Walter confided: "I have to do some awful close figuring to make ends meet, and then they don't meet." To his father, Walter reported: "We were paid off today but all the money is spoken for before I get it almost."[7] Walter is less the carefree consumer than a frazzled budgeter calling on all the financial arts he knows. Despite his money worries, Post felt that the debts he incurred were beneficial for achieving the life he and Lilly wanted. Comparing the costs of renting a house versus boarding, Post conceded that a few more years of boarding would have enabled the couple to put aside $150 of his salary at a savings bank. "But now we have $202.80 worth of furniture," he countered. "And we might have had to use some of the money in the Bank so you see we are ahead a good deal."[8] It is an interesting logic. Though the Posts still owed money on their furniture, Walter regarded their debt as a form of savings, and he recognized that the liquidity of a bank savings account was to him a constant temptation to fritter money away on insubstantial expenditures. This is the kind of thinking that legitimated installment buying when it became more widely available in the 1920s.

Post's letters end abruptly in the fall of 1896. As the economy sank into a deep recession, Walter lost his job with the railroad. He and Lilly left town owing money to their doctor, a dentist, a sewing machine agent, and Walter's brother, Charlie. The young family moved to Grand Rapids, Michigan, then, a few years later, to South Bend, Indiana, where the Posts lived out the remainder of their lives. No letters from these years appear in the archives. Reading the young Walter Post's letters, however, brings alive a saying of the late nineteenth-century celebrity preacher Henry Ward Beecher: "If a young man will only get in debt . . . and then get married, these two things will keep him straight, or nothing will." It was a familiar joke, an acknowledgment that although rules such as "don't go into debt" are necessary, there have to be permissible ways of bending, and sometimes breaking, the rules. Post's letters also call to mind the words of Artemus Ward, the mid-nineteenth-century humorist, who was fond of telling audiences, "Let us live within our means, even if we have to borrow money to do it."[9]

The story of Walter Post challenges much that Americans know about the history of household finance. Often, the expansion of consumer credit in postwar America is seen as a radical departure from a thrifty past, when Americans rarely got into debt and generally lived within their means. "People have changed their view of debt," wrote John Kenneth Galbraith in *The Affluent Society*, an obituary for thrift published in 1958. "Thus there has been an inexplicable but very real retreat from the Puritan canon that required an individual to save first and enjoy later." Forty years later, historian David Tucker agreed with Galbraith, arguing in *The Decline of Thrift in America* that "installment buying required a moral revolution against the Puritan ethic." Most famously, Daniel Bell asserted in *The Cultural Contradictions of Capitalism* that "the greatest single engine in the destruction of the Protestant ethic was the invention of the installment plan, or instant credit."[10]

That Americans have "changed their view of debt" is not only a view held by scholars; it is also an article of faith in popular writing about American personal finance. Pundits and social critics often look at debt through the lens of what I call the myth of lost economic virtue, the belief that the invention of modern consumer credit brought down the curtain on a golden age of financial prudence. The perception that Americans have fallen from a state of economic grace is a powerful myth. It accords with available evidence, such as newspaper reports of rising indebtedness and personal memories of how one's parents managed their money. It offers simple explanations for how we got to where we are, sometimes portraying Americans as victims of exploitive credit card companies, sometimes placing the blame squarely on Americans themselves, faulting them for character so weak that they would trade wholesome thrift for consumer excess.

In recent years, the myth of lost economic virtue has figured prominently in calls for a nationwide revival of the virtue of thrift. The leader of this movement to curb Americans' fondness for borrowed money is David Blankenhorn, founder and president of the Institute for American Values. An unabashed cheerleader for thrift, Blankenhorn would like to jumpstart a national social movement away from debt-financed hyperconsumerism back to an earlier age when financial husbandry was a cherished social ideal. To get Americans there, Blankenhorn calls for the revival of National Thrift Week, a 1920s-era celebration of financial prudence that lost momentum after World War II. It would make an interesting doctoral dissertation to examine why the Hallmark Card Company, the world's largest greeting card company, chose to develop thirty-five different Hallmark cards for a made-up occasion called Administrative Professionals Day (April 27) but nothing for the extant National Thrift Week, which quietly was retired in 1966. Hallmark knows its reasons. But Blankenhorn wants twenty-first century Americans to give thrift a chance.[11]

David Blankenhorn is not a crank. He is a sober critic pushing a serious agenda. In fact, I second Blankenhorn's insistence that thrift is not the same thing as stinginess, that its boundaries are capacious enough to include an ethic of altruism and environmental stewardship. And who could oppose making savings accounts more desirable and accessible to low- and middle-income households? But as a historian I part company with Blankenhorn when he bases his campaign for thrift on rhetoric that conjures up a golden age of saving. In books and speeches, Blankenhorn claims that "the idea and practice of thrift has been a robust part of the American vision of economic freedom and social abundance." Thrift, he says, is "a quintessentially American virtue."[12] Here, the activist's desire for a usable past elides a great deal of contrary evidence.

Tellingly, Blankenhorn's favorite story about thrift is taken not from life but from Hollywood. It is the romance of George Bailey, director of the Bedford Falls Building and Loan Company, in Frank Capra's 1946 film *It's a Wonderful Life*.[13] In this beloved film classic, Bailey suffers an existential crisis that is resolved within the context of the Building and Loan's fight to survive the heartless profiteering of the town's villainous banker, the dour, wheelchair-bound Henry Potter. For Blankenhorn, Bailey's idealistic efforts to help working men secure homes on the basis of mortgages financed by their own collective savings represent the ethos of thrift at its best. Who could fail to respond warmly to the idealism of the self-sacrificing George Bailey, played so endearingly by a young Jimmy Stewart? But as a depiction of historic American attitudes about thrift, debt, and credit, Capra's film is an insufficiently rich version of the subject. I once heard a historian say, with a twinkle in his eye, that historical interpretations are like bathing suits: what they reveal can be interesting, but what they conceal is crucial. Hidden by Capra's image of American financial wholesomeness is evidence that runs contrary to the myth of lost economic virtue—-evidence such as the credit history of Walter and Lilly Post.

Of course, the story of the Posts is just an anecdote. Suppose that the Posts' finances were unusual for their time. In that case, their story might be less useful than the fictional story of George Bailey for making generalizations about how an earlier generation of Americans handled its money. So let us use the Posts' balance sheets as a jumping off point to consider several questions relevant to discussions of why contemporary Americans incur so much debt. How much debt did American households have before modern consumer credit made it easier to get credit? What influence did a thrift ethos have on economic decision making in earlier periods of American history?

How Much Debt Did Past Americans Have?

Walter and Lilly Post's finances do not fit the standard declension narrative often applied to American thrift. But how typical were they? Walter seemed to think they were an exception to the rule. In his letters, he portrayed himself as the *thriftiest* of the dozens of clerks in the St. Paul office where he worked, clerks who were occasionally fired for drunkenness, gambling, or having their wages garnished by persistent creditors. Walter may have exaggerated his thriftiness, if only to justify himself to his parents, but the ease with which he went into debt to pursue his goals makes one wonder. How many households like the Posts' were there in a time that David Blankenhorn and others characterize as a golden era of American thrift?

The short answer is that we do not know for sure. But the evidence suggests that the Posts were well within the norm for Americans of their era. More than that, historical records reveal a river of red ink flowing through the balance sheets of past American households, running wider and deeper at times than the levels seen today. This may seem hard to believe. After all, the secular trend for consumer indebtedness since the late 1920s has been steadily up. Looking at the rising line of indebtedness in Federal Reserve historical charts, it is natural to extrapolate the line *backwards* from its starting point until one infers a time when households must have used very little credit at all. But it would be a mistake to assume that 1928, the first year the Federal Reserve collected data on credit volumes, is an appropriate baseline for measuring the later history of household indebtedness. The absence of carefully collected statistical data on debt before 1928 should not be understood as meaning that there was no debt.

Celebrated cases come to mind. The Pilgrims financed Plymouth Colony with money borrowed at 30 to 70 percent interest. It took the colonists twenty-eight years to retire the loans, which means few of the original colonists lived to see their debts repaid. The same can be said of Thomas Jefferson, who lived most of his life at the mercy of creditors. When Jefferson died in 1826, his estate owed $107,000, a sum that today would be over $2 million. It is not an exaggeration to say that the American way of life has always been predicated on debt.

The first general estimate of the nation's household indebtedness that I am aware of was made by the orator and statesman Edward Everett during the Panic of 1857. Everett blamed that economic crisis on "a mountain load of debt" taken on by governments, businesses, and citizens. Everett estimated the nation's total household indebtedness in 1858 to be $1.5 billion, or $300 per household. The figure was nothing more than an educated guess based on Everett's personal observation and experience. But he would not be the last nineteenth-century observer to note that Americans had a "natural proclivity to anticipate income, to buy on credit, to live a little beyond our means."[14]

A more meticulously compiled estimate was made thirty years later by the United States Census Bureau, and it confirms that Walter and Lily Post were not alone in financing their household on credit. The 1890 Census survey of personal debt was a response to agitated demands for information from various populist groups—Grangers, labor unions, Single Taxers, Greenbackers, Christian Socialists, and others—who alleged that the indebtedness of farmers and workers had reached such an amount that it was doubtful whether Americans could produce enough wealth to pay back the interest, much less the principal. Thus, Congress directed the Eleventh Decennial Census to "collect the statistics of, and relating to, the recorded indebtedness of private corporations and individuals."[15]

For the purposes of later historians, it would have been wonderful if the Census Bureau had been able to comply with its charge. But the undertaking was simply too large, too intrusive, too expensive, and too unprecedented. In the end, Census officials decided to calculate the private debt of the nation on the basis of public records for private real estate mortgages.[16] Mixing hard figures on mortgages with round numbers and educated guesses as to other types of household debt, Census Superintendant Robert Porter and his staff estimated that the *minimum* private debt of the people of the United States in 1890 was $11 billion.[17]

If the Census figure is accurate, it would apportion to each American household in 1890 about $880 of debt. That amount was nearly twice the $475 average annual wage of nonfarm workers that year.[18] In today's money, $880 would be equivalent to about $109,000.[19] The figure is an average, which means some owed less than this amount and some owed no money at all. But some owed more. Census officials admitted that their figures almost certainly underreported the true amount of household debt. After all, they could hardly estimate the people's *unrecorded* debts, the debts owed to pawnbrokers, loan sharks, retailers, friends, and family members. In other words, the Census statisticians had no way to estimate debts like those owed by Walter and Lily Post. Still, taking the Census figure as it stands, the estimate of $880 per household is hard to reconcile with the view that massive indebtedness is a phenomenon peculiar to the late twentieth century, or that the lure of instant money is something new in American life. On the contrary, it reminds us that in the so-called Golden Age of Thrift, Americans were familiar with debt on a scale roughly comparable to today. Money, as a journalist put it in 1876, "[was] shouting itself hoarse in the effort to get itself loaned."[20]

Historians now recognize that high levels of indebtedness are part of the enduring fabric of the American experience. Since I raised questions in *Financing the American Dream* about the willingness of nineteenth-century Americans to go into debt, other historians have contributed to the construction of a counternarrative to the myth of lost economic virtue. The titles of their monographs summarize the new view: *Republic of Debtors; Navigating Failure; Born Losers; Debt's Dominion; In Hock; A Culture of Credit.*[21]

Still, many questions remain. Comparisons of debt and savings between the postwar era and earlier periods in American history are tricky, because the data available is asymmetrical. The need is great for an economic historian to update Oliver Goldsmith's pioneering study of nineteenth-century saving and indebtedness, work that is now more than a half-century old.[22] Until we have better data, arguments about how much debt Americans carried in past eras must be considered provisional.

How Influential Has a Thrift Ethos Been?

If the story of Walter and Lilly Post suggests that debt was a familiar experience for nineteenth-century Americans, it also calls into question another aspect of the myth of lost economic virtue: the belief that thrift is, as David Blankenhorn claims, a "quintessential" American virtue. What can be said about this belief?

It is certainly true that, for a long period of American history, thrift was part of a package of virtues promoted by religious, educational, and business authorities for the moral improvement of American citizens. When researching his 2008 book, *Thrift: A Cyclopedia*, Blankenhorn had no trouble at all finding an abundance of pro-thrift primary sources, beginning with Benjamin Franklin's popular pamphlet *The Way to Wealth* and extending through the heyday of National Thrift Week.[23] For about a century, from the 1820s through the 1920s, a gospel of saving was preached, promoted, and pushed on American society in ways that were part of the bourgeois program of character formation and that contrast with today's near silence on the subject.

"What do you know about 'thrift'?" I asked my eleven-year-old daughter one day on our way to her school. "Thr-i-ft..." she repeated slowly, hefting the word in her mouth. "I don't know," she said after a pause. "I never heard that word before." This is an extraordinary statement. My daughter's public school offers advanced math, science, and literature, as well as programs for sex education, patriotism, conflict resolution, and many other worthy ends. But, to my knowledge, there is no instruction in money management. Blankenhorn is right when he says that a cultural apparatus that once existed for the promotion of thrift in the United States has been almost entirely dismantled.

But to concede this point is not to agree that thrift is deeply rooted in American life and history. If thrift were an ingrained practice, there would be no need for thrift propaganda. The reality is that thrift in the past was never the only game in town, as Jackson Lears and others have made clear.[24] Thrift in the nineteenth century was an embattled ideal. It competed against the cards, dice, and drink of the sporting crowd. It went up against the appeal of fashion in a fluid society in which display was an essential form of asserting one's identity and sizing up others. In middle-class households like the Posts', thrift could be overwhelmed by the status-striving of people who were supposed to be improving themselves. Benjamin Franklin's Poor Richard, the most widely quoted financial authority in American history, may have said, "He who goes a-borrowing goes a-sorrowing," but this maxim competed with Beecher's quip about the value for a young man of getting into debt. Another nineteenth-century epigram maintained, "One never becomes rich until he is in debt." This is similar to Mark Twain's report of a man overheard to say, "I wasn't worth a cent two years ago, and now I owe two millions of dollars." P. T. Barnum, one of the century's greatest advocates for thrift, told audiences the story of an old Quaker who had said to his son, "John, never get trusted, but if thee gets trusted for anything, let it be for 'manure,' because that will help thee pay it back again." Benjamin Franklin Butler, a Union general during the Civil War and later the governor of Massachusetts, summarized his financial advice for young men this way: "Buy improved real estate, partly for cash, and partly for small notes."[25]

Borrowed money was, after all, credit, which in nineteenth-century America was a valued necessity. Credit built communities; it got young men started in life. Credit staked the pioneer's homestead, enabled immigrants to obtain a business, allowed businessmen to enlarge their plans, and knit borrower and lender together in bonds of mutual dependency. "Credit to a man," declared business journalist Freeman Hunt, "is what cream is to a nice cup of coffee."[26] Hunt's jocular tone was made possible by attitudes toward credit that he could take for granted. A century earlier a pro-credit ethos had appeared that viewed lending and borrowing as a barometer of public morality, the exact measure of the soundness of the social state. This is the conclusion of Jennifer Baker who, examining writers as diverse as Cotton Mather, Benjamin Franklin, Royall Tyler, Charles Brockden Brown, and Judith Sargent Murray, finds that "writers within all these social and intellectual circles [Puritan, Yankee, southern agrarian, revolutionary] imagined new modes of financial speculation and indebtedness as a means to build American communities and foster social cohesion."[27] After the Revolution and continuing into the early twentieth century, credit was an emblem for the unity and coherence of society as a whole. In the language of the day, people did not "borrow money." Rather, they "got trusted."

Lamentations for the death of thrift promotion downplay or ignore these other formative messages that circulated widely in nineteenth-century America. If economizing is a "quintessential" American value, even more so is an optimistic alacrity to try out new tools of finance.

It may be tempting to join Blankenhorn and others in wanting to revive an older rhetoric of thrift. But before distributing reprints of Franklin's *The Way to Wealth*, we might ask how helpful those old thrift sermons actually were. They were none too effective, the evidence suggests. In the writings of nineteenth-century foreign travelers to the United States, "thrifty" is not a description applied to Americans very often. Alexis de Tocqueville, commenting on the desire for physical gratifications in the United States, all but predicted the rise of the easy payment plan: "As [the American's] ultimate object is to enjoy, the means to reach that object must be prompt and easy or the trouble of acquiring the gratification would be greater than the gratification itself."[28] If we turn our attention away from money management to the predominant economic activity of the nineteenth century, which was farming, it is clear that the thrift ethos was usually abandoned for a "get rich quick" mind-set. Domestic and foreign observers expressed shock at the American practice of "land killing," a reckless exploitation of soil fertility that led to scruffy, rundown farms, exhausted lands, and expensive relocations farther west. In a masterful book on the subject, Yale historian Steven Stoll notes that "the entire republican project was predicated on the waste of land."[29] So much for thrift as a quintessential American virtue.

The power of a thrift ethos in earlier eras of American history is easily overrated. Thrift mattered in the past, to be sure. But it mattered more to the moral elites who wrote money management books than it did to others. Benjamin Franklin knew as much. At the end of Father Abraham's anti-debt harangue in *The Way to Wealth*, Franklin has Poor Richard observe, "The People heard it, and approved the Doctrine, and immediately practiced the contrary."[30]

Why Do Americans Go into Debt So Much?

As a historian, I think it important to look for immediate, proximate causes behind surges in American indebtedness. But ultimate causes need to be considered, too. This point was lost on me when I first began thinking about the problem of American household finance. That is because in the beginning of my work on the subject, I fully subscribed to the myth of lost economic virtue. I believed that, before the rise of modern consumer credit, people rarely went into debt and always lived within their means, that a thrift ethos had been dismantled by an industry that profited from people's short-sighted desires for instant gratification. This metanarrative in my head short-circuited any search for the ultimate causes of the problem of excessive debt, a problem I erroneously considered to be a recently adopted habit. Then I met the Posts. Their budgets pointed to an illuminating historical context for Americans' present-day love affair with borrowing. Discovering this context made it easier to understand how American households got to where they are today: contrary to what most believe, the American debt wish of the 1990s and 2000s did not appear out of nowhere, nor was it unprecedented. We should want to know why and how Americans piled up so much debt in the latest cycle of debt-financed über-spending. But the historical perspective sketched here raises other interesting questions. For starters, why have Americans *always* been willing to boost their spending with money and goods on loan?

A decade of excellent historical work on this problem now makes it possible to replace the worn-out myth of lost economic virtue with a new narrative of American household finance more attentive to the roots of contemporary indebtedness. The new story is writ small in the following reminiscence, which I came across when studying the debate over installment buying in the 1920s. Most people romanticize the money management of previous generations. But this man remembered that while growing up on a "midwest wilderness farm" he had come into contact with credit buying on numerous occasions: "First, when my mother bought her sewing machine; second, when my father bought his reaper; third, when the family purchased a piano; fourth, when I bought my first good suit . . . ; and fifth, when I purchased my *Encyclopaedia Britannica* in place of the college education that was beyond my reach."[31] Here in a nutshell is a reliable history of American household finance. It is a story of small experiments with borrowed money encouraging people to take larger risks. It is a story of newly arrived immigrants learning about a strange American custom called "getting trusted" and enthusiastically adopting the practice of "buy now, pay later." It is a story of one generation improving its lot in life with loans and inspiring the next generation to go further. Sometimes the story of American indebtedness cuts against the grain, as when memories of crushing debt for one's parents inspire thoughts in a son or daughter of "Never again!" But most of the time over the past four hundred years, Americans have felt reasonably satisfied with the utility of Twain's "beautiful credit." If the new story needs a name, we can call it the domino theory of American debt.

The cultural force pushing the dominos is, in a word, optimism. We have no history of this prevailing American emotion, but a rough typology can be made. To begin with, there is the unassailable buoyancy of some borrowers who, like Broadway's Little Orphan Annie, believe "the sun'll come out tomorrow, bet your bottom dollar." Some may believe that emotions are culturally constructed, but this kind of optimism owes more to brain neurochemicals than to cultural currents and is probably equally distributed across all populations. Some people see the sunny side of life; others do not.

More unique to the United States is the pious optimism of "mind cure" thinking that has been so influential in American life since the early nineteenth century. Mind cure religions celebrate the power of positive thinking. Encapsulated in proverbs such as "As a man thinketh, so he is," mind cure applied to money teaches that there are no rewards without risks. To the hesitant borrower, mind cure says, "Just believe—the money will come!" In the magisterial *Land of Desire,* historian William Leach argues that mind cure is the religious worldview animating American consumer culture, a suggestive explanation, I think, for Americans' consistent willingness to bet on the future.[32]

Thirdly, there is the optimism produced by the world's first economy to deliver prosperity to the millions. In *The New Basis of Civilization* (1907),

Simon Patten, professor of economics at the University of Pennsylvania's Wharton School of Business, famously argued that the New World's material abundance was replacing economies of scarcity and the fearful negativism of thrift-oriented cultures with a fresh mental outlook that was more generous, warm, artistic, and upbeat. Patten's predictions about the difference high-level consumption would make on human nature were overly rosy. But the main thrust of his argument has been revived and updated recently by Jackson Lears, who agrees with Patten that economic abundance inspired in Americans new understandings of the human psyche and what it is capable of. According to Lears, American optimism made indebtedness seem less threatening and credit a more attractive possibility. Migrants to the New World brought with them traditional notions of thrift grounded in a pessimistic psychology of scarcity. Their cautious prudence demanded a strict conservation of money and energy, but in the United States an effervescent economy generated new psychologies of abundance. Old-world thrift did not disappear but was reimagined and repurposed. Previously, when wealth creation was considered to be difficult, if not impossible, thrift had meant saving money and staying out of debt. But the democratization of wealth-creating opportunities generated new, more optimistic, and demanding expectations for the thrifty self. Formerly it had been enough to hide one's savings under the mattress. In the new dispensation of abundance, however, thrift came to mean much more than simple saving. Now the thrifty were expected to save *at interest,* keep a budget, borrow responsibly, comparison shop, repay loans on time, and be mindful of other wealth-generating opportunities. The new high-performance ethos of thrift was based on optimistic assumptions about what humans are capable of and the good that can come to them. This optimistic psychology of abundance, Lears insists, did not lead to a hedonistic consumer culture, as critics often allege. Rather, American optimism produced lifestyles characterized by more energy, self-discipline, and belief in the generative power of finance than ever before thought possible.[33]

The Frenchman quoted at the beginning of this essay credited Americans with inventing credit. Am I now claiming that Americans invented optimism, too? One could point to the theme parks of Walt Disney, upbeat fairy tales like *The Wizard of Oz,* and nonfiction bestsellers like Norman Vincent Peale's *The Power of Positive Thinking* to support a view that, yes, Americans, going back a century and more, have been a fundamentally optimistic people, more so perhaps than others. But all three of the cultural artifacts just mentioned have done well in overseas markets, too. In truth, we do not yet have the comparative evidence we need to know whether and to what extent the American debt wish traces back to a unique cultural propensity to optimism. But we should be open-minded to the possibility. If cultural determinism is a dated belief, this does not mean that all social populations have the same emotional and personality makeup. My claims for the power of optimism are meant to be suggestive, not taken as demonstrated facts.

Still, I can think of one more attestation to the power of optimism in American life, and that is the eternal hopefulness of debt's detractors. Predictably, reliably, in the aftermath of every financial devastation, critics of the American way of debt come once more unto the breach proclaiming a lasting revival of American thrift.

So it was more than a century ago when Superintendent of the Census Robert Porter predicted that the publication of statistics on real estate mortgage debt would "bring the people to their sober senses." Bemoaning a decade of "debt-creating mania," Porter confidently announced that a new era of "retrenchment and debt-paying" was at hand. That was in 1890. Echoes of Porter's words were heard again in the aftermath of the 2008 financial meltdown. Voices from all points of the ideological spectrum proclaimed game over for America's indebted consumers. National Public Radio's Daniel Schorr predicted Americans were seeing "the end of an era," when patriotism was defined by pledging allegiance to the mall. Daniel Leonhardt of the *New York Times* wrote that "the psychology of spending and saving" had permanently shifted. He seconded the opinion of pollster John Zogby, who reported that his surveys showed "a fundamental reorientation of the American character away from wanton consumption and toward a new global citizenry in an age of limited resources." With her finger on the zeitgeist, Oprah Winfrey declared that a new frugality was heralding the return of older ways of thrift. "Remember layaway?" she asked viewers in the fall of 2009. "That is where we are heading."[34]

In the short term, these optimists may have been right. But in the long run, will Americans give up their historic debt wish? I wouldn't bet on it.

Notes

1. James Salter, *There and Then: The Travel Writing of James Salter* (Berkeley, CA, 2005), 123.
2. Dennis Cauchon, "Leap in U.S. Debt Hits Taxpayers with 12% More Red Ink," *USA Today*, May 29, 2009, http://www.usatoday.com/news/washington/2009-05-28-debt_N.htm.
3. See chapter 10 in this volume by Silke Meyer, "Economic Agents and the Culture of Debt."
4. Mark Twain and Charles Dudley Warner, *The Gilded Age: A Tale of Today* (1873; New York, 1985), 193.
5. Walter T. Post letters, box P1040, Minnesota Historical Society, St Paul, MN.

6. Massachusetts Bureau of the Statistics of Labor, *Fourth Annual Report* (1873), 414.
7. Post letters, to Charlie, January 20, 1896; to his father, April 2, 1895.
8. Post letters, to his father, April 2, 1895.
9. Beecher quoted in P. T. Barnum, *Dollars and Sense* (New York, 1890), 49–50; Charles Farrar Browne [Artemus Ward], *Artemus Ward in London* (New York, 1867), 71.
10. John Kenneth Galbraith, *The Affluent Society* (New York, 1958), 200; David Tucker, *The Decline of Thrift in America* (New York, 1991), vii-ix, 99–155; Daniel Bell, *The Cultural Contradictions of Capitalism* (New York, 1976), 21.
11. Templeton Press, *Bring Back Thrift Week: A National Celebration of Forgotten Virtues,* http://www.bringbackthriftweek.org.
12. David Blankenhorn, Barbara Dafoe Whitehead, and Sorcha Brophy-Warren, *Franklin's Thrift: The Lost History of an American Virtue* (West Conshohocken, PA, 2009). Quotes are from the Templeton Press web site, http://www.templetonpress.org/book.asp?book_id= 135.
13. The working title for *Franklin's Thrift* was originally *It's a Wonderful Life: Essays in American Life.* See the description of the book at http://www.templetonpress.org/book.asp?book_id= 135.
14. Edward Everett, *The Mount Vernon Papers* (New York, 1860), 167–68.
15. U.S. Department of the Interior, Census Office, *Report on Real Estate Mortgages in the United States at the Eleventh Census, 1890* (Washington, DC, 1895), 3. For analysis of the debt controversy, which centered on western farm mortgages, see *Banker's Magazine* 42 (January 1888): 502–3; Daniel R. Goodloe, "Western Farm Mortgages," *The Forum* 10 (November 1890): 347–55; J. P. Dunn, Jr., "The Mortgage Evil," *Political Science Quarterly* 5 (March 1890): 65–83.
16. "Private" real estate mortgages included farm acreage, city lots, and some mortgages for commercial purposes, but excluded mortgage debt of "quasi-public" corporations such as railroads and public utilities. Robert P. Porter, "Public and Private Debts," *North American Review* 153 (November 1891): 610–12.
17. Census Office, *Report on Real Estate Mortgages,* 102.
18. Estimate of debt per household computed from data on households in U.S. Bureau of the Census, *Historical Statistics of the United States from Colonial Times to 1970* (Washington, D.C., 1975), 1:41. Average annual wages for American workers are reported in *Historical Statistics of the United States,* 1:165.
19. Census Office, *Report on Real Estate Mortgages,* 102. There are many ways to compute the relative value of money in one year compared to another. Here the figure is computed in terms of affordability based on unskilled wage rates. See "Seven Ways to Compute the Relative Value of a U.S. Dollar Amount—1774 to Present," http://www.measuringworth.com/uscompare.
20. Charles Barnard, "A Hundred Thousand Homes: How They Were Paid For," *Scribner's Monthly* 11 (February 1876): 479.
21. Lendol Calder, *Financing the American Dream: A Cultural History of Consumer Credit* (Princeton, NJ, 1999); Bruce H. Mann, *Republic of Debtors: Bankruptcy in*

the Age of American Independence (Cambridge, MA, 2002); Edward J. Balleisen, *Navigating Failure: Bankruptcy and Commercial Failure in Antebellum America* (Chapel Hill, NC, 2001); Scott A. Sandage, *Born Losers: A History of Failure in America* (Cambridge, MA, 2005); David A. Skeel, Jr., *Debt's Dominion: A History of Bankruptcy Law in America* (Princeton, NJ, 2003); Wendy A. Woloson, *In Hock: Pawning in America from Independence through the Great Depression* (Chicago, IL, 2009); Rowena Olegario, *A Culture of Credit: Embedding Trust and Transparency in American Business* (Cambridge, MA, 2006).

22. Raymond Goldsmith, *A Study of Saving in the United States,* 3 vols. (Princeton, NJ, 1955), 1:699.

23. David Blankenhorn, *Thrift: A Cyclopedia* (West Conshohocken, PA, 2008).

24. Jackson Lears, *Rebirth of a Nation: The Making of Modern America, 1877–1920* (New York, 2009), 65–71.

25. Epigram quoted in Clarence Wassam, *The Salary Loan Business in New York City* (New York, 1908), 11; Twain and Warner, *The Gilded Age,* 193; Barnum, *Dollars and Sense,* 50; Butler quoted in *The Nation,* September 15, 1887, 205.

26. Freeman Hunt, *Worth and Wealth* (New York, 1856), 363.

27. Jennifer Baker, *Securing the Commonwealth: Debt, Speculation, and Writing in the Making of Early America* (Baltimore, MD, 2005), 2.

28. Alexis de Tocqueville, *Democracy in America* (New York, 1899), 2:623.

29. Steven Stoll, *Larding the Lean Earth: Soil and Society in Nineteenth-Century America* (New York, 2002), 36.

30. Benjamin Franklin, "Poor Richard Improved, 1758," *Benjamin Franklin: Writings,* The Library of America (New York, 1987), 1302.

31. Charles Connard Hanch, "The Case for Installment Buying," *The Forum* 77 (May 1927): 660.

32. See chap. 8, "Mind Cure and the Happiness Machine," in William Leach, *Land of Desire: Merchants, Power, and the Rise of a New American Culture* (New York, 1993).

33. Simon Patten, *The New Basis of Civilization* (New York, 1908); Lears, *Rebirth of a Nation,* 65–71.

34. Porter, "Public and Private Debts," 614, 618; Daniel Schorr, "Age of American Consumerism May Be Over," *All Things Considered,* November 13, 2008, http://www.npr.org/templates/story/story.php?storyId= 96970075; David Leonhardt, "Buying Binge Slams to Halt," *New York Times,* November 11, 2008, http://www.nytimes.com/2008/11/12/business/economy/12leonhardt.html; John Zogby, *The Way We'll Be: The Transformation of the American Dream* (New York, 2008), 23; Winfrey quoted in Eric Dash, "The Last Temptation of Plastic," *New York Times,* December 6, 2008, http://www.nytimes.com/2008/12/07/weekinreview/07dash.html.

Index

Note: The letter 'n' following the locators refers to notes cited in the text. Likewise, the letter 'f' refers to figures, and the letter 't' refers to tables.

Hamburgische Patriotische Gesellschaft, 42

Hansen, Alvin, 205, 206

Haydon, Benjamin, 227

Hermann Tietz department stores, 134

Heuss, Theodor, 46

Higher Education Act (U.S., 1965), 207

Hirai Yasutaro, 80n13

hire purchase, 86–87, 94, 98

Hire-Purchase Credit Control Order (UK, 1938), 185, 186, 189

historical contextualization of American indebtedness, 13–14, 263–65

home equity loans, 63, 79n2

Home Mortgage Disclosure Act (U.S., 1975), 216n35

Horioka, Charles, 9, 13, 79n2, 258

House Banking and Currency Committee (U.S.), 207

household indebtedness, 244, 245–48t, 249–51

   disposable income and, 2, 157–58, 158t, 169, 249

   economic growth potential of, 219n59

   in France, 31, 173, 194, 194t

   in Germany, 31, 194t, 258

   historical record of in the U.S., 263–65

   in Japan, 258

   optimism in the U.S. and, 268–71

   overindebtedness, 201–2, 230, 239n24

   in the UK, 31, 194t

   in the U.S., 31, 194t

   U.S. Census Bureau and, 264–65

   women and, 194

   see also bankruptcies; consumer debt; mortgage loans

household wealth, 243, 244, 245–48t, 251–52, 253t

House Subcommittee on Consumer Affairs of the Committee on Banking and Currency (U.S.), 122

housing, 35, 254, 255

Housing Loan Corporation (Juutaku Kin'yuu Kouko, Japan), 249, 254

housing loans, see mortgage loans

housing prices, 249

Howard, Christopher, 204, 207

HSBC, 167

Hunt, Freeman, 267

Hyman, Louis, 11

identity numbering system, national, 139, 140–41

income

   credit cards as, 211

   discounting of, 114, 117, 120, 123

   ratio of household indebtedness to, 2

independent retail credit, end of, 167–68

industrial development, 185

"industrial insurance policies," 88–89, 92

inflation

   credit rationing and, 31

   "creditworthiness ratio" and, 189–90

   finance charges and, 27–28, 164

   "free credit" and, 173–74

   National Credit Council and, 185

informational privacy, see privacy, informational

informational rights, see privacy rights

information collection, 131, 144, 149, 153n35

information model of consumer protection legislation, 145

information sharing, repayment and, 159

informed consent for data collection, 148

In Hock (Woloson), 265

INSEE (Institut National de la Statistique et des Études Économiques, France), 31

installment credit, 9

   debt as savings and, 261

   deregulation of Japanese consumer credit, 77

   self-governing subjects and, 136–37